PEACE, WAR
AND WHITEHALL

DEDICATION

For Kate

FIELD MARSHAL
LORD GUTHRIE

FOREWORD BY
HRH THE PRINCE OF WALES

PEACE, WAR
AND WHITEHALL

A MEMOIR

OSPREY PUBLISHING
Bloomsbury Publishing Plc
Kemp House, Chawley Park, Cumnor Hill, Oxford OX2 9PH, UK
29 Earlsfort Terrace, Dublin 2, Ireland
1385 Broadway, 5th Floor, New York, NY 10018, USA
E-mail: info@ospreypublishing.com

www.ospreypublishing.com

OSPREY is a trademark of Osprey Publishing Ltd

First published in Great Britain in 2021

A catalogue record for this book is available from the British Library.

ISBN: HB 9781 4728 5232 8; eBook 978 1 4728 5229 8; ePDF 978 1 4728 5230 4; XML 978 1 4728 5231 1

21 22 23 24 25 10 9 8 7 6 5 4 3 2 1

Map by www.bounford.com
Index by Zoe Ross

Typeset by Deanta Global Publishing Services, Chennai, India
Printed and bound in Great Britain by CPI (Group) UK Ltd, Croydon CR0 4YY

Osprey Publishing supports the Woodland Trust, the UK's leading woodland conservation charity.

MIX
Paper from
responsible sources
FSC® C020471

To find out more about our authors and books visit **www.ospreypublishing.com**. Here you will find extracts, author interviews, details of forthcoming events and the option to sign up for our newsletter.

Contents

I am delighted that Field Marshal Lord Guthrie has decided to write his memoirs. Having been Colonel of the Welsh Guards for the past forty-six years, I saw at first hand Lord Guthrie's inspiring leadership when he commanded the First Battalion in Berlin and South Armagh from 1977-1980.

These memoirs recount his remarkable forty-two year career that culminated in his appointment as Chief of the Defence Staff, and the first Welsh Guardsman to become head of the Armed Services. It is a record of extraordinary service to the Regiment, the Army and our nation. Lord Guthrie's period of service covered a demanding era in the Army's history, a time of great social change as well as enormous challenges both in the United Kingdom and abroad.

The memoirs are full of humour, reflecting not only the enduring ethos of Welsh Guardsmen, but of Lord Guthrie himself. Anecdotal and unassuming, the memoirs capture the spirit of adventure and the gift of friendship that Lord Guthrie joined the Army for, as well as the pressures of high command.

They also have a strong educational value for anyone who wishes to develop the leadership qualities and personal attributes for a successful career in the Armed forces. He took great care of the men and women under his command and was always sympathetic to the demands faced by Service families.

Field Marshal Lord Guthrie is rightly regarded as the 'Father of the Welsh Guards.' His legacy to the Regiment and Armed Services has been profound. These memoirs are an enduring tribute to a remarkable career.

Preface

Major General Richard Stanford, CB, MBE,
Regimental Lieutenant Colonel, Welsh Guards

Regiments of the British Army are defined by our people. Acts of valour and heroism are studied by the generation currently serving, traditions are passed on, and the great achievements of our forebears are held up as exemplars to follow.

As part of this process, we all look at those who have reached the highest ranks in the army, people who have not only shaped the ethos and *esprit de corps* of the Regiment but of the army as well.

As Welsh Guardsmen, we are greatly privileged to count Field Marshal Lord Guthrie of Craigiebank as the shining light in the history of our Regiment to date. This book is an important record of a part of the history of our Regiment.

The Welsh Guards were formed on 26 February 1915. Field Marshal Charles has served for 61 of our 105-year history: over half the life of the Regiment. He has shaped so much of how our Regiment operates, our ethos and values. He has mentored and trained a generation of officers and non-commissioned officers. He is the Regiment's first officer to reach the rank of Field Marshal.

This excellent memoir of Field Marshal Charles's life recounts many of the experiences of his service, from young platoon commander to Chief of the Defence Staff. Throughout these pages the reader will recognise a great leader who has always cared for those under his command. He stands out as someone who, as a commander, has delegated matters to those he trusts and lets them get on with it. Micro-management is not his way. He has allowed people to learn and develop through making genuine mistakes, while at the same time stamping out incompetence and unprofessionalism. Throughout his career he has been the best of the group; he has commanded and led the best and most professional organisations, be it at platoon, company, battalion, brigade or army level. Those around him have enjoyed working for him and as a result they have thrived.

Such is the modest nature of Field Marshal Charles that he does not fully account for his achievements in developing and encouraging officers who have served under him. The Welsh Guards have had more officers promoted to the rank of Brigadier and above than any other single battalion regiment over the last 50 years. A brigadier is a one-star rank. The Regiment can boast 23 stars – an extraordinary achievement. Many of us who have reached these ranks have been influenced, trained and mentored by Field Marshal Charles.

More broadly within the army, a large number of officers who have served under him have gone on to reach the highest ranks, including Chief of the Defence Staff. This is a combination of Field Marshal Charles picking a strong team around him, as well as developing and training those serving under him. He is an excellent judge of people, with the courage of his convictions to give people a second chance.

There are few officers who have commanded at every level in the army from platoon to army level. Field Marshal Charles has done so during a fascinating period of British history. He joined the British Army in 1959, when Britain's influence was shrinking around the world, and he left in 2001, when that influence was once again expanding. He has served in Aden, Northern Ireland, Cyprus, Kenya, Germany, UK and the New Hebrides. He was General Officer Commanding 1st British Corps when the Soviet Union collapsed and the Cold War ended.

Subsequently, he was closely involved in bringing Eastern European countries into NATO as part of Partnership for Peace. He was closely involved in the Northern Ireland peace process when he was Chief of the General Staff. He was Chief of the General Staff during the UN and NATO operations in Bosnia, and he was Chief of the Defence Staff during the wars in Kosovo and Sierra Leone. He oversaw the modernisation of the army from the Cold War years and shaped the way the army operated, updating doctrine from the Cold War and the streets of Northern Ireland to the conflicts in the Balkans and Sierra Leone. He retired from the army as Chief of Defence Staff in 2001, before the Iraq and Afghanistan wars.

Not only is Field Marshal Charles a Welsh Guardsman, but he also served in the SAS, was Colonel Commandant of the Intelligence Corps and Colonel of The Life Guards. In the latter role he found out rather publicly at the Trooping the Colour parade in 2018, when he was unceremoniously turfed off his horse having fainted under the weight of his uniform and helmet, what many of us discover in less eye-catching circumstances – that we joined the Foot Guards, rather than the Horse Guards, for a reason.

This record of Field Marshal Charles's life has been a great opportunity for people to reconnect, reflect and share stories of our times working for him. Among many other officers, I have had the good fortune to serve Field Marshal Charles. He has developed his subordinates; he has tolerated our mistakes; and he has ensured that no one around him takes life too seriously. He is an extraordinarily impressive man. Everyone who has ever served with him knows that.

He and his wife Kate make a wonderful team and we are so grateful to finally have his many stories, anecdotes and experiences recorded for generations who follow in his footsteps as Welsh Guardsmen.

Date	Rank	Command	Remarks
25 July 1959	Second Lieutenant	Commissioned into the Welsh Guards	
1 June 1961	Lieutenant	Platoon Commander and Assistant Adjutant, London and British Army of the Rhine	
25 July 1965	Captain	Adjutant, 1st Battalion Welsh Guards, Aden	
1966	Captain	Troop Commander, 22 SAS	Served in Aden, Persian Gulf, Malaysia and East Africa
1968	Acting Major	G Squadron Commander, 22 SAS	Persian Gulf and United Kingdom
1970	Major	Prince of Wales Company, 1st Battalion Welsh Guards*	Münster, West Germany

*Prince of Wales Company became The Prince of Wales's Company after HRH The Prince of Wales reviewed the Company on 23 June 1980 and remarked, "I would like this Company henceforth to be known as The Prince of Wales's Company."

Date	Rank	Command	Remarks
1973	Major	Military Assistant to the Chief of the General Staff, General Sir Michael Carver	
1974	Major	Second in Command, 1st Battalion Welsh Guards	London and Cyprus
31 December 1975	Lieutenant Colonel	Brigade Major, Household Division	Appointed MVO (in 1984 reclassified as LVO) following 1977 Silver Jubilee
1977	Lieutenant Colonel	Commanding Officer, 1st Battalion Welsh Guards	Berlin and Northern Ireland
31 December 1979	Colonel	Northern Ireland	Appointed OBE
1980	Colonel	Commander, British Forces New Hebrides	Awarded Queen's Badge of Honour for the New Hebrides
	Colonel	Military Operations in the MOD	
31 December 1981	Brigadier	Commander, 4th Armoured Brigade	Münster, West Germany
1984	Brigadier	Chief of Staff, 1st British Corps	Bielefeld, West Germany
18 January 1986	Major General	General Officer Commanding, 2nd Division and North East District	York

Date	Rank	Command	Remarks
24 November 1987	Major General	Assistant Chief of the General Staff	
2 October 1989	Lieutenant General	General Officer Commanding, 1st British Corps	Appointed KCB in 1990 New Years Honours list
7 January 1992	General	Commander, Northern Army Group and British Army of the Rhine	ADC to HM The Queen on 13 July 1993
13 July 1994	General	Chief of the General Staff	GCB in Birthday Honours, 1994
2 April 1997	General	Chief of the Defence Staff	
2001	General	Retired from the army	
June 2012	Field Marshal		Promoted by HM The Queen

List of Illustrations

All uncredited images form part of the author's collection. All Crown Copyright images are released under the terms of the Open Government Licence v3.0: http://www.nationalarchives.gov.uk/doc/open-government-licence/version/3/

PLATE SECTION IMAGES

Being awarded the Army Rugby Cup by General Sir David Peel Yates.

All togged up as Head of School, 1957.

As Head of School at Harrow with HRH The Prince Philip and HM The Queen, 1957.

Harrow vs Wellington, 1957.

Army Officer Selection Board, 1957.

Captain Poldark, Aden 1966.

The remains of the Parsi cemetery overlooking Aden. (© Ka Wing Chan, https://www.flickr.com/photos/chan_kawing/27031261 102/in/photostream/)

Commanding Prince of Wales Company in Belfast, 1971.

Our wedding day, 11 September 1971.

General Sir Michael Carver on a visit to the Swedish Army, 1973. (Crown Copyright)

Leading the procession on the return from HM The Queen's Silver Jubilee Thanksgiving Service, 1977. (Crown Copyright)

Schleswig-Holstein, November 1977.

My 40th birthday party, 17 November 1978.

St David's Day in Berlin, 1979. (Crown Copyright)

South Armagh, winter 1979/80. (Crown Copyright)

A visit to South Armagh by HRH The Prince of Wales, 1979. (Crown Copyright).

Margaret and Denis Thatcher in South Armagh, 1979. (Crown Copyright)

The 'Coconut War', 1980. (Photo by Alain Dejean/Sygma via Getty Images)

The rebels were a formidable foe.

Handing out medals, 1986. (Crown Copyright)

With Her Majesty The Queen Mother, 1987. (Crown Copyright)

Judging the Gurkha curry competition, 1987.

With my counterpart from the Russian Third Shock Army, 1992. (Crown Copyright)

Elements of the Royal Armoured Corps, First Gulf War, 1990. (Crown Copyright)

Princess Diana visits the British Army of the Rhine, 1992. (Crown Copyright)

A visit to Fort Knox, 1993.

The Calgary Stampede, 1993.

With Robert Cranborne, Parliamentary Under-Secretary of State for Defence, 1993.

Observing tanks from the 17/21st Lancers live firing in Canada. (Photo: Sgt Mark Webster RLC/MOD/Open Government Licence version 1.0)

Meeting the US Secretary of State for Veterans' Affairs, Togo D. West, 1994. (Crown Copyright)

Dancing with the Bulgarian Minister of Defence's wife, 1994.

Qaboos bin Said, Sultan of Oman, 1995.

Flying above the Al Hajar mountain range in Oman, 1995.

With Nicholas Soames, Minister of State for the Armed Forces, at the Helles Memorial, 1995. (Crown Copyright)

Chatting to new recruits in the South African Defence Force, 1996.

On the flight home from South Africa with Richard Stanford, 1996.

Chairing the Executive Committee of the Army Board, 1996. (Crown Copyright)

The author, Admiral Sir Jock Slater and Air Chief Marshal Sir Richard Johns, 1996. (Crown Copyright).

Michael Portillo with senior advisers, 1996. (Crown Copyright)

With the Speaker of the House of Commons, Betty Boothroyd, and
 Edward Garnier, Shadow Attorney General, in 1999. (Crown
 Copyright)
A visit to the Royal New Zealand Army, 2000. (Crown Copyright)
The magnificent Black Watch, 1997.
George Robertson, Lord Carrington and Denis Healey. (Crown
 Copyright)
A visit to Svalbard, 1999.
With Tony Blair and George Robertson in 1998. (Crown Copyright)
Kate and I with the US Chairman of the Joint Chiefs of Staff,
 General Hugh Shelton, and his wife Carolyn, in 1999. (Crown
 Copyright)
A visit in 2000 to the valley of death in the Crimea.
A visit to the BAME recruiting team, 1999. (Crown Copyright)
With President Menem of Argentina, 1998. (Crown Copyright)
The Monument to the Fallen of the Falklands War, Buenos Aires,
 1998. (Crown Copyright)
Speaking at a leadership conference, 1999. (Crown Copyright)
Shaking hands with a splendid veteran from the Crete campaign of
 1941.
With Tony Blair during the crisis in Kosovo, 1999. (Crown
 Copyright)
A Royal Navy Lieutenant Commander bringing me up to speed,
 May 1999. (Crown Copyright)
At Trooping the Colour, 1999. (Crown Copyright).
Ehud Barak, Prime Minister of Israel, and General Shaul Mofaz,
 Chief of the Israeli General Staff in 1999. (Crown Copyright)
One for the ladies, 1999. (Crown Copyright)
Firing the Israeli light machine gun, 1999. (Crown Copyright)
A briefing by Israeli senior officers, 1999. (Crown Copyright)
Clambering aboard the Merkava in 1999. (Crown Copyright)
The view from the Golan Heights in 1999. (Crown Copyright)
With the Commander of the People's Liberation Army (PLA).
 (Crown Copyright)
Outside the 'Forbidden City', Beijing, 2000.
A visit to Chateau Pomerol with Hugh Shelton, US Chairman of the
 Joint Chiefs of Staff, and General Jean-Pierre Kelche, Chief of the
 French Defence Staff, in 2000.

President Musharraf of Pakistan. (Crown Copyright)

Admiral Boyce, my successor as Chief of the Defence Staff, on my right in 2000. (Crown Copyright)

Training for Trooping the Colour, 2000.

With Brigadier David Richards and Peter Westmacott, Foreign and Commonwealth Under-Secretary of State. (Crown Copyright)

Horses of The Life Guards at Trooping the Colour in 2000. (Crown Copyright)

With President Eduard Shevardnadze. (Crown Copyright)

Inspecting the Passing out Parade at Sandhurst, 1999. (Crown Copyright)

With Harry Legge-Bourke at the Welsh Guards Memorial in the Falklands, 2000. (Crown Copyright)

General Hugh Shelton presents me with the award of an Officer of the Legion of Merit in 2001. (Crown Copyright)

A Farewell to Arms.

'Civvy Street' beckons.

With Lord Robertson and Lord Carrington, 2001.

Playing tennis; a perfect antidote to the stresses of a busy working life.

The Gold Sticks, 2009. (Crown Copyright)

Welsh Guards on the Queen's Birthday Parade in 2008. (Crown Copyright)

With the Prince of Wales in 2013 during the Walk on Wales.

Enjoying a happy retirement with Kate, 2014.

MAP

Prologue

'*The Pharaoh's chickens*'

THE ADEN EMERGENCY 1963–67

Aden was a protectorate of the British Empire. It is now part of Yemen. In 1963–67 there was an armed insurgency against British Forces stationed there.

*The Parsi cemetery above the town of Aden's
Crater district, May 1967.*

By midday, the three bodies laid out in the shadow of the Tower of Silence in the Parsi cemetery had been picked clean. The vultures, known locally as 'the Pharaoh's chickens', their bellies full, soared above us in tight circles searching for the next ride from the thermals rising from the ridge of the crater.

My squadron commander's last words to me before the operation came back to me:

Charles, full marks for imagination. It could just work. The rebels won't suspect even the SAS to lie up in the Parsi cemetery. But we must know what's going on in the warrens inside Aden's Crater district. You'll have a clear view. I don't envy you. The heat will be fierce, every bit of shadow will count, and water resupply will be difficult. It will be hard graft, but you'll have a vulture's eye view of things.

He turned away from the map that we had been poring over. A wintry smile crossed his face as he gazed at the Jebel's desolate landscape.

I had been a troop commander in the SAS for six months, but we had yet to venture into the foetid alleyways of Aden from the mountainous Radfan region. Every tribesman thought himself a sultan there, and would snipe away at leisure before scuttling back amongst the rocks.

Some time before I arrived, an SAS patrol had been ambushed in the Al Hajaf hills. Two of them had been killed. Their mutilated bodies were recovered, but their heads later appeared on public display in the town of Sana'a in Yemen.

As the time drew closer to Britain's formal withdrawal in June 1967, the Federal Regular Army (FRA) and the police, mindful of retribution and the settling of scores, switched their allegiance. A group of skilled assassins also began targeting our Special Branch officers and their contacts.

Our tactics had to change to meet the rising levels of rebel violence and aggression. The Regiment had begun to conduct its first urban counter-terrorism operations in Aden town. They became known as *Keeni-Meeni* jobs, a Swahili phrase used to describe the sinuous, unseen movement of a snake in long grass.

"Charles, I leave it to you," my squadron commander said. "But I want you and your men to blend into the local scenery, establish an observation post (OP) and report back what's going on in the old quarter in the Crater district. The British withdrawal from Aden has become quite messy. You have 48 hours to come up with a plan."

By luck, I'd had a chance conversation with Kaamran, a Zoroastrian. The Zoroastrians, who follow the Parsi religion, came from India to join the British Garrison and administration after Indian Independence in 1947.

Kaamran worked as a trusted handyman around our base. His cousin had recently died and he told me that, in line with custom, his cousin had been laid out in the Parsi cemetery at last light at a *Dakhma*, or Tower of Silence. This was a circular raised structure built for excarnation – that is, the leaving of bodies to be cleaned of all earthly impurities by scavengers or vultures. It was, he said, an individual's final act of charity.

The Parsi cemetery was a place of reverence. It was unvisited, spooky, certainly macabre, and built on the lip of Aden's Crater district. It immediately struck me as a good place to play dead and blend in with the local scenery. We looked pretty cadaverous anyway after six weeks in the Radfan, and we could keep a close eye on any mischief below. Given my orders to get cracking within 48 hours, I wasted no time.

We conducted a final kit check before we set off, and I thought about my fellow patrol members. An SAS patrol would normally comprise four members: a demolitions expert, a signaller, a linguist and a medic. Like most in the SAS, they were self-sufficient, strongly individualistic but utterly reliable in a group.

Narayan, a Fijian, was broad of limb, impossibly strong and wonderfully calm. He had just one limitation in that he snored like a stampede – a potentially fatal failing in a close observation post.

Jock was a Highland Scot, the son of an estate gamekeeper. Jock's intuitive feel for ground, distance, fieldcraft and marksmanship was characteristic of his kith and kin. With a

9mm pistol, he could put six rounds through a playing card at 15 yards. As I was later to discover in Dhofar, he was a good deal less squeamish than me.

The last member of the patrol was Wigley, a North Wales man from my own Regiment, the Welsh Guards, a man of few words with a hint of 'otherness' that you often find in the peoples of the desolate and rugged area of Snowdonia. With a thumbs-up from the helicopter pilot, we embarked for the short hop to our drop-off point some 2 miles short of the Parsi cemetery. We began our *Keeni-Meeni* approach.

The furnace-like heat of the day had barely lessened. It must have been close to 50 degrees Celsius as we clambered over boulder after boulder to reach the lip of the crater. The path, built by the Persians at the height of the Parthian Empire in around 100 BC, was nothing more than rubble. The climb was quite the hardest physical challenge that I have ever had to endure in my military career. I was alarmed to see that, by the time we reached the cemetery, we had drunk most of our water. Resupply was not for another 24 hours.

Over 60 years have now passed since the Parsi cemetery and my time in Aden. It was described then as the Last Battle of the British Empire. Though my memory has become a little hazy, I have never forgotten those days in Aden. They were formative in my career, and what I learned there was as relevant then as it was when I became Britain's Chief of the Defence Staff (CDS).

I learned a great deal about soldiering. I learned what keeps soldiers happy and motivated, and that the profession of arms, regardless of the ever-growing impact of technology, is essentially one of human endeavour.

Above all, I learned that to manage and lead others, you must first learn how to manage yourself.

No blueprint exists on leadership. A few principles hold true: courting popularity ends in failure; so does using the power of your rank or position. A lot will depend on the situation in which you find yourself and the time-honoured adage of knowing your audience. Using personal influence is fine, but to do that effectively, you need to know what makes different people tick. You have to be able to sniff the wind and be astute to what is being said and the things going on around you.

If I am proud of anything in my own leadership style, it is that I have inspired people to grow. I have seen officers and non-commissioned officers with whom I have served go on to achieve fulfilling careers.

As it turned out, Aden was far from being the last battle of the British Empire. In 2020 we are still raking over the embers of what became known as 'The Great Game', with the formation of the East India Company in 1600.

As my career has progressed, I have observed and played my part in helping Britain retreat from its empire with as much grace as possible, and to find a new role in the world.

I have been reluctant to write my memoirs, not least because I have been extremely fortunate, and I had no wish to break the 'Omerta' – the code of silence – in an honourable profession where many have lost their lives, or continue to suffer to this day the physical and mental scars of service to their country.

I should also add that I am on record (*Daily Telegraph*, 19 April 2000) as saying, "When I retire I certainly will not be writing my memoirs. I'm sick of generals who write about their experiences in the Army. It's a betrayal and should not be allowed. I'll never write about my career and I don't think others should either."

Now that I am in my 82nd year, I feel the time has come to write about the good fortunes of my life and career without betraying the confidences of others. Memoirs are different from autobiography in the sense they do not need to be chronological. But they do have to have a certain flow, otherwise the reader will find themselves hopping about wondering what decade they are in. There were periods in my career that I consciously chose to leave out because they were plain dull – Assistant Chief of the General Staff (ACGS) was one; or because they added little to a reader's enjoyment or curiosity. My time as Corps Commander in the British Army of the Rhine (BAOR) differed little from my period as a brigade or divisional commander. The big step, and one which I decided to write about, was my appointment as Commander-in-Chief BAOR and Commander Northern Army Group. With a British, Dutch, Belgian and German corps under command, as well as 3rd US Corps in reserve, I became as much a diplomat as a soldier.

My 42 years in the army were spent during a fascinating, troublesome and complex period in our nation's history. It was a time of great social change, when the old certainties and innate conservatism of the British Army had to change as well. I was privileged to be part of that change and to make the army as professional as possible when money was invariably scarce. Our country has become fairer and more tolerant. I was always mindful that the conditions of our soldiers, both men and women and their families, had to mirror those of society. We have come a long way since the day I joined the army to overcome prejudice and bigotry.

Despite my reluctance to write anything down, my family, friends and my Regiment have convinced me that I have good stories to tell, and some common-sense advice to share.

For those who wish to build a career in the army, or make a success of their lives, I hope this may be helpful.

I have also had the privilege of meeting an eclectic range of characters who taught me how to do things and, on occasion, how not to do things.

Above all, I have written these memoirs for my descendants. I am proud to be a field marshal and I trust that they, too, will be proud to have had a field marshal in their family.

Harrow

Harrow 1953–1957, more than just the sum of its days.

Fate, as I have often found, is a matter of choice, not chance. It was only towards the end of my time at Harrow in 1957 that I found myself having to take the first real choice of my life. To humour myself during my skirmishes with academic classwork, I had become an avid reader of C.S. Forester's *Hornblower* books, the fictional adventures of a Royal Naval officer in the Napoleonic Wars. Contemporary films like *In Which We Serve* starring Noel Coward, and Anthony Quayle in *The Battle of the River Plate* further sparked my enthusiasm for a career in the navy. Like Anthony Quayle playing Commodore Harwood, I saw myself on the bridge of HMS *Ajax* giving orders to engage the German cruiser *Admiral Graf Spee* and keeping true to Nelson's dictum before the battle of Trafalgar, "No Captain can do very wrong if he places his ship alongside that of the enemy." I sought the spirit of adventure, travel, sport and the friendship of like-minded people.

In those days, there was no such thing as a careers master, let alone careers advice. Harrow's masters might give you a steer but that was about it. Many boys would join the professions of their fathers or, if they were from the landed gentry, had little ambition beyond a leisured life running their estates. My father was a successful businessman, but I had no inclination to be something in the City. I had expressed my interest in a naval career to Major Jim Morgan, known as 'Monkey' Morgan. 'Monkey' reputedly had only one testicle, though how anyone knew that I never found out. Monkey taught me mathematics, and he also ran the School Combined Cadet Force (CCF).

The Harrow CCF, as in most traditional public schools, sought to encourage its pupils to join one of the services. Many of my friends had lost their fathers in the Second World War. It was understandable that they should seek the spirit of their lost fathers in a service career. Monkey arranged for me to go and visit the navy in Portsmouth. A university friend of his was now Captain of HMS *Dainty*, a Daring-class destroyer.

HMS *Dainty* didn't strike me as a promising name for a destroyer, and my visit quickly dispelled any idea I might have had of standing on a ship's bridge, enveloped in a duffel coat, peering through a pair of Barr and Stroud naval binoculars and sinking the enemy. The Captain, whose name I cannot remember, was a sparse figure with a shock of marmalade-coloured hair.

Monkey Morgan had told me that the Captain had been on the Arctic convoys during the war. The Captain's laconic manner, and his eyes that appeared fixed on some far point on the horizon, suggested difficult and trying times in his past. After he had asked me a little about myself and if I had any family members who had served in the navy, he remarked that we should now go and see where the action took place.

The action, if you could describe it as such, took place below the waterline. As we made our way down into the bowels of the ship, I noted the grey but largely cheerful faces of the ship's crew. Two huge boilers and two steam turbines dominated the engine room. I dimly remember the Captain firing statistics at me: "Displacement 4,000 tons, new Squid anti-submarine mortars, 34 knots, enough fuel oil to take us to Malta and back…"

I was at a loss for words and mumbled, "How do you command the ship when engaging the enemy?"

"Well, that's the easy part," he said. "More or less down to pressing a few buttons and radar fire control, Bofors 40mm cannon and 21-inch torpedoes. I sit down here and let the gunnery and weapons officers get on with it. Not too troublesome, really."

I took the train back to London knowing that the navy was not for me. I wanted excitement, my reach to exceed my grasp, and though many years later as CDS I was full of admiration and respect for Britain's Senior Service, I realised then my temperament was not really suited to it.

In the evening of my memory, I often return to Harrow. I had been to a prep school which had close links to Winchester College. My father was a Wykehamist and naturally was keen that I should follow him there. My prep school Headmaster with admirable foresight persuaded my father that Harrow would better suit my talents, adding that he did not see me in later years in the higher reaches of the judiciary or tax planning. That was a little unfair to Winchester, which has produced many fine soldiers.

Harrow School's ethos was then, as it still is today, "To prepare boys for a life of leadership, service and personal fulfilment". As I penned these memoirs, I thought about those principles and how they had formed my life after Harrow.

Until the age of 15, I was no different from most boys: argumentative, unkempt, the usual maddening teenager. Beating and 'fagging' (the running of errands for senior boys) was still going on at Harrow in the '50s. Both practices died out soon after.

My contemporary and close friend to this day, Dale Vargas, who went on to teach and become a housemaster at Harrow, and who wrote *The Timeline History of Harrow School*, said that fagging developed at the great public schools to teach boys how to treat their servants fairly at home. As we never had servants, the arcane practice was lost on me.

On the cusp of 16, I was, however, beaten for some trifling misdemeanour by the head of house, who was 18. He didn't amount to much as a leader or head of house, and I think he just wanted to establish his authority over me. It is an odd thing to say that I was indebted to this individual. Not because he forced me to wake my ideas up, but because it awoke in me a belief that I was to carry throughout my career: that the inappropriate use of authority is a false step.

Like many boys, I drew great personal fulfilment through sport, particularly rugby football. It has remained with me throughout my life. With the arrival in 1950 of A.L. Warr, an Oxford blue and England International, Harrow Rugby enjoyed a remarkable revival, unbeaten in 1954. We lost just one match in 1955 and 1956 when I captained the team, playing alongside Robin Butler, who was later to become Head of the Home Civil Service under Prime Ministers Thatcher, Major and Blair. Playing competitive sport taught me all the usual attributes of teamwork, communication, resilience and losing with grace. It also gave me the priceless gift of friendship and a much better understanding of how to instil confidence in others.

Everyone needs a hinterland, a backdrop to their lives apart from the love of family and friends, which gives them somewhere to travel to in life's uncertain moments. My love of drama and music started at Harrow, where the tradition of the annual Shakespeare play in the Speech Room started as a result of a German bomber dumping its bombs on the school in 1940. The Speech Room's roof was blown off, giving Harrow's legendary Head of Drama, Ronnie Watkins, an opportunity to replicate the Elizabethan open-air Globe Theatre.

My first foray as an actor was as Peaseblossom in *A Midsummer Night's Dream*. I was dressed rather suggestively, attracting whistles from the boys and a kiss on the lips from Blossom, played by James Fox, whose acting talent marked him out for the later stardom he went on to achieve.

My fondness for opera, which came later in life, was inspired by Harrow's preference for large-scale choral works. After morning Chapel, the whole school would trudge across to the Speech Room to rehearse in our choral unison role. Many years later, while commanding my Regiment on a particularly demanding operational tour in South Armagh, I was listening one evening in my room to 'The Chorus of the Hebrew Slaves' from Verdi's opera *Nabucco*, quite oblivious to the fact that we were under mortar fire from the IRA. Amusingly, and to my unintentional credit, word went round the Regiment that the commanding officer was a pretty cool hand if he could listen to opera while under mortar fire. 'The Chorus of the Hebrew Slaves' was to become my first choice of record when I was invited by Sue Lawley as a guest on *Desert Island Discs* in 2000, when I was CDS.

Harrow may not have been particularly enlightened in its outlook in the 1950s, but it did allow boys a considerable amount of freedom and responsibility in how the school's daily business was run. The masters were there to teach, and the housemasters there to ensure their individual trains kept on the tracks. But they rarely interfered.

The Headmaster in my time was Dr James, a double first in classics, and known as 'Jankers'. He was politically astute, a fine delegator, and seemed to know exactly what was going on without apparently leaving his study. His study reflected his temperament: neat, low-key and conservative. He had the gift of appearing to have time for everyone.

Before my final year, Dr James called me in to his study and asked if I would like to be Head of School. We had struck up a rapport because he seemed to think that, as captain of rugby, I knew what was going on in the school. He would often call me in to his study for a chat to hear, as he described it, "the news from the bazaar". I enjoyed these chats as it allowed me to miss lessons.

I remember on one occasion the worthy but uninspiring school chaplain knocked on the door, peering round to say, "Headmaster, may I have a word about next Sunday's sermon?"

Jankers replied, "Not now, Chaplain. By all means pop in later, but I'm talking to Guthrie about something much more important."

Ironically, it was more important. The Headmaster said he would like me to organise the Queen's visit the following term – the Lent term of 1957. It was the first time the Queen had visited the school, and she was the first monarch to do so since King George V. Like any good delegator, the Headmaster set clear expectations with advice that the Press should be kept at arm's length, that no boy should be seen snivelling in the corridors, and that time spent in rehearsal would ensure success.

The Headmaster had a pathological distrust of journalists, particularly those from the *Mail* and *Express* whose sole purpose, he thought, was to unearth any scandal they could. Given the visit's importance – Prince Philip was to accompany the Queen –

I knew we had to work in partnership with the Press, an experience which served me well throughout my army career.

The visit was considered sufficiently newsworthy to be filmed by Pathé News, the popular producer of film and newsreels at the time. Bob Danvers-Walker, the unmistakable 'Empire' voice of Pathé News, gave a characteristically upbeat commentary to the day's events, though he was a little lost in his commentary when I arranged for the Queen and Prince Philip to watch the boys milking cows in the school farm.

I overheard Prince Philip remarking to one boy, "Used to this at home, are you?" to which the boy replied, "Not exactly, Sir, we live in Belgravia."

The day finished in the Speech Room with the boys singing 'Forty Years On', one of the great traditional Harrow Songs. At the end I called for "Three Cheers for Her Majesty!" The response was resounding.

It was a demanding task for a 17-year-old boy to organise such a visit, but I was thankful for the ordeal, as exactly 20 years later it was left to me to organise much of the ceremonial for the Queen's Silver Jubilee celebrations while serving as the Brigade Major (Chief of Staff) for The Household Division. The Queen reminded me at the time of the Silver Jubilee that she had met me before and recalled her visit to Harrow with affection. She had, she said, been intrigued to see what life was like in a boys' boarding school.

Not all aspects of Harrow life were deemed opportune. Flogging and fagging, the former ceasing in the 1970s and the latter phased out in the 1980s, were not part of Her Majesty's visit programme.

For role models on leadership and courage, Harrow was blessed. We had produced seven prime ministers, including Peel, Palmerston, Baldwin and Churchill, and the first Prime

Minister of India, Jawaharlal Nehru. Fifty-five Harrovians fought at Waterloo under Wellington, Britain's greatest military commander, who has always been a hero of mine.

Banners of the 19 Old Harrovian winners of the Victoria Cross hung in the Harrow War Memorial building. Just under half of the 2,917 Harrovians who served in the Great War were killed or wounded.

Field Marshal Alexander of Tunis, an Old Harrovian, was an inspiration. His son, Brian, was a contemporary of mine. Leadership and courage were in the fabric of the institution and I could not help but absorb its weave.

Like most school corps at the time, the Harrow Rifle Corps was unimaginative and unenlightened, with a dreary emphasis on drill, cleaning belts, polishing shoes and the parade ground.

It is a rule of thumb of mine that boys who flourish in their school corps are a menace if they go on to pursue a career in the services. The head of house who had beaten me when I was 16 encouraged me to join the corps, saying, "No boy will be the worse in the after-life for being able to change step and slow march properly."

That might be true enough, but I have always felt that school sport, at whatever level, was a much better preparation for leadership, team-working and instilling confidence.

There is a rather touching scene in the film *Young Winston* when the Headmaster of Harrow, the Revd James Welldon (played by Jack Hawkins) accepts Churchill into the school even though Churchill had submitted a blank exam paper. Welldon's foresight gave Harrow its greatest son, and a sense that anything and everything was possible.

Churchill returned most years to attend Harrow Songs in the Speech Room, even in 1942 when our fortunes in the war seemed bleak. As Churchill himself said of Harrow Songs,

"They shine through the memories of men... they cheer and enlighten us... they are, on the whole, the most precious inheritance of all Harrovians."

When I was CDS, a politician remarked to me that the army placed too much emphasis on singing, music and bands, and we should get rid of a good many to save money. I firmly put him down, telling him that regimental bands and stirring marching music were fundamental to a soldier's morale and sense of belonging.

I had tea with Winston Churchill in the Headmaster's study on one occasion when I was Head of School. Inevitably, he asked me what I intended to do with my life. It was before my forlorn visit to Portsmouth and I replied that I had set my heart on a naval career. A faint smile crossed his face, but he said nothing in return.

By my last term at Harrow, my thoughts had turned towards a career in the army. My uncle, Victor Llewelyn, had served in the Welsh Guards and said he would have a word in the right ear. Victor's first cousin, Desmond Llewelyn, went on to become Q: "Now pay attention, 007", in the early Bond films.

The right ear belonged to Colonel Luke Dimsdale OBE MC, who commanded the Regiment. Colonel Dimsdale was a direct descendant of Catherine the Great's personal physician, Thomas Dimsdale. He had pioneered the prevention of smallpox by inoculation, and had been invited to Russia to inoculate Catherine the Great. For his service to the Empress, Dimsdale received, in today's money, £2m, an annual pension of £150,000 and £500,000 in expenses. He was also made a Baron of the Russian Empire.

The interview process could not have been more different from my experience in the bowels of HMS *Dainty*. I was taken to lunch at the Guards Club in Charles Street, Mayfair, by Christopher Thursby-Pelham, known affectionately as 'Thirsty-Pelican', and Peter de Zulueta who was equerry to Prince Philip, the then-Colonel of the Welsh Guards. As I was plied with gin and tonic after gin and tonic, my answers to their questions became increasingly incoherent. I remember saying I wanted to play rugby for the Welsh Guards and win the Army Cup. I was sick on the train back to Harrow.

A few days later, I received a letter from Colonel Dimsdale informing me that the Welsh Guards would be delighted to accept me as an officer, provided that I passed the War Office Selection Board for Sandhurst and that my exam results that summer were "along the right lines".

I showed the letter to my housemaster, Johnny Greenstock, an Oxford triple blue who had also played cricket for Worcestershire. Needless to say, he was much more interested in sporting prowess than academic performance. We both agreed that "along the right lines" meant anything above a straight fail. I was keen to pass selection for Sandhurst as soon as I left Harrow. I was determined to get on with my life and make my mark.

Many years later, I became President of the Harrow Association and I was invited to introduce the guest speaker at the Churchill Songs at the Royal Albert Hall in 2009. Some 6,000 Harrovians and their families were present. The guest speaker was a star of stage and film and an Old Harrovian, Benedict Cumberbatch. I made rather a hash of my introduction and introduced him as Benedict 'Cumberbitch'.

Afterwards, I made my apologies to Benedict, who said to me, "But Field Marshal, how clever of you to refer to me as Cumberbitch. My adoring female fan club are known as Cumberbitches."

2

The Welsh Guards

*A family Regiment that has given me so
much over my life.*

I am proud to be a Welsh Guardsman. I joined the Regiment
in 1959, and when I said farewell to regimental soldiering
just over 20 years later after my time as commanding officer
ended, it was a dispiriting moment. The Welsh Guards had
become a second family. They gave me the lasting gift of
friendship. They taught me how to lead.

There are many fine regiments in the British Army with
proud records, but there is no better soldier than a well-led
Welsh Guardsman. There is a healthy rivalry in the British
Army, and army contemporaries would fiercely defend their
own regiments. I would respond, and I believe this to be true,
that to understand the formidable fighting spirit and character
of the Welsh soldier, you only have to look at the Welsh rugby
team. On their day, with their tails up and the Welsh *hwyl*
focused, they are unbeatable. The Welsh temperament may
be mercurial and things can go awry pretty quickly, but they
respond well to a steadying hand and consistent leadership.
The officer who shouts, or who is susceptible to histrionics
and is inconsistent in his personal dealings, will fail.

My two years at the Royal Military Academy, Sandhurst, from 1957 to 1959 taught me a good deal, except for practical experience. The rigours of my Harrow schooling had stood me in good stead. I smile when I read of some former public school pupil who ends up doing 'time', remarking that prison was really quite manageable if you'd been to an English public school. I did not find Sandhurst too taxing, but it gave me a sense of where my strengths and limitations lay. I made many good friends, a number of whom went on to the highest reaches of the army. I played for the academy rugby team and became a much better horseman. I developed a healthy regard for Guards non-commissioned officers who more or less ran the place and took a genuine pride in educating and training Britain's future officers.

There was time for fun as well. I took great delight in running the gauntlet of returning to Sandhurst before first parade after visits to London to attend deb parties, or see my girlfriend in my beloved Ford Anglia. On the night before the Passing-Out Parade, this nearly saw the end of my army career before it had started. I had returned to Sandhurst in the early hours with a contemporary and good friend, John Wilsey. To our dismay, we found the doors locked to our college. John, who went on to become a four-star general with a flair for covert operations, spotted a route to our rooms up a couple of drainpipes and along a thin ledge to an open window. My parents, none the wiser for the early-morning escapade, beamed with pride as I was commissioned in the Welsh Guards.

I have never been a great admirer of Napoleon, though I am sympathetic to his much-quoted riposte: "I know he's a good general, but is he lucky?"

On joining the Welsh Guards, and in my formative years in the Regiment, I was indeed lucky. I served under some fine commanding officers. They had all conducted themselves with courage and distinction in the Second World War. I think it was because of this wartime experience that they went out of their way to educate young officers through personal example. After all, they had been young officers in the war. Nobody stood on ceremony then. Everyone, whatever his rank, was part of a common endeavour.

All the Regiment's senior officers were different characters and all had different attributes, but I learnt something of lasting value from each. Their willingness to talk to, listen to, and guide those under their command never left me. I was also fortunate in having an outstanding platoon sergeant when I took command of my first platoon of men. He was called Sergeant Bill Elcock. He was a proud Shropshire man, and I could not have asked for a better man to help me understand the men under my command and avoid the usual pitfalls that trip up young officers.

My desire for travel and the spirit of adventure was met early on. I had only been in the Battalion a few months when we were transported by air to Libya for *Exercise Starlight One*. We were part of 1st Guards Brigade, and the airlift was the biggest air transportation exercise since the war. Before Colonel Gaddafi's *coup d'état*, Libya was ruled by King Idris I. The king had seen what had happened in Egypt when Nasser overthrew the monarchy. He saw the US and the UK as his insurance policy.

My admiration for the British Eighth Army in the Second World War's North Africa campaign grew as I saw at first hand the conditions they had fought under. The heat of the day was gruelling, the nights glacial, the terrain a torment for a young officer's map-reading skills. We finished the six-day exercise with a brigade dawn attack on the Jebel Akhdar, a mountainous plateau 3,000 feet up in north-eastern Libya.

What I did learn from the experience was how tricky it is to move troops to an assembly area within given time limits over harsh terrain. It was a useful lesson. The Guardsmen, most of whom had never been abroad, were pretty cheery throughout and even more so when they were given 24 hours' rest and recuperation in Benghazi. As one Guardsman said to me rather laconically as we boarded the flight home, "Quite a bit more lively than Merthyr Tydfil on a Saturday night, and a few tidy women. Mind you, the beer wasn't too swift." ('Tidy' is a Welsh expression for good-looking.)

John Miller, my first commanding officer, finished his period of command after Libya. He had won the DSO for his leadership and the MC for bravery during the Normandy campaign in 1944. Behind a carapace of a studied reserve, resulting, I think, from an unhappy childhood and fierce wartime experience, he was the kindest and most supportive of men.

He had a rather disconcerting habit of taking an inordinately long time to answer a question. He would often sit with the young officers at lunchtime and I might ask a question. He would appear to ignore it, which was unnerving, and then five minutes later would say, "Now, Charles, in answer to your earlier comment..." He had the great gift, a rare quality amongst those holding senior commands, of not insisting that everyone had to be busy all the time. "There's a time and place to be busy, to have a sense of urgency and that's at the sharp end in battle", he once remarked to me, before going on to say, "You're showing promise as a horseman, and I want you to concentrate on your riding a bit more. I have a couple of horses I can lend you."

The loaned horses were a good deal slower than his Olympic thoroughbreds. His command – "Now, follow me"– was unsettling.

I was honoured to give the address at John's memorial service at the Guards Chapel in 2006.

Everything I joined the army for – travel, sport, excitement and friendship – was plentiful in the early 1960s. After John Miller's advice, I did concentrate on both riding and polo, and we won the Combermere Cup at the Guards polo club in 1960. The Colonel of the Regiment, Prince Philip, captained our foursome. Besides myself, the other two players were Richard Watt, whose son, Reddy, was to become an outstanding polo player and my Adjutant in Berlin and South Armagh, then later a four-star general; and Mervyn Fox-Pitt, uncle of the successful Olympic rider, William Fox-Pitt. Prince Philip, hugely competitive and energetic, kept me up to the mark, shouting whenever he missed a shot, "Where the hell's Guthrie?"

Rather more was expected of me when it came to rugby. I had captained Harrow and played for English Schoolboys. I had joined a Welsh regiment whose nation drew inspiration and self-confidence through the success of its rugby team. The Army Rugby Cup began in 1907, and from the time of the Regiment's formation in 1915 and the end of the Great War when the competition began again, we have won the cup 13 times and been runners-up 12 times. In the years that I played, 1960–64, we won the cup three times, once in 1963 under my captaincy. Of course, being a good rugby player doesn't make up for being a good officer, but it gives you a certain amount of standing in the bazaar. And as I have said to many young officers, any sport that adds to your resilience and leadership skills has to be a good thing.

An unexpected benefit from my time as a young officer in Chelsea Barracks was an introduction to opera. There was a need for extras at the Royal Opera House (ROH) for the big productions. Queen Victoria, many years before, had declared that the extras were too weedy looking and the ROH should use strapping Guardsmen from London's barracks. Equity, the UK trade union for the creative arts, didn't like the idea at all, but at the time their hands were tied. Usually, around 25 volunteers were required. The going rate was 30 shillings (£32 in today's money) for two hours and 50 minutes. Anything above three hours in length was double the money. A quiet word with the production team's electrician to "short the fuse" meant we invariably went over three hours.

It was a great privilege and fun to be in an opera like Puccini's *Tosca*, with the legendary Maria Callas and Tito Gobbi where, as extras, we acted as the firing squad. Maria Callas made quite an impression on me. She gave it her all. As a Guardsman said to me before we made our appearance, "Goodness me, Sir, she looks all done in. I hope we're not going to get as knackered as that." I have had a lifelong love of opera ever since.

We had begun a three-year tour of Germany in November 1960 as part of 4th Guards Brigade. We were based in Hubbelrath, Düsseldorf, originally home to the Wehrmacht's 64th Flak Regiment. We were part of the newly created Allied Command Europe (ACE) mobile force, ready to deploy quickly to any of NATO's flanks to head off any Soviet aggression. To test this concept, we provided the British contribution to a huge exercise in Greece in October 1962 with our NATO partners from the USA, Belgium and West Germany. I remember talking to a German officer who had fought on the Eastern Front who had me spellbound as he described placing anti-tank mines under the Red Army's tanks as they overran the German trenches.

It was my first joint exercise with our allies. It was by no means plain sailing. Once again, I saw the challenges of moving large numbers of troops to the right place at the right time and with the right equipment. I also observed the difficulties in building multi-national teams. Fortunately, I had good cause to remember the lessons learnt years later when I became Chief of Staff in the British Army of the Rhine (BAOR) in Germany.

The Regiment was again blessed with a commanding officer who, despite his enormous size and obvious lack of fitness, knew his profession. His name was Vivian Wallace, affectionately known as the 'Bomber', a sobriquet he had earned because of his ability to throw hand grenades long distances with unerring accuracy. Vivian, like John Miller, had fought with great courage in the Normandy campaign.

Vivian also took the time to talk to young officers, and he once took me and a brother officer to dinner at his favourite restaurant near the barracks. He ordered his customary dish of Chateaubriand, an enormous serving of about 2 pounds of fillet steak with rich Béarnaise sauce, usually sufficient for at least three or four people. We were three.

The head waiter politely enquired, *"Natürlich, Herr Colonel, ist das Chateaubriand für drei Personen?"* to which the Bomber replied, *"Nein, Dummkopf, für eine Person!"*

For some time after that, and rather unfairly to an otherwise highly professional officer, there was a photograph of the Bomber wearing his 53-inch Sam Browne belt above the pudding trolley at the Guards Depot Officers' Mess at Pirbright in Surrey.

In June 1963, Peter Leuchars took over command from Vivian Wallace. Peter was one of the finest officers I have served under. Before he joined the Welsh Guards, he had won an exhibition to read history at Balliol College, Oxford. He had also fought with distinction and some degree of luck in the war. A shell failed to explode under him, he was shot in the chest, and a German paratrooper's gun jammed in the nick of time.

Peter was a brilliant trainer and set up the Leuchars Cup, an inter-company patrolling competition testing teamwork, endurance, fieldcraft and platoon spirit. The competition was to prepare us for our operational tour of Aden in 1965. It remains an annual event, subject to the Regiment's commitments. Peter went on to be a major general but he should have gone much higher. He was rather a loner and apt to speak his mind to senior officers. In my experience, there is no harm in speaking your mind to senior officers, but only once you have earned their trust and you know you are on solid ground.

Travel and the spirit of adventure, and in one instance misadventure, carried on throughout 1963 and 1964. The mid-summer of 1963 saw me in Norway on a training exercise where I managed to contract meningitis. Fortunately, a Norwegian doctor recognised it for what it was, and I was casevaced to London. I recovered quickly enough.

I spent an enjoyable three weeks getting over my setback with my mother in Menton on the French Riviera before re-joining the Regiment. They were fortuitously also in Southern France as guests of the French Army. The year ended with an exercise in Schleswig-Holstein near the Baltic coast. The icy Baltic wind and freezing rain were numbing.

The year 1964 saw a return to public duties in London as we prepared for the Regiment's 50th anniversary and an operational tour in Aden the following year. We did, however, squeeze in a memorable two months' training with the Canadian Army at Camp Wainwright, Alberta. On this occasion, we spent our R&R at the Calgary Stampede and

Rodeo. Several Guardsmen had a crack at the rodeo and one, the Battalion's scrum-half, hung on to his bucking horse for 60 seconds – most accomplished horsemen last half the time – before he was hurled to the ground. It was his first time on a horse, and he was cheered to the rafters.

So ended my carefree days as a Welsh Guards subaltern. In 1965, I was appointed Adjutant, the principal staff officer responsible for the Battalion's daily administration and discipline. By then, I saw I could make a go of things and a successful army career was within my grasp.

As I look back on those formative years as a young officer, I realise how much I owed to Welsh Guards officers, non-commissioned officers and Guardsmen who, by example, taking a personal interest, or through observation, instilled in me the confidence to master my profession. When I was selected for promotion to Lieutenant Colonel and a command appointment, I had the privilege of choosing the SAS or the Welsh Guards. I never gave it a moment's thought.

3

Aden

*1st Battalion Welsh Guards deploys to Salerno
camp in the Crown colony of Aden as Britain
announces its formal withdrawal. In the power
vacuum that developed, chaos ensued.*

Aden was a lost cause and not worth the life of a single Welsh
Guardsman. The Regiment's experience there, however, was
not a lost cause. The young officers and non-commissioned
officers found their time in Aden exciting and formative.
For the Guardsmen, many of whom had never left the UK
before, it was just as exhilarating, with the frisson that they
were facing an unpredictable but real threat from the tribal
guerrillas. All great regiments, like great institutions, develop
a collective memory from which they draw their strength and
build resilience. Aden gave us the leaders to face the challenges
of the next two decades, particularly in Northern Ireland.

I also owe a great deal to my time in Aden. I was appointed
Adjutant, the Battalion's principal staff officer, a role which
put me at the centre of things. More importantly, I worked for
a commanding officer, Philip Ward, whose gifts and qualities
far transcended those of a soldier. Philip's influence on my

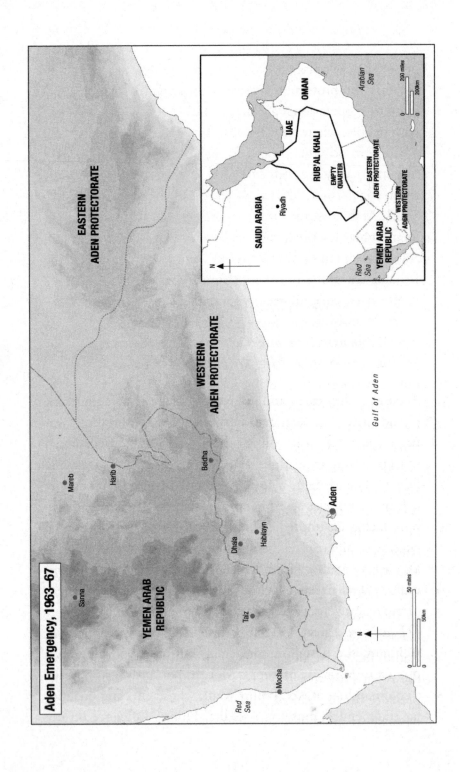

Aden Emergency, 1963–67

personal development and career was profound. He taught me that the profession of arms was a great deal more than mastering operational art. It was how you treated and dealt with people, whatever their position or rank, that mattered.

Close to 60 years on, most people do not know (or have forgotten) why we were in Aden, a British Crown Colony from 1937–1963, located in the south of Yemen, and the South Arabian seaboard in the first place. Rudyard Kipling memorably described the area as, "the unlit barrack-stove". Aden was an important coaling and refuelling station to secure Britain's sea routes to the jewel in the Crown that was India. It also had a magnificent natural harbour. It became a hub for trade and was sometimes described as the Hong Kong of the Middle East. Similar to Gibraltar, Britain's gateway to the Mediterranean, Aden was a strategically important staging-post and a port of regional importance.

Britain should have left Aden when we granted India independence in 1947. But as always, events overtook us. First, there was the abortive Suez operation in 1956 after President Nasser of Egypt seized the Suez Canal from Britain and France. Ironically, it was our closest ally, the US, who called our bluff on our pretensions to remain a world power. Suez was of great strategic importance to the West. Growing Russian influence was also a threat. We could not afford to lose Aden, a key military base, as the Cold War between the Soviet Union and the West took hold.

The emergence of Arab nationalism under President Nasser's messianic leadership, and his broadcasts from Cairo Radio, led to an alliance between the tribal sheikhdoms of the Aden Protectorate and the colony of Aden. The British presence became more than just a pebble in the shoe of Arab nationalism and Soviet ambition.

Things took a turn for the worse when the ruler of Yemen, the Imam, was overthrown in an army-led coup in 1962. Egyptian troops arrived to consolidate the coup with dirty tricks and assassinations orchestrated by the Soviet KGB. These, ironically, were all under the direction of their British agent, Kim Philby. What then occurred was a proxy war between Britain and Egypt, backed by Soviet Russia. Ironically, 50 years on, Yemen remains the site of a proxy war between two protagonists: Saudi Arabia and Iran. The battleground was the desolate but dramatically beautiful mountainous territory lying between the Gulf of Aden and Saudi Arabia.

Philip Ward was right. The British withdrawal from Aden was not worth the life of one Guardsman. It was not the first time, nor will it be the last, that British soldiers would have to fight for a lost cause while politicians rack their brains for a viable exit strategy.

It was into this uncertainty that the Welsh Guards deployed in the autumn of 1965 to relieve 2nd Battalion Coldstream Guards at Salerno camp in Little Aden. The Battalion was part of 24th Infantry Brigade under Brigadier Richard Bremner. 45 Royal Marine Commando was also part of the Brigade.

The contrast between Chelsea Barracks and Little Aden was stark. Although the Battalion was in pretty good shape on arrival thanks in no small part to the previous commanding officer, Peter Leuchars, a wonderful trainer of men, we needed to acclimatise to the fierce heat and assault on our senses. My orderly (batman), Drummer Weaver, thought we were still on public duties in London. He took enormous pleasure in starching my shorts, to such an extent that they stood up of their own accord. He would come in each morning at 6am with a cup of tea, bring his feet loudly to attention and salute my shorts, exclaiming, "Morning Sah, all's well East of Suez. Shorts: stand easy!"

This period of relative calm as we got used to the enervating heat was short-lived. There was always trouble afoot somewhere during Britain's withdrawal from its colonies. This time it was Tanzania and a mutiny in the Tanzanian army. 45 Royal Marine Commando, who were engaged in fighting the rebels north of us, were redeployed at short notice by HMS *Bulwark* to Dar es Salaam to bring the mutiny under control.

The Battalion moved to the sharp end to replace 45 Commando. Our operational area now became the Radfan, a desolate mountainous region with a terrible beauty; it became the battleground for British troops.

The Radfan was some 80 miles north of the town of Aden. Our companies and platoons were spread out over a large area to contain the Qutaibi tribesmen. Ill-equipped and poorly organised, the tribesmen were, nonetheless, born fighters known as the 'Red Wolves'. Harry Cockerill, an SAS veteran of Aden, described them: "They will never surrender in battle. They will endure shocking wounds and will prefer to die on their own rather than seek aid. They know the place like the backs of their hands, and just a few can hold up a battalion."

One of the key chokepoints was Dhala, a town 5,000 feet up on the ancient trade route linking Aden and North Yemen. The Qutaibi were nominally subject to the Emir of Dhala. The tribesmen had historically regarded it as their right to exhort payment from travellers using the road. The Emir of Dhala, Shafaul ibn Al Amiri, knew his days were numbered and went out of his way to keep in with us.

We also had British political officers who spoke fluent Arabic to help us garner intelligence and find our way amongst the tapestry of tribal leaders. Most of these political officers were courageous, professional and dedicated. After distinguished war service they gave the rest of their lives to colonial service in Southern Arabia.

But dedication and obsessiveness can be two sides of the same coin. Some became world-weary, their judgement unbalanced. Others were straight out of Graham Greene's novel *A Burnt-Out Case*, whisky-soaked and prone to loosening-off a burst of Bren-gun fire for the hell of it as twilight descended. They often came up with fanciful schemes, doomed to failure despite the best of intentions, such as encouraging the tribesmen to grow tomato plants. The tribesmen were solely interested in acquiring AK47s, and those were in plentiful supply from Soviet Russia and its proxy, Egypt.

I paint a picture that would be only too familiar to a British soldier serving on the Khyber Pass in the 19th century. But I do so with the recognition that the Radfan, though equally inhospitable, was a magnificent place for Guardsmen to learn their trade. Soldiering did not come much harder than amongst the high peaks, jagged cliffs and deep wadi gorges. The air temperature in the shade hovered around 45 degrees Celsius and the nights were bitterly cold. For the junior leader, whether he was a newly joined subaltern, podgy and pasty from Sandhurst, or a newly appointed lance corporal in charge of eight Guardsmen, the experience was invaluable. It was not by chance that three outstanding future Regimental sergeant majors – Emlyn Pridham, Tony Davies and Ray Evans – played out their formative years in Aden.

It is something of a generalisation, but in my experience there are two types of senior officer in the British Army. There is the 'Monty' type (Field Marshal Montgomery of Alamein) who masters the operational art, the ideal battlefield commander; and then there is the 'Alex' type (Field Marshal Alexander of Tunis) who through personal example, calmness and consistency, instils confidence in those around him and inspires unbreakable loyalty.

Philip Ward, our commanding officer in Aden, was unquestionably of the 'Alex' school of soldiering. He was unfailingly courteous, wonderfully mannered and put everyone at their ease, regardless of position or rank. Philip taught me how important it was that it was not just the people under your command that you had to worry about. A good commander also had to manage sideways and upwards. Philip made a point of getting on with our Brigade Commander Richard Bremner whose son, Charles, was later to join the Regiment. When we left Aden, Philip presented Richard with a much-prized symbol of the Welsh Guards, a silver dragon.

Philip, however, was far from being a soft touch and expected the highest of standards. Those who let him down, and it was usually because of a lapse of manners or indifference to others, were removed.

Philip created a garden outside the Officers' Mess and I sometimes felt that he was more interested in how the garden was getting along than our operations in the Radfan. But there was method in his desire for an attractive garden. As Churchill said, "We shape our buildings, and afterwards our buildings shape us." The garden gave a human face to the business of soldiering. It was always a point of interest for our visitors and an opportunity for Philip to charm them away from the routine of a dry military briefing.

I was glad, however, when Battalion Headquarters moved to a tented camp at Habilayn in the Radfan. Philip's garden was entirely dependent on camel dung for fertilisation. If the coastal breeze was in the wrong direction, the Mess became almost uninhabitable. I don't think Philip realised this, as he was billeted in a villa belonging to British Petroleum some 3 miles away.

I also had to remonstrate with him over his use of Guardsmen in detention for gardening. I would often catch him chatting away quite merrily with them about the garden. I had to remind him that they had been put in detention for good reason.

It seems hard to believe now, but our year-long tour in Aden was unaccompanied. There was no leave allowed back to the UK. The Guardsmen invariably chose Mombasa on Kenya's coast for their rest and recuperation.

I had hoped to travel somewhere agreeable with a friend, James Emson, who was serving with the Parachute Regiment, but this plan was thwarted when James broke his ankle jumping out of the bedroom window of his paramour, an attractive Australian nurse. The Matron was a disciplinarian who took a very dim view of her charges being distracted from their duties. She would inspect their quarters unannounced for any sign of fun and games. With a badly broken ankle, James was of no further use to the Parachute Regiment; he transferred to The Life Guards, where he had a distinguished career.

Philip then asked me to travel with him to Ethiopia, a country of ancient cultural and historical significance, for our break from Aden. For some reason that escapes me, we were asked to call on the Emperor of Ethiopia, Haile Selassie. This was to take place after Philip and I had seen the various sites of antiquity and the source of the Blue Nile in Lake Tana.

To cut a lengthy story short, our car broke down in the middle of nowhere and we had to be rescued by a contingent from the Ethiopian Army. With the car back on its wheels, Philip handed the equivalent of 50p to an Ethiopian who he thought was the mechanic. The man looked aghast. We later discovered he was the head of the army, sent by Emperor Haile Selassie to ensure we had safe passage.

We were only a few months into our tour when the British Government announced a complete evacuation of Aden by November 1967. British promises were no longer seen as credible. The hearts and minds campaign became irrelevant. An atmosphere of mistrust quickly took hold. The British Army did not know whom to rely on: were the police now quietly siding with the rebel factions to avoid retribution when we left? Was Aden's Federal Regular Army truly with us?

A half-century later, the West repeated its mistakes when the US announced its withdrawal from Afghanistan. Deception and double-dealing filled the vacuum as the irreconcilable factions sought to shore up their interests.

It was fertile territory for the Egyptian-backed National Liberation Front and its partner in mayhem, the Front for the Liberation of South Yemen to sow chaos and confusion. As Philip Ward said, "It had become quite impossible to tell who was friend or foe."

Philip's calmness and consistency saw us through a very difficult period. Guardsman Harry Holland was awarded the Military Medal (MM) for his bravery during an ambush; Sergeant Tom Edwards was also awarded the MM for coolness under fire. Peter Williams, who commanded No. 2 Company, had considerable success with his coat-trailing tactics, which were designed to draw the dissidents into battle. The remainder of the tour became largely a defensive war, though we always took the fight to the rebels if they let their guard down.

As in most military campaigns, we had our fair share of visits from senior officers. These were always fielded with great style by Philip Ward, each visitor returning to Whitehall full of praise for the Welsh Guards. Only one visit went rather awry when we were visited by the Director of Military Operations. Philip thought it would be a good idea for him to visit our forward headquarters in the Radfan, which was run by George Richmond Brown.

George was a man of great charm who took over from me as Adjutant and, in later life, started the travel company Corfu Villas. I sent George a signal to warn him of the visit. I am not sure what George understood by the title of Director of Military Operations, but he took it upon himself to show the General the cookhouse, the latrines and the tented accommodation. The General, a rather gruff Yorkshireman, returned to our Battalion Headquarters muttering to Philip, "A bit of an oddball you've got up there in the Radfan. He just wanted to show me the shit-house."

And so our tour in Aden drew to a close in the autumn of 1966. Philip Ward, true to his word, brought back the Battalion to the UK without the loss of a single Welsh Guardsman. The next year the colony descended into chaos and civil war between the rival factions who sought ascendancy after Britain's formal withdrawal.

If we learnt any lessons from our withdrawal from Aden, we soon forgot them. Events 40 years later in Basra, Iraq, sadly proved that.

Our time in Aden marked the Regiment's half-centenary since our formation in 1915. Our experience and success there meant we could look forward to our next 50 years with confidence, pride and indomitable humour.

4

The SAS

Only when you learn how to manage yourself,
can you lead and manage others.

I have always kept my own counsel about my time serving
with the SAS. However, I cannot ignore in my memoirs what
was an integral and formative part of my career. In part, I
have written my memoirs to help those serving now, and
in the future, to become better soldiers and better leaders.
Experience was undoubtedly the most valuable thing I had
to offer.

My time in the SAS from 1966 to 1970 helped me in
both respects, and for that I shall always be thankful. The
SAS motto, 'Who Dares Wins', has become so well-known
and so overused as to become almost mock-heroic. And yet,
during so many times in my career, the motto served me well.
This chapter has no tales of derring-do, nor of me triumphing
against seemingly impossible odds. For some reason, I can
only recall the funnier moments, some of the stranger
characters with whom I served, and scenes where the bizarre
and fanciful – not for the first or last time in my career –
became almost commonplace. It all began in the summer of
1966 when I took SAS Selection.

SAS SELECTION

The SAS sergeant instructor was grinning as I made my way to the checkpoint at the summit of Pen y Fan in the Brecon Beacons. It was the first major test of my stamina in SAS Selection. I had to complete the course known as the 'Fan Dance' in under four hours, carrying my rifle and an A-frame canvas rucksack weighing 55 pounds. The rucksack's weight was usually made up of bricks, but I had been given a Larkspur A13 radio to carry. As I glanced at my watch, I saw that I would complete 'The Dance' with 20 minutes to spare. I was about to find out why the sergeant instructor was grinning as he said, "Well done, good effort and with time to spare. Just let me see if you've got the right kit in your rucksack."

I laid down my rucksack and opened it for his inspection. He gave it a cursory look before saying, "Well, that radio's not much bloody good to us without the antenna. Waste of a trip. Better get straight back to the start point at the Storey Arms and pick one up. You've got three and a half hours."

Fortunately, I had been tipped off that this was all part of Selection. The SAS instructors would throw in 'sickeners', extra tests to test mental determination and to see if you would throw the towel in. Many did. But as I got to the start point, the Storey Arms, there was a vehicle waiting and a friendly face telling me to hop in.

I cannot remember all that much else about Selection. The brain masks the memory from less agreeable moments in one's life. I do, however, recall the separate part of Selection known as 'Officers' Week'. This was designed to test potential SAS officers in their ability to think straight and creatively while sleep-deprived and under pressure. Of course, the real test was to see whether you caved in before experienced

SAS troopers who would tear your plan apart, often with scoffing comments.

The details of the plan I had to present are long forgotten, but not the remarks made by one rough-hewn SAS non-commissioned officer in the front row who, turning to the troopers behind him, said in a thick Glaswegian accent, "Ye dinnae want this bozo leading youse lot. It would'nae be a fair scrap."

I was not going to be put off too easily by a few deliberately provocative comments. I had set my heart on joining the SAS since I came across them operating in Aden when I was Adjutant of the Welsh Guards. Much as I had loved my time in the Regiment, there was something missing, an itch that had to be scratched before it was too late, and when the time spent at a desk far outweighed the time spent leading soldiers.

The SAS seemed to think I was made of the right stuff, though I was lucky to avoid the part of Selection known as 'Green Hell'. This was the jungle phase of Selection lasting four weeks and, more than any other phase of Selection, allows instructors to see if you have really got what it takes to win your SAS wings; however, the Regiment was running hot in Aden and short of officers.

In the late 1960s, the SAS was looked upon with some scepticism, a haven for mavericks, and a little irregular for most officers – quite unlike today, where time serving with Special Forces is a well-travelled path to high command.

After a few days' leave, I was warned off to deploy to Aden to join the recently formed G Squadron, drawn from the ranks of the Guards Independent Parachute Company. Until the formation of G Squadron, the SAS comprised just three other operational sabre squadrons with a total active fighting strength of around 120 men.

Before I left for Aden, I also had to be trained up in a dedicated skill. Apart from being patrol commander, I also became the patrol medic. The other three patrol members would be the signaller, linguist and demolition expert. In reality, you had to be competent in all areas, though after my days at Harrow grappling with French and Latin, I paid lip-service to learning any language. If I knew then what I was to discover three months later in Aden, that the first call on my medical skills was to perform a circumcision – not part of the syllabus for aspiring SAS medics – I might have taken my language training a little more seriously.

My medical training was largely spent in the A&E department of St Mary's Paddington. It was intense and, given the hospital's proximity to London's less gentrified boroughs, particularly busy at weekends. After I passed my initial test learning about drugs, trauma management, and advanced first aid, I was more or less thrown into the crash theatre.

It was all far removed from *Doctor in the House*, the Ealing comedy film of the 1950s, though the in-house senior surgeon put in charge of my training was not unlike the gruff, tetchy Sir Lancelot Spratt in the film. I remember him inviting me to do a cutdown on an Irishman's leg. A cutdown is an emergency procedure where you have to cut through the layers of skin to expose a deep vein through which you can insert a cannula to start pumping essential fluids. I was rather taken aback to learn that the patient had died a few hours later, but then relieved to hear that the cause of death was post-traumatic shock, unconnected to my cutdown.

I also spent time in the Maternity Ward where I was taught the duties of a midwife and how to deliver babies. This, as I was later to discover in Malaya, was the most useful part of my training. There were other compensations, as the nurses, mainly from Australia, New Zealand and South Africa, were easy-going and companionable.

ADEN

I arrived in Aden to be met by the Regiment's second-in-command, Peter Walter. Peter was the original fighting animal. By the time I met him, he had already won the MC and Bar for bravery. A friend who served with him in the Malayan jungle once remarked that Peter was a liability at night because he would "fight in his sleep". Rules and regulations were for guidance only, but he was dedicated to practical hard training. He was known as 'The Rat' for his grit and resourcefulness; although his appearance – with slightly buck teeth, darting black eyes and a messy moustache – did little to dispel the image. I got on very well with him. He was straight, loyal, never dissembled and would back you to the hilt whether you were right or wrong. In return, he expected the same.

I knew Aden pretty well by then, having served there with my Regiment just 18 months before. The whole thing had become a mess as soon as the British Government had publicly announced its intention to withdraw from Aden. This emboldened the Marxist rebels from Yemen, who quickly ramped up the movement of arms and guerrillas from their Yemeni bases in the north. It was clear that they were also receiving money and support from countries under Soviet control, particularly East Germany.

Rival tribal factions across the region added to the chaos. It was chaos that the SAS had become only too familiar with as we became the eyes and ears, and occasionally the fighting fists, of the British withdrawal from empire.

In his characteristic no-nonsense style, Peter Walter briefed me as to what was expected. I remember being slightly unnerved by the experience, as he didn't believe in maps. "Too bloody tiresome", he would say before referring to a sand model he had built of the area in the Radfan in which we were to operate. He kept the model outside his office and would only brief people in the heat of the midday sun. "Adds a bit of realism", he said. "Damnably hot out there, you know. Best get used to it."

Our task was to establish observation posts from which we could observe enemy movement, report back and direct artillery fire if we saw a guerrilla patrol. The terrain, with its jigsaw of rocky outcrops and obscure wadis (valleys or dry riverbeds) lent itself to effective concealment.

The climate, however, with its merciless heat (the temperature would often reach 50 degrees Celsius) meant we needed 2 gallons of water each a day. That meant resupply by helicopter, so concealment was invariably short-lived.

There was a rather strange happening as dusk fell one evening. One of the tribesmen, friendly to our cause and accompanying our patrol, pressed his ear to the ground. I asked him, *"Madha Tafiel?"* ("What's up?") He replied to my astonishment that three horsemen were approaching from the east across the Rub'Al Khali (the empty quarter). He added that he thought they were young men, possibly boys. He was true to his word, as some half an hour later, four boys no more than 15 or 16 years of age, appeared on horseback. One of them said in English, "We look for English doctor." I raised my hand, to which the boy, reverting to Arabic, asked if he could be circumcised.

This caused a lot of hilarity amongst my troopers who said I should "give it a go". Rather to my shame I declined, despite the suggestion from one trooper who said, "Don't worry, Boss, I'll hold it for you, you just cut away." Some time later, I had a look at the detailed medical handbook given to me at St Mary's Paddington and discovered it was a surprisingly simple procedure.

There was just one close brush with death. I was with my eight-man patrol in two Land Rovers driving into the town of Aden to pick up provisions for a patrol upcountry. The next thing I remember was landing upside down in a large crater after hitting a landmine. I was dazed and bruised but no one was seriously injured. The terrorist was not so fortunate. He had been sitting high up in a palm tree which acted as his firing point. The blast area from a bomb is notoriously difficult to predict, but it had blown him clean out of the palm tree onto a metal railing below, where he lay impaled.

The Union Jack was lowered for the last time in Aden in November 1967. The SAS's involvement in the Middle East was over – for a brief period of time.

I look back on my time in Aden with mixed feelings. I learnt a great deal about soldiers and soldiering, but our withdrawal was a troublesome and unsatisfactory affair. As Julian Paget, a former Coldstream Guards officer and military historian, wrote in his study of Aden, "It was difficult to find a political or national cause that was worth fighting and dying for, and of none was that more true than the politically, militarily and geographically isolated patrols of the SAS during those last days in the Radfan."

Postscript to the Parsi cemetery
During my last few days as the CDS, I was in Oman to visit Sultan Qaboos, a friend and staunch ally of Britain. I took

myself off to see Oman's empty quarter, the vast desert plain covering most of central Oman. I watched as an ibex, the wild mountain goat, was picked clean by a pair of vultures. It was a vivid reminder of my patrol in the Parsi cemetery where we saw little except the grisly sight of vultures stripping clean the laid-out corpses.

MALAYA

The original SAS volunteers made their reputation in the desert in the Second World War and in the jungle during the Malayan Emergency. Since then, everyone serving in the SAS has been expected to train and operate beneath the jungle canopy. Freddie Spencer Chapman's book *The Jungle is Neutral* is true in a sense. But it takes you quite a bit of time to master your surroundings and learn to live in an unforgiving environment.

I was certainly pretty nervous when told that, after Aden, I was to deploy to northern Malaya to track down Chin Peng and his Malay and Chinese guerrillas.

Chin Peng was the long-time leader of the Malayan Communist Party and the Malayan National Liberation Army. He was a determined anti-colonialist and nationalist for whom it was difficult not to have a degree of respect. He had a huge influence on Malayan politics until his death in Thailand in 2013 aged 89. He had fought bravely against the Japanese occupation of Malaya and had then led the guerrilla insurgency in the Malayan Emergency 1948–60, fighting against us and Commonwealth forces in an attempt to establish an independent socialist state.

Malaya won its independence in 1957, but communism was sweeping across South East Asia, and the West, fearful of its insidious effects, was determined to combat the threat. That was what led the USA into the ruinous Vietnam War.

The conduct of the Malayan Emergency, thanks to the redoubtable Gerald Templer, a former four-star general and High Commissioner in Malaya, was one of the few outright British successes. Churchill appointed Templer, whose tactics against Chin Peng and his guerrillas are often held up as a blueprint in handling counter-insurgency. It was Templer who famously said, "The answer lies not in pouring more troops into the jungle, but in the hearts and minds of the people." Templer sought political and social equality for all Malayans, granting citizenship to all Malayan residents, including around 1.1 million ethnic Chinese, the main source of communist support. The Malayan Emergency was declared at an end in 1960.

Chin Peng, however, was not one to give up too easily. After a few years in exile, harbouring his grievances and plotting his return, he waged a second campaign, from 1968 to 1989, to replace the government with a socialist one. It was clear he was masterminding operations from southern Thailand, where he had been given sanctuary. Once again, the SAS were called upon to regain the initiative and take the war to those threatening Malaya's post-independence stability.

First, I had to be trained in jungle warfare. I had missed out on the 'Green Hell' part of SAS Selection when we were needed in Aden. It seemed that most of the likely action was going to take place in northern Malaya, bordering on Thailand. It was mountainous jungle, with peaks between 5,000 and 7,500 feet. Just moving from A to B is a constant, draining effort, quite apart from the snakes and other creepy-crawlies you had to put up with. It was impossible to say you could get to a certain point by a certain time as you had no real idea of how long it was going to take you.

The bamboo jungle was the most difficult kind, almost impenetrable and growing in thick clumps. You would do well to cover 200 yards in a day. Secondary jungle was not much better; it was where the open, primary, jungle had been cut down, opening it to sunlight where things grew at an alarming rate and bugs, ticks and mosquitoes flourished.

The final claim on one's sanity was clothing. You had just two sets: one dry set for wearing at night, and one that was soaked through from the previous day's efforts, which you then put on again just before first light. It was quite a test of one's morale.

A training camp was set up and, once again, my mentor was Peter Walter. For Peter, the jungle was home from home. There was little classroom work; Peter was a great advocate of training without (as he liked to put it) "swimming trunks or water wings". Peter took us straight out to the jungle and for three weeks taught us everything we needed to know to operate effectively. He taught us how to operate in patrols where visibility, unlike in the Radfan, was severely restricted; how to navigate; survival skills; and how to estimate your position by using pacing. In essence, that meant once a soldier knew how many paces it took him to walk 10 yards, he could start to measure with reasonable accuracy the time and distance travelled on a map.

In the jungle it is the small stuff and self-discipline that matter. Adding a drip line to my night shelter meant rain would flow to the ground rather than on me; wrapping the wooden handle of my parang (machete) in tape ensured it wouldn't fly out of my hand when cutting through the jungle; selecting sites away from streams meant you wouldn't be swamped when they quickly overflowed during the rainy season; and the importance of keeping oneself clean and alert, so I could walk blindfold to have a pee during the night (a more important skill now that I am 82 than it was at the age of 30 in 1968).

We were also taught how to see things in layers. I remember on my first couple of days looking no more than a couple of feet away, mainly at the ground or directly above me, to see whether something nasty was lurking. To overcome this, I was taught to focus on something 6 feet away, scan to the left and right, then move my line of sight on another 5 feet or so. Soon it became second nature and I was looking 30 feet away, and things began to stand out from the green blob.

Ironically, the only time I lost my temper was six weeks or so later when we were on a real patrol trying to find and pin down Chin Peng. Jock was the patrol tracker, just in front of me. Jock, the son of a Highland ghillie, was superb at layering and spotting potential danger 30 or 40 feet away, but he never paid any attention to the branch immediately in front of him, which he would push to one side. This would then swish back, catching me in the face. After a day of swishing, I'd had enough, and words were exchanged. We remain great friends to this day.

There was one great advantage to jungle warfare: you could have a straight, undisturbed eight hours of sleep. The only things that moved at night were the scourge of insects, and as I learned to live with the jungle, they were not too much of a problem. I drew the line, however, at eating snake. Tinned sardines became my staple diet for the patrol's duration; curiously enough, they are a food that I still return to 40 years on if I find myself looking sideways in the mirror with a growing sense of alarm.

Our long-range patrols to hunt down Chin Peng and his guerrillas were fruitless. His guerrillas were always one step ahead of us, and I dare say they had the support of some of the poor local villagers. Chin Peng was a charismatic leader, not unlike the North Vietnamese leader Ho Chi Minh. I doubt Chin Peng was in the Malayan jungle himself – he would have been in his mid-40s in 1968 – but his influence on guerrilla operations remained pernicious. The local villagers were smiling and gracious, but not inclined to betray the whereabouts of Chin Peng's guerrillas. He died in Bangkok in 2013, his 90th year.

As patrol medic, I found myself rather busy delivering babies and handing out aspirin. It astonished me what aspirin could do; it was the perfect palliative for local tribespeople. That was all to the good in winning 'hearts and minds', but it did little to help us in our endeavours. My mother was rather surprised to receive a postcard from me saying that I was in good spirits and had now delivered half a dozen babies. I was proud to add that no baby had died in childbirth.

Rest and recuperation in Kuala Lumpur, the Malayan capital, was a dead loss. I strolled into the Intercontinental Hotel, reputedly full of Pan-Am air hostesses. I should have taken a good long look at myself beforehand. White, gaunt and covered in welts from leeches and insect bites, I must have been an unattractive sight.

KENYA

There is an inscription on the clocktower at the SAS HQ in Hereford taken from James Flecker's verse play *The Golden Journey to Samarkand*, with its haunting lines, "We are the Pilgrims, master; we shall go always a little further... Across that angry or glimmering sea... But surely we are brave who take the Golden Road to Samarkand."

I was now 30 years old and had served in nine different countries. I had joined the army to travel and to embrace the spirit of adventure. But 30 years of age, false milestone though it is, carries a little uncertainty. After four years of a peripatetic life, I wanted to return to England to see my family and friends. I also had to study for entrance to the British Army's Staff College.

But, as so often in life, it wasn't quite to be, as events in East Africa wrested my plans away from me. In the event, I was glad things turned out as they did; 1969 was quite a year.

Kenya was a familiar pattern of events, similar to those I had seen in Aden and Malaya. British colonial rule had come to end, with Kenya winning her independence in December 1963. Jomo Kenyatta, born to Kikuyu farmers, was an anti-colonial activist who became Kenya's first Prime Minister and then appointed himself as President. He had been charged by Britain's Governor with masterminding the Mau Mau uprising against British rule, which we had suppressed. Kenyatta was convicted and imprisoned, and then exiled until 1961.

On his release he led his party, the Kenya African National Union, to victory in the 1963 election. He then oversaw the transition of Kenya into an independent republic. Smooth transition from colonial rule to independence was invariably a mirage.

Kenyatta had a number of headaches to contend with, some of his own doing, but others because of tensions over which he had little control. First, he favoured his own tribe, the Kikuyu, for whom all key government positions and lucrative contracts were reserved. Second, there was understandably a degree of animosity towards him from the white settler farmers who ran the wealthy agricultural sector, and from Kenyan Indians who ran a great deal of the day-to-day commerce. On top of that, he had to tackle Somali separatists in the North Eastern Province.

Kenyatta, like many anti-colonialist activists, retained an affection for his former colonial rulers. He was a pragmatist, and he realised that without British support, tacit or direct, his grasp on power was likely to be shaky.

It is a characteristic of autocratic rulers that they see plots everywhere, cabals emerging, assassination attempts imminent; so, Kenyatta decided he needed greater protection. As an ironic footnote to the British withdrawal from colonialism, he approached the British Government.

The planning and conduct of the job of protecting Kenyatta was handed to the SAS. The mandate was in the gift of a man called Bruce McKenzie. McKenzie was the only white man in Kenyatta's government, serving as his Minister of Agriculture, and he brokered the deal with the British Government.

Bruce McKenzie bore a startling resemblance to Les Dawson, the mutton-chopped comedian. But there the similarity ended. South African by birth, he was a rough diamond, but a remarkable man. He had joined the RAF and had won the Distinguished Service Order (DSO) and Distinguished Flying Cross (DFC) during the Second World War. He emigrated to Kenya in 1946 and became a prominent farmer, much respected by the other white settlers.

He earned the trust of Kenyatta who realised that, for the time being, he needed to keep the settlers onside. Bruce was also one of life's fixers. I was never quite sure if he worked for MI6, South African intelligence or Mossad, quite possibly all three, as well as being a minister and advisor to Kenyatta.

Bruce became a good friend, invited me to the occasional party in Nairobi, and was always a source of sound advice. He encouraged me not to get too close to the white settlers as they would compromise my position of trust with Kenyatta.

Bruce McKenzie met his end several years later in extraordinary circumstances, reminiscent of a Bond film. During Operation *Entebbe* in 1976 (a successful counter-terrorist hostage rescue mission at Entebbe airport in Uganda), he persuaded Kenyatta to allow the Israeli Air Force and commandos to have access to Nairobi airport to refuel and gain intelligence. Idi Amin, the deranged President of Uganda, who was in league with the Palestinian terrorists, bided his time to get his revenge. Two years later, Amin presented McKenzie with a carved wooden statue of a lion as a gesture of reconciliation. Inside the statue was a bomb with a timer. As McKenzie flew over the Ngong Hills in Kenya, the bomb exploded. Kate and I remain close to his widow, Christina, who by coincidence was the niece of David Stirling, the SAS's founding father.

My first task was to train up Kenyatta's bodyguard and a special company of the Kenya Armed Forces. The job was a sensitive operation. I wore the uniform of the Kenya Armed Forces, holding the rank of Assistant Superintendent of Police. The Kenya Armed Forces and bodyguard had to come from Kenyatta's own tribe, the Kikuyu, but it was left to me to select the right people. Of course, there were any number of volunteers as it was a prestigious position to hold. I rather wished I had put together a module as part of the selection process on being a waiter and guard at state banquets. At the first state banquet, where I was responsible for security, I dressed the bodyguards as waiters, but it did not go well. Unused to such extravagant food and fine wine, they all got blind drunk and hoovered up most of the canapés before the dinner.

Such was the sensitive nature of the task that John Slim, then commanding 22 SAS and son of Field Marshal Bill Slim, came to visit. He briefed Kenyatta personally on all the security arrangements. On one occasion, John left me with his briefcase, which contained his pistol and top secret documents. I decided to have lunch in a Chinese restaurant with one of my troop commanders, Alastair Morrison, who was later to win the MC and public fame for his role in the successful rescue of hostages at Mogadishu, Somalia, in 1977. Sometime after we left the restaurant, we both realised we had left John's briefcase in the restaurant. We raced back, our feet barely touching the ground, to rescue the briefcase and our careers. Fortunately, it had been left untouched.

Alastair remains a close friend and enjoys reminiscing with me about our rather racy social life in Nairobi when we weren't on duty. The British head of the Presidential Bodyguard, a policeman called Alex Pearson, held wonderful parties. Alastair has reminded me that a girl broke a plate over my head to everyone's amusement as she felt I had stood her up in favour of someone else. We were rather spoilt for choice. It was the 'swinging sixties' in London; and Nairobi was no different. I have no recollection, although Alastair does, of a party where he and I had to reproduce the sounds of *Macbeth* using saucepans and traditional Kenyan drums.

There was serious unrest on the borders with Somalia and South Sudan. I was sent to observe and report back on what was going on. We were an eight-man patrol in two Land Rovers, entirely self-sufficient for a lengthy time in the wilderness. I remember the sheer majesty of my surroundings, the seemingly vast African skies and wildlife which roamed freely around us. The patrol, however, was memorable for two incidents, neither of which was related to anything military.

We were up in the North Eastern Province of Kenya, close to the border with Somalia. Every night we slept on the ground close to the Land Rovers. We had to keep our wits about us, not so much on the lookout for aggressive tribesmen, but for lions and rhinos which might wander in a little too close for comfort.

Something rather smaller than a rhino, however, wandered into my ear while I was asleep. I woke up the next morning as though a brass band were playing in my head. After a few hours of this, I was slowly going potty. One of my patrol members rather unhelpfully suggested he would try to dig the thing out with his bayonet. I knew there was a missionary post run by nuns some 200 miles south-east of us at Loiyangalani on the edge of Lake Rudolf (now Lake Turkana). I knew it would have some rudimentary medical centre. We drove for what seemed hours, arriving at the Mission just after dusk. A nice nun poured warm oil into my ear. The bug – a red locust – fell out, and to my great relief the brass band in my ear stopped playing.

I was eternally grateful to the nuns and, many years later, in one of life's fortuitous coincidences, I was able to repay their kindness. At the time, I was Chief of the General Staff (CGS) and received a letter from the Mission asking my support to buy a fishing boat for them. I was only too happy to help and sent the Mission a personal cheque for £700.

They named the boat the *Saint Charles* and sent me a picture of it on Lake Turkana, much to my sons' amusement. I kept in touch with the Mission and asked how the fishing enterprise was going, and could I do anything else to help.

I received a reply telling me that the boat had been a roaring success. As it happened, it was rather too much of a success. The fishermen were making far too much money, upsetting the fragile balance of the local economy and spending it all on drink.

A couple of weeks later, a much larger animal presented us with a more formidable challenge. We had been in the rough for some time and were dirty, dusty and smelly. We found a watering hole, took off our clothes and jumped in, washing away the weeks of grime and grit. We were gently dozing away, content in our cleanliness, when suddenly the sun disappeared.

I looked up to see a huge bull elephant, which had not taken kindly to finding us in his watering hole. A trooper, a Cumbrian of reiver ancestry called Tom, glanced at me, picked up his rifle and said in his Cumbrian dialect, "Eh, what? Bloody 'ell, booger off, I'll drop him, naw matter."

I gave his suggestion a split second of thought before deciding that I could not guarantee which way the elephant might fall in his death throes. If the elephant had landed on us, I doubt we would have survived. Anyway, it was a magnificent beast and hardly his fault that we were in his favourite spot. I made up my mind and told my fellow patrol members to pick up their rifles and, on my command, fire a single shot into a tree on the edge of the watering hole. The crack and thump did the trick, and the elephant, looking a little perplexed, gently padded away.

After we returned to Nairobi, I received notification that I should return to the UK in the spring of 1969, to take over from Murray de Klee as G Squadron Commander. Alastair Morrison joined me, eventually taking over himself in 1970.

We had one final exercise in northern Norway in the mid-summer of that year with a fortnight off at the end in the Norwegian archipelago, near to Tromsø. My Norwegian sojourn in the summer of 1969, in the company of athletic and sun-kissed Norwegian women, was my last hurrah of the swinging sixties.

My soldiering with the SAS came to an end in December 1969. I was to return to my Regiment in Germany, as part of the British Army of the Rhine (BAOR) and prepare for an operational tour of Northern Ireland. From a personal level, I also needed time to prepare for the Army Staff College examination, a prerequisite if I were to succeed in higher command and staff appointments.

I have never lost touch with the SAS. Over the period of my career in the army, the SAS had become a key strategic asset and was no longer seen by the rest of the army as a haven for talented mavericks shunted off for unruly behaviour. Like any great and successful organisation, it has had to guard against the blight of institutional arrogance. Other parts of the army have equally important roles to play, though they may not seem as glamorous. I always encourage soldiers and officers to have a crack at SAS Selection if they feel it is within their grasp. It is tough; anyone who says differently is either a liar or a fool.

I was privileged to become Colonel Commandant of the SAS. I sanctioned their deployment to Sierra Leone in 2000, despite political misgivings, when I was CDS. It was a vicious episode linked to the trade in 'blood diamonds' and where we were up against the drug-crazed West Side Boys. I write about this in a later chapter.

Soldiers often ask me what I learnt from my four years in the SAS. I reply that I learnt how to be a soldier. This does not mean that I learnt to master my profession. Far from it. But it gave me the confidence in higher command to take decisions that the ordinary soldier could carry out. I understood their world. This allowed me to concentrate on what I should be doing as a general and not getting waylaid by operational tactics.

I have seen too many senior officers who have reached the top because they did very well at Staff College, or had been brilliant administrators, but when they were in the field commanding a brigade or a division, felt they had to position every machine gun or tank. I have seen it happen. To have acquired that confidence in myself as a soldier, I remain indebted to the SAS.

5

Germany

*My introduction to the British Army of the Rhine
(BAOR), a life not unlike the cantonments in India
during the Raj.*

A contemporary and friend of mine from Harrow who went
on to pursue a career in commercial law spent all his working
life in the same office in Cheapside in the City of London.
He made a lot of money and just occasionally I envied him
his sedentary but stable existence. His was a life of 'known
knowns'. But I have always had an appetite for variety and a
change of tempo. I had just spent two years in the Malayan
jungle, the searing heat of Aden and in equatorial Kenya.
London in 1969 and the Regiment's move to Münster,
Germany, in 1970, was a welcome change of pace. I was able
to catch up with old friends and make up for lost time.

Ten years had passed since I last served in BAOR and the
change was striking. Not in a military sense: that was to come
a decade later when Lieutenant General Sir Nigel Bagnall
took over as 1st British Corps commander and injected some
much needed vigour into an operational strategy which had
become hidebound and defensive.

The change was most marked in West Germany, where the post-war economic miracle, the *Wirtschaftswunder*, was visible in every aspect of life. We were no longer an army of occupation. West Germany was now a host nation and our allies in deterring any Soviet aggression. The non-fraternisation policy of the 1950s and early 1960s was a thing of the past. I remembered with horror how a contemporary and friend of mine in the Regiment was sent back to the UK after he was seen holding hands with a German *Fräulein*.

It was also noticeable to everyone that the local population were enjoying a better standard of living than we were back home. Everyone's first impression was of cleanliness and efficiency. The Guardsmen were well off; Local Overseas Allowance almost doubled their wages, and buying a car was tax-free.

With inflation, industrial unrest and a floundering economy in the UK, service in Germany became an attractive option. The Welsh Guards recruited largely from South Wales, which was beginning to suffer from the decline in the traditional industries, particularly coal-mining. The army offered excitement and a chance to get away from what seemed a bleak future. Shortly after we arrived in Münster in March 1970, I remember a Guardsman saying to me in that special Cardiff dialect, after he had spent a night out in the historic old town with a full wallet, "Lush place this is, very tidy. I like it here."

There remained some distinct cultural differences, and it was not until I returned to Germany in 1982 as a brigade commander that social interaction with the Germans became more evident. Despite that, they never quite got our sense of humour and our love of dogs. The tank regiments would put berets on their dogs with radio headsets, close the hatches down, and drive through German villages. Obviously, the drivers could see where they were going through their armoured windows, but the Germans would look at the dogs in the command hatches, shake their heads and mutter, "The mad British! How can we rely on them as allies when they have dogs commanding tanks?"

It was a happy time for the Regiment, which was part of 4th Guards Armoured Brigade commanded by Brigadier Sir Ian Jardine. Ian had won the MC for bravery in hard fighting towards the end of the Second World War. He had nothing to prove except to ensure the wellbeing of his brigade with its historic provenance. I was given command of Prince of Wales Company, known as 'The Jam Boys', a sobriquet we earned because, historically, its officers paid for an extra ration of jam as additional sustenance for their taller men.

Our commanding officer was James Malcolm, whose father Billy had commanded the 2nd Battalion in the Second World War. James's elder son, Sandy, later commanded the 1st Battalion in Northern Ireland in 1996. James was just the right man to command a family regiment at a relatively benign time in its history. At the time there was a rather hackneyed expression at the end of every married officer's confidential report to say, provided it was the case, that "He was ably supported by his charming and vivacious wife". In James's case, it was perfectly true. James and his wife, Heather, were a wonderful team.

James gave me a good deal of time off to study for entrance to the Staff College. It wasn't a particularly stiff examination, but it had to be passed if I was to progress to the higher reaches of the army. I had failed it once, largely because my time in the SAS didn't lend itself to studying of any kind except for the operation in hand. At the back of my mind was also the precedent of Harrow where I was head boy and Captain of Rugby, but did little to stretch the academic examiners.

I was blessed in the officers who served with me in Prince of Wales Company. They were an eclectic and talented bunch.

I rarely found I had to say, "If you haven't got anything to do, I'll find you something to do." All of them became ushers at my wedding to Kate and one, Christopher Drewry, became my brother-in-law and a three-star general.

Young officers can take a little time to settle into their regiment. One officer, David Mason, joined us just two months after we arrived in Münster; his highly individual style persisted in competing with operational requirements. An impending visit by General Sir David Fraser, a Grenadier and known by most as 'Fraser the Razor', filled me with trepidation as David Mason was tasked with leading a platoon attack and showcasing our newly learned skills as mechanised infantry. I envisaged my career going up in smoke.

David obviously realised the importance of the occasion. He found his stride without apparent effort and delivered a textbook example of how to lead four armoured personnel carriers to his objective. General Fraser turned to me and said, "Well done, Charles! Very promising young officer you have there. I congratulate you on training him so well." I was speechless with astonishment, but David was indeed promising. He later proved that on operations in Oman, where he won the Sultan of Oman's Bravery Medal.

The problems in Northern Ireland were beginning to make their presence felt, and they affected the routine of the BAOR training cycle. This was no bad thing. Training had become far too much of an accustomed routine, and the major BAOR exercises were neither challenging nor memorable.

The routine was frequently punctuated by the Guardsmen's nervousness of wild boars. Many thousands of these beasts, some of them weighing 250 pounds or more, roamed around the training areas, and their behaviour was unpredictable.

The response by some of the Guardsmen was to dig pits everywhere, hoping to trap one. They never succeeded.

For the Guardsmen, the real value of a BAOR posting was the wonderful opportunities for sport, particularly skiing and adventure training. Many Guardsmen had never ventured out of Wales. *Exercise Snow Queen* in Bavaria was a wonderful holiday for them, quite unlike anything they had experienced before, where they were taught to ski, their sense of daring emboldened by the strong Bavarian Bockbier,

Another adventure training trip, canoeing down the Rhine in full spate, nearly ended in disaster as the Guardsmen, passing a nudist camp on one of the river's banks, deliberately capsized their canoes in their attempt to get a better handle on things.

For my part, I made the most of my tax-free red Alfa Romeo as I travelled back to the UK to cram up on various courses for the Staff College examination and, more importantly, to try to win the hand of Kate Worrall. I had been best man to my closest friend from the Regiment, David Lewis, who had married Kate's younger sister, Sue.

This relatively carefree existence soon came to an end in March 1971 when the Battalion was deployed to 39 Brigade in North Belfast, in what became known euphemistically as 'the Troubles'. There were some who thought it was a distraction from proper soldiering in countering the Soviet threat in West Germany.

Northern Ireland certainly kept the army's blade sharp, but only at a junior leadership level.

By the time I returned to Northern Ireland eight years later in 1979, the strategy of no casualties and minimum force had blunted the army's offensive spirit and meant that its step had begun to falter.

6

Belfast

*The Troubles began in the late 1960s with a
campaign by the Northern Ireland Civil Rights
Association to end discrimination against the
Catholic minority by the Protestant majority.
The IRA quickly exploited the perceived
political, police and military bias against the
Catholic community. Violence descended
on the province.*

The spring of 1971 in Northern Ireland was a period of both reward and regret. As I look with affection at the photograph of Prince of Wales Company in North Belfast, I remember the enjoyment of commanding on operations close to 120 men, all of whose names I knew.

But 1971 was also a year of regret as the descent into violence took on a momentum of its own. There was a good chance that the Troubles could have been ended earlier that year. The political decision to introduce internment without trial on 9 August, which seemed to be directed solely against the Catholic community, was a disaster. The army was told to take a tougher approach. Some elements of the army took the bait without much idea of what that might mean, or how it would play into the IRA's hands.

Six months after the Battalion left Belfast, 'Bloody Sunday' took place in Londonderry. Any chance of establishing a lasting peace was lost.

Operation *Banner*, lasting 38 years, was the longest operation in the army's history. It came to an end with the Good Friday Agreement on 2 December 1999 when I was CDS and Tony Blair was Prime Minister. Some 300,000 troops had served on Op *Banner*, 763 of whom had been killed and 6,116 wounded as a direct result of terrorist action.

Our experience in Northern Ireland was a mixed blessing. It later helped the British Army when we intervened in the murderous disintegration of Yugoslavia in the 1990s. But it dulled our senses when we came to Iraq in 2004 where, despite the extraordinary courage of individual soldiers, our senior commanders often appeared hidebound by too much peacekeeping. The 'soft hat' approach we had used in Northern Ireland led to the army losing control of the city of Basra. Our allies, particularly the US, became openly critical of our unwillingness to grip security in the city, and our lack of offensive spirit.

The year 1971 was the Battalion's first operational tour in Northern Ireland. I'm not sure we knew what to expect. A rather earnest brigadier came to brief us, after which he asked if we had any questions. A brother officer and to this day a close friend, Jamie Robertson, raised his hand and said, "Sir, are you by any chance wearing a toupee?"

Our brigade commander in North Belfast was a gritty and controversial figure. Brigadier Frank Kitson, later General Sir Frank Kitson, who is now 94 at the time of writing and only gently fading away, was a warrior from our retreat from empire. An original thinker, Kitson had won an MC in Kenya during the Mau Mau uprising and a bar to his MC in the Malayan Emergency. A lot of people were frightened of him. He was laconic and forensic and would fix you with an expressionless stare which most people found disconcerting. I think it was all part of an act to test your mettle. He certainly instilled confidence in the soldiers; but perhaps less so in the Catholic community.

I got along fine with Kitson, I suspect because we had both been on operations in the Malayan jungle, and I had come across equally challenging figures during my time in the SAS. This was all good news for Prince of Wales Company, because Kitson gave us the task as his Brigade reserve force. That meant we were the first to tackle any incident, shooting or riot in the Brigade's area of responsibility. They were challenging but exciting times.

The Brigade comprised eight battalions, substantially larger than a normal peacetime brigade. Kitson would hold a weekly conference for key staff, members of the Royal Ulster Constabulary (RUC), and the battalion commanders. I was included as the Brigade's reserve commander.

It paid to have your wits about you at those weekly conferences. One commanding officer, a languid cavalryman, was asked by Kitson what he felt his Regiment had achieved that week.

The commanding officer drawled, "Well, Sir, we've had a successful week. We found a radio."

I realised that was not going to play out too well. Kitson looked at him for a second or two, like a leopard surveying his prey, then pounced. "A radio, you say? What type of radio? What is the frequency range? How is it adding to our intelligence picture?"

The commanding officer shrank back in his chair, murmuring that he thought it was quite a big radio.

Belfast was becoming increasingly febrile. Armed gangs had all but taken over large swathes of the city. Londonderry was no better. Both cities were showing the scars of conflict. The death toll of soldiers, civilians and members of the IRA was rising fast.

By the early summer, the various Protestant associations took to the streets during the 'marching season' to mark King Billy's victories against the Catholic King James. That added to the turmoil. The Northern Ireland Government at Stormont just wavered; and that was enough to convince the IRA's leadership that more violence would lead to more concessions. It was classic insurgency tactics.

I was determined to remain non-partisan and that Prince of Wales Company should earn a reputation for impartiality. In this we succeeded. We were tasked to deal with a Protestant demonstration in central Belfast near the Divis Tower, a hideous 1960s building which was often the focus of tension between the Catholic and Protestant communities. Ian Paisley, then in his mid-40s, had already made his mark as a rabble-rousing demagogue; it would be almost another 40 years before he showed signs of statesmanship. In the meantime, he was bellowing through a tannoy, doing his best to stir things up.

The Catholic community in the nearby Falls Road area were gathering. I remember the words of one Guardsman who was standing near me as I surveyed the scene. "Fuckin' drama merchant, that bloke Paisley, ain't he."

I persuaded Paisley to desist, and he duly departed.

Shortly afterwards we were visited by General Sir Michael Carver, the newly appointed CGS. Carver was a remarkable man in many ways. He had commanded an armoured brigade in Normandy in 1944–45 at the age of 29, but he was notoriously peppery and not given to small talk.

One of the men, I think L/Cpl Griffiths 56*, came up with a colourful gem: "Well, for a general, he was a bundle of fuckin' laughs. Looked like a moose that had been kicked in the bollocks, didn't he." Ironically, 18 months later I went on to serve as Carver's Military Assistant after I had finished Staff College. I did not regale him with that anecdote.

A few days later we had to put down a major riot by the Protestant community in the unlikely named Snugville Street, a side-street off the staunchly loyalist Shankill Road. It was all chaotic – a cacophony of noise, confusion, petrol bombs, bottles, rocks and other missiles.

A self-styled community leader came up to me and said, "Major, your presence here is causing extra tension. If you and your soldiers would just withdraw, I'm sure things will calm down."

I was having none of that. There were around 250 rioters, soused with drink and hell-bent on wanton vandalism. I stood my ground and said, "The people you claim to represent are rioting. They were rioting before we arrived, so it has nothing to do with our presence. Tell them to go home, or we will disperse them – by force if necessary."

I can recall only part of the subsequent sequence of events. I later thought of the Duke of Wellington's remark after

---

*In Welsh Regiments where surnames like Griffiths, Jones, Thomas, Owen and Williams are commonplace, soldiers are often referred to by their last two army numbers.

Waterloo that the history of a battle is not unlike the history of a ball: "One can have an overall sense of what happened, but no individual can recollect all the little events or the order in which they occurred."

Snugville Street was no Waterloo, but we put the riot down with great professionalism and no little dark humour. It also helped that Prince of Wales Company had quite a few members of the Battalion's rugby team which had won the Army Cup in 1970 and 1971, just a few days before we deployed to Northern Ireland. The RUC, whose reputation for even-handedness was questionable at that time, were nowhere to be seen.

I had the overriding impression that many of them enjoyed rioting and fighting for no particular reason. That was confirmed a week later when a man came up to one of my platoon commanders and said, "Was it youse Welsh boys involved in that dust-up we had last week on the Shankill? Fockin' great fight, that was. Enjoyed that, so we did."

There was one other incident during these riots that has stuck in my mind. Lance Sergeant Williams 75, whom I had occasion to bust down a rank quite regularly during his time in the army, was proficient in his handling of one of the Company's 'pigs'. The 'pig' was a heavily armoured 1-ton Humber personnel-carrier with a snout-like appearance. It was a lumbering vehicle, fitted with a 400-volt electric shock switch to repel unwanted boarders. L/Sgt Williams' pig appeared to break down, and was immediately surrounded by rioters trying to rock it over. At this point Williams switched on the voltage, sending them howling and running away in outrage. Then, he calmly started the pig and drove away out of trouble, grinning with delight.

The battle of Snugville Street was a wonderful fillip for company morale. As we returned to our base at the disused factory at Carnmoney, I remember Warrant Officer 2nd Class 'Gazang' Ellis, one of the Company's memorable characters, saying to me, "The boys did us proud today, Sir. Good Welshmen all of them, plenty of spirit, got stuck in but kept a tight grip on themselves."

I was proud of how they had conducted themselves in trying conditions. More importantly, it demonstrated to the Catholics that the Welsh Guards were impartial in their dealings with the warring communities. The Battalion's reputation was immeasurably enhanced. Prince of Wales Company suffered no casualties throughout our tour.

If I had any lingering thoughts about returning to the SAS later in my career, that tour in Northern Ireland commanding Prince of Wales Company put paid to them. I was determined to remain a Welsh Guardsman and command the Battalion.

The political decision to impose internment without trial on 9 August undid much of the good work the army had done in the earlier part of 1971. Before 9 August 1971, 31 people were killed; in the rest of August 35 more died. Another 150 lost their lives before the end of the year. In 1972, the death toll of soldiers, IRA and civilians rose to 500, by far the bloodiest year of the Troubles.

There was one event during our tour for which I remain eternally grateful. I was minded before the start of the tour to ask Kate Worrall to marry me on my return from Northern Ireland.

I was busy enough during the tour, but in the uncertain hours early one morning, wakeful and restless, I realised I had better get on with things and make my intentions clear.

The following evening, I waited for my turn to use the welfare telephone. We were all allowed two minutes a week to telephone family and loved ones.

I had two minutes to change the course of my life. I rang Kate with more than a touch of apprehension. My radio operator, who had to be close by at all times, pretended not to listen as I told Kate I loved her. I also asked her to meet me at 8.30am the following morning at Heathrow, the start of a four-day break (R&R) from operations. Kate replied that was impossible as she had a meeting. I remember my words to her: "Well, cancel it. I've got something to ask you that can no longer wait." I put the phone down.

Many years later, when I was a guest on *Desert Island Discs*, I chose Stevie Wonder singing 'I Just Called to Say I Love You'.

7

Military Assistant to the Chief
of the General Staff

Mastering the labyrinthine ways of the MOD.

"My senior Military Assistant, David Ramsbotham, thinks you are the right man for the job. If you fail, I can always sack you."

I looked at General Sir Michael Carver's face for just a hint of encouragement, but his expression, as always, was deadpan.

I had travelled up that day from the Staff College with a fellow officer and good friend to be interviewed for what was the plum job for students leaving the Staff College. I was recently married, which was in my favour. My fellow student in the running was a bachelor, and it was thought his mind might drift elsewhere in the evenings or, worse still, at the weekends. The office of the CGS is hard work at the best of times. With Michael Carver as CGS, there was no room for compromise or concessions to feelings.

My year spent at the Staff College was also my first year of marriage to Kate. We spent the first four months at the Royal Military College of Science at Shrivenham, which was part of the Staff College syllabus. Most of the scientific lectures were a little above my head.

I was given one project on which to lead, and that was to develop a method for riot control using hypodermic needles. The aim was to fire a projectile to put rioters into a deep slumber. It seemed a pretty daft idea then, and equally fanciful now. I was told the scheme would not work, although I was given high marks for presentation and originality of thought.

Our first married quarter was 157 King's Ride. It is strange how your first married address remains indelibly printed in your mind. It was unmodernised, damp and cold. I bought some paraffin heaters to jazz the place up a bit, but we just ended up stinking of paraffin. Kate, by now, knew what she had let herself in for.

The Staff College course itself is competitive. You are observed, marked and graded all the time. The instructors are some of the brightest lieutenant colonels in the army. I was pleasantly surprised to see that my broad operational experience to date, and my time in the SAS, allowed me to do well.

Most of my contemporaries on the course seemed to have done precious little in their careers. Northern Ireland had not really kicked off, and what experience they had was limited to a few desultory exercises in north-west Germany. I learned the art, during group discussions, of listening carefully to everyone's point of view and then summarising the salient points to the syndicate, tempered with a thought of my own born from personal experience.

I had captained the Army Rugby Team, so I put myself forward to captain the Staff College Rugby Team, but not before I had changed the fixture list to ensure we had an unbeaten season. This was much to the delight of the Commandant, Patrick Howard-Dobson, who was a rugby fanatic. I knew the army well enough by then. Its unwritten culture and the importance of gamesmanship was best expressed in Henry Newbolt's famous poem 'The Vitai Lampada':

The Gatling's jammed and the Colonel dead
And the Regiment blind with dust and smoke.
But the voice of a schoolboy rallies the ranks,
"Play up! Play up! and play the game!"

As I look back on my career, my two years as Military Assistant (MA) to the CGS were as formative as my time in the SAS. I learnt how the army worked, how the Ministry of Defence (MOD) worked and how the top civil servants operated. I learnt as much from Michael Carver on how not to do things as how to do things. A cold fish and fiercely clever, he had no emotional intelligence and had the unnerving habit of giving you complex briefs as he left the office for lunch: "I want next year's financial projections for BAOR by 3pm." As anyone who could give me such information was likely to be at lunch as well (sandwiches at the desk did not become the norm until the late '80s), I found these short-order requests to be unsettling.

Even to this day, I still have the occasional dream of the austere figure of Carver standing over me, handing me a pile of papers with the words, "I should like a *précis* of these so I can brief the Prime Minister." He would think nothing of telephoning his aide-de-camp (ADC) late on a Friday evening when the ADC was in the country for the weekend, ordering the unfortunate man to bring him his fountain pen which he had left in the office.

It does you no harm to work for such an individual, however disagreeable it may seem at the time. A hard taskmaster teaches you a good deal more than someone who is amiable but indecisive. Still, I regret often returning home in the evening to Kate on a short fuse.

Carver had won an immediate DSO for his leadership at the battle of El Alamein in 1942, and at 29 was the youngest brigade commander in the British Army. Field Marshal Montgomery, no soft touch himself, said of Carver, "This officer thinks there is nothing but dead wood between him and the Chief of the Imperial General Staff."

Carver was devoid of sentimentality. I attribute that to his wartime experiences and the fact that his family, previously wealthy and of some standing, had been badly affected by the Depression. This allowed him to take hard decisions without emotion concerning the future structure of the British Army and the Reserves.

It was little comfort to those of us at the time who were looking for more benign leadership from the top. The three most senior officers in the army were called Carver, Hackett and Fraser 'The Razor'. Those names conjured up an unsettling vision of a triumvirate of ruthless butchers.

The MOD at the time was blessed with some colourful and eclectic characters. None was more lively than Harry Dalzell-Payne. Harry was then a colonel on the Northern Ireland desk and one of the most gifted officers of his generation. The Troubles were now in full swing and Carver found that most of his time was spent on the province, particularly after the disaster of 'Bloody Sunday'.

"Fetch Dalzell-Payne immediately. Find his location. Why is he not at his desk?" Carver would say.

Much of the time, Harry's desk was at Crockfords, the casino in Curzon Street, Mayfair. I liked Harry and kept my own counsel as to his whereabouts. I would put a telephone call in, and Harry would dash back in complete command of his brief.

Harry had an extraordinary ability to spend the evening carousing until the small hours, then get into a cold bath where he would go to sleep. None the worse for wear, he would then give politicians and senior officers a brilliant summary of how things stood in the province. Sadly, it all caught up with him in the end. As a divisional commander in Germany, laden with debt, he was caught out trying to import a horse-box full of port without paying tax. Harry was never found guilty but there were any number of senior officers who wanted to pull him down. The Army Board had no option but to ask him to resign. It was the end of a dazzling career. Harry bounced back in Boston and New York where he built a successful career in financial services. We kept in touch, often over a jolly lunch, until his death in 2018.

I would not wish, however, to appear churlish or ungrateful about Carver. He was a remarkable soldier with an extraordinary intellect. He may not have expressed thanks or asked after me or my family once during my time in his service, but he helped my career immeasurably. In his own inimitable way, he was ferocious but fun.

Carver's successor as CGS was also a fighting soldier with a fine war record. But there the similarity ended. General Sir Peter Hunt was a Seaforth Highlander whose career, after the war, was largely spent in the Far East. He was a man of natural warmth and avuncular temperament. His time in the Tropics had taught him to take life at a different pace to Carver, though he was every bit as competent.

If Carver got things done through sheer intellect, Hunt got the same results through the loyalty and the affection he inspired. He had a black Labrador called 'Pudding' which would accompany him around the MOD. Hunt had never served in the MOD and was not used to its byzantine ways. After my year with Carver, I was well placed to guide him through the labyrinth.

Some years previously, when he had been knighted and was serving as General Officer Commanding (GOC) Far East Land Forces, Hunt had asked his ADC to book him on to a cruise holiday. "Please don't book it using my rank," he said. "I really just want some peace and quiet."

The ADC duly booked the holiday without mention of Hunt's rank of General, but slipped up about the knighthood.

Unfortunately, he was paged at a reception desk by an announcement asking for "Sir Peter Hunt."

Shortly afterwards, a socially ambitious American approached him exclaiming, "Excuse me, but did I hear that right? Are you Sir Hunt, a genuine English Sir?"

Hunt, not missing a beat, replied, "Good gracious, no! There must be a spelling mistake on the passenger list. My name is Sid."

The disappointed American left him alone after that.

Inevitably the story got around, and thereafter he was known affectionately by his colleagues as 'Sid'.

I never dared call him 'Sid' myself, but he probably wouldn't have minded too much if I had – in fact, he would probably have laughed. He was a charming man, and a very fine CGS.

I was to serve a further ten years in the MOD, including six years as CGS and CDS. I gave my staff strict instructions never to arrange meetings on a Friday afternoon, and that everyone should have left the office by 5pm for the weekend.

8

Cyprus

*The Turkish invasion of Cyprus in July 1974
put an end to Greek Cypriot ambitions of the
Hellenic Republic of Cyprus. The Welsh Guards
deployed to Cyprus in October 1975 as part of
the United Nations (UN) peacekeeping force.*

The Cyprus emergency was not the first or last time that I found myself involved in the dampening down of the embers of the British Empire. I scoured the Turkish Army's positions to the north of the United Nations buffer zone known as the Green Line with my binoculars, and saw the distinctive red flag of the Turkish Republic with its white star and crescent fluttering in the early morning breeze.

Standing next to me was the Brigade Commander, British Forces Cyprus. He seemed to be flapping rather more than the Turkish flag. When he had learned that his final posting was to be in the idyllic setting of Cyprus, I doubt he had imagined that he would find himself facing a Turkish parachute brigade.

The evening before I had introduced myself to the Turkish General. He had snowy white hair and held himself well. His

almond-shaped eyes and quizzical smile exuded calmness.
I discovered that he had fought with the Turkish Brigade
as part of the UN forces in the Korean War. Over a bottle
of Yakut, Turkey's lively red wine, he made it clear that
he had no intention of progressing further south than the
UN-monitored Green Line which divided the Greek and
Turkish forces.

I remember his words even now: "Even if the Turkish
Cypriot community did not exist, Turkey would not have left
Cyprus to Greece, but we must defend our peoples here from
Greek nationalism." He went on, "Please remember, Colonel,
as members of NATO since 1952, we take our obligations
seriously to the member states. We do not want to fall out
with the British. We both suffered at Cape Helles in 1915
when we fought each other to the death."

With the Turkish General's words echoing in my mind, I
felt able to reassure the British Forces Brigadier that there was
no cause for alarm. He was unused to being at the sharp end
of a potential crisis, having spent much of his career on the
staff or in the MOD.

Deep down, I think the British Army had, in its collective
unconscious, a fear of the Turkish Army after the disastrous
Gallipoli campaign in 1915. "That's all very well, Charles," the
Brigadier remarked, "But Johnny Turk is a tough customer.
You only have to look at how they treat their own soldiers."

At the time there were rumours that Turkish officers beat
their soldiers on the soles of their feet, and any soldier caught
asleep on sentry was shot on the spot. I think that might have
been true in the Korean War, but their adversaries then were
the Chinese People's Volunteer Army. Falling asleep on sentry
with thousands of Chinese 'volunteers' swarming all over you
could indeed have fatal consequences.

Being awarded the Army Rugby Cup by General Sir David Peel Yates. The Welsh Guards won the cup 1962–64.

All togged up as Head of School, 1957.

As Head of School at Harrow, 1957, HRH The Prince Philip, Duke of Edinburgh, on my left; Her Majesty is clearly enjoying her visit.

Harrow vs Wellington, 1957: Simon Clarke from Wellington, who later played for England, making his break. Robin Butler (later Lord Butler of Brockwell, Cabinet Secretary and Head of the Home Civil Service) on my left.

Army Officer Selection Board, 1957: one of these unlikely looking lads has a field marshal's baton in his knapsack.

Captain Poldark,
Aden 1966.

The remains of the Parsi cemetery (1998) overlooking the town of Aden where I holed up with my SAS patrol in 1967. (© Ka Wing Chan, https://www.flickr.com/photos/chan_kawing/27031261102/in/photostream/)

A happy memory during the Troubles: commanding Prince of Wales Company in Belfast, 1971.

Our wedding day, 11 September 1971.

Keeping a watchful eye as Military Assistant to the Chief of the General Staff, the fearsome General Sir Michael Carver, on a visit to the Swedish Army, 1973. (Crown Copyright)

Leading the procession on the return from HM The Queen's Silver Jubilee Thanksgiving Service at St Paul's Cathedral, 7 June 1977. (Crown Copyright)

The loneliness of command, Schleswig-Holstein, November 1977.

My 40th birthday party, 17 November 1978. The junior officers are acting as Mess waiters.

No sign of spring, St David's Day in Berlin, 1979. My good friend and mentor, Major General Sir Philip Ward, hands out the leeks. (Crown Copyright)

The Troubles: South Armagh, winter 1979/80. The Regimental Sergeant Major, Emlyn Pridham, a wonderful man and friend, is on my left. (Crown Copyright)

A morale-boosting visit to the Regiment in South Armagh by our Colonel, HRH The Prince of Wales, 1979. (Crown Copyright).

South Armagh, Christmas 1979. Mrs Thatcher in full swing accompanied by her husband, Denis.
(Crown Copyright)

Jimmy Stevens and the rebels in the 'Coconut War', 1980.
(Photo by Alain Dejean/Sygma via Getty Images)

The rebels were a formidable foe,
armed to the teeth.

Handing out medals: an enjoyable
duty as Colonel Commandant of the
Intelligence Corps, 1986. (Crown Copyright)

With Her Majesty The Queen Mother on her visit to York Minster, 1987. (Crown Copyright)

The army marches on its stomach: judging the Gurkha curry competition, 1987.

Exchanging pleasantries with my counterpart from the Russian Third Shock Army, 1992. (Crown Copyright)

Elements of the Royal Armoured Corps in plain sight, First Gulf War, August 1990. (Crown Copyright)

A tonic for the troops: a visit by Princess Diana to the British Army of the Rhine, 1992.
(Crown Copyright)

A visit to Fort Knox in Kentucky, adjacent to the US Bullion Depository of 'Goldfinger' fame, 1993.

The Calgary Stampede in full 'Ben Hur' mode, 1993.

With Robert Cranborne, Parliamentary Under-Secretary of State for Defence, at the Calgary Stampede – some light relief from a visit to watch the British Army on live-firing exercises in Canada, 1993.

No substitute for realistic training: observing tanks from the 17/21st Lancers (the Queen's Royal Lancers from 1993) live firing in Canada. (Photo: Sgt Mark Webster RLC/MOD/Open Government Licence version 1.0)

Meeting the US Secretary of State for Veterans' Affairs, Togo D. West, 1994. (Crown Copyright)

Duty dancing with the Bulgarian Minister of Defence's wife, 1994.

A great ally of Britain and a good friend, the remarkable Qaboos bin Said, Sultan of Oman, 1995.

Spot the helicopter: flying above the Al Hajar mountain range in Oman, 1995.

A day of remembrance: with Churchill's grandson, Nicholas Soames, Minister of State for the Armed Forces, at the Helles Memorial on the Gallipoli peninsula, 1995. (Crown Copyright)

Chatting to new recruits in the South African Defence Force undergoing parachute training, 1996.

I don't think my words of reassurance had much effect. The Brigadier remained as fearful as a cat in a tree. I, however, was delighted to be in Cyprus after what had been a demanding two years as Military Assistant to the Chief of the General Staff. Time spent more or less desk-bound in the MOD doesn't lend itself to keeping fit, and I cherished my time in Cyprus with all that it had to offer. Although I was second-in-command of the Battalion, I enjoyed the rank (and increase in pay) of a lieutenant colonel. This was because the Battalion was divided into two with different responsibilities.

The commanding officer, Peter Williams, Battalion Headquarters and two companies were part of the United Nations forces; they wore the UN blue beret. I was in command of my old company, Prince of Wales Company, and Support Company. We were part of British Forces Cyprus, and we wore our normal Welsh Guards khaki beret. Ostensibly, I was in charge of the UK Sovereign Base area of Dhekelia. The other Sovereign Base area was at Akrotiri, where the RAF were to be found taxiing gently around the airbase.

If all this sounds rather muddling, it probably was. The British colonial policies of divide and rule to prevent action (whether Greek or Turkish) against colonial rule was always going to be messy. Britain had annexed Cyprus into the British Empire after the Ottoman Empire, or Turkish Caliphate, collapsed after the Great War, where it had sided with Germany.

There was bound to be trouble. At that stage northern Cyprus was 80 per cent ethnic Greek. As we unravelled ourselves from empire at the end of the Second World War, the National Organisation of Greek Cypriot Fighters (EOKA) saw their chance to end British colonial rule and unify Greece and Cyprus (Enosis).

The Turkish Cypriots who made up quite a bit of the population of southern Cyprus were having none of this. Fighting and 'ethnic cleansing' on both sides became an unpleasant feature of the emergency running throughout the 1950s and 1960s, despite Cyprus winning its independence in 1960.

After the Greek coup, supported by EOKA in 1974, Turkey invaded in July 1974 and again in August that year; 150,000 Greek Cypriots were expelled from the North and 60,000 Turkish Cypriots moved northwards to replace them. UN forces remain in Cyprus today to keep the peace.

If the Brigadier Commanding British Forces was windy, the General Officer Commanding Near East Land Forces was as steady as a lighthouse. Corran Purdon was an Irish-born commando who took part in the St Nazaire raid where he had won the Military Cross. He was subsequently imprisoned in Colditz Castle.

Purdon did not stand on ceremony and stripped his grand GOC's villa of most of its pictures and furniture, replacing it with gym equipment. Needless to say, he was a fitness fanatic. He took me to task about the size of one of my sergeants. I batted this away saying that the sergeant had been the Battalion's scrum-half when the Welsh Guards had won the Army Rugby Cup two years before.

Purdon thought the Welsh Guards were marvellous. He was a warrior. He enjoyed our sense of humour and our shared Celtic heritage. It doesn't seem so funny now, but it made me chuckle at the time when he visited the officers' quarters and asked one of the officers how he found the accommodation.

The officer, who had a similar manner to Private Godfrey in *Dad's Army*, replied, "Well, I have to say the loos are too far away, rather maddening in the middle of the night."

Purdon, without missing a beat, said, "Well, I suggest you pee in the basin then." Purdon's son, Tim, later commanded the Welsh Guards in Northern Ireland in the mid-1990s.

Cyprus was a brief but sunny interlude in my career. After two months I was recalled, on promotion, to London to take up the position as Brigade Major to the Household Division. Despite its ambiguous title, Brigade Major, it carried with it the rank of substantive lieutenant colonel.

The Cyprus embers have not died out. On 20 July 2020, the 46th anniversary of Turkey's invasion, President Erdogan of Turkey made a belligerent speech calling for "a permanent solution to the island dispute, and equal rights over the island's natural resources".

Turkey still has 30,000 troops stationed in the north. Hopes of reunification between Turkish and Greek Cypriots remain fanciful.

9

Brigade Major, The Household Division

And I heard someone cry,
"Clear the front for the Guards!"
And the Guards came through.

ARTHUR CONAN DOYLE

I have had enough practice to consider myself a reasonably accomplished horseman, but as I rode to St Paul's Cathedral for HM The Queen's Silver Jubilee Thanksgiving Service, I was just a little anxious. My charger, a horse called Amarillo, would rear up alarmingly at the sound of bells.

It was no occasion to be unhorsed. As the procession approached the church of St Clement Danes in the Strand, I could hear the church bells beginning to sound. But I had not expected on that windy and overcast morning of 7 June 1977 that 1 million people would be lining the streets of London to cheer Her Majesty as she made her way in the Gold State Coach to St Paul's Cathedral. Amarillo may have hated bells, but she loved the applause of the crowds. My journey passed without any dent to my pride. I was not so fortunate 41 years later as I rode back down the Mall to Buckingham Palace after Trooping the Colour.

I had joined a family Regiment, the Welsh Guards, but in doing so I joined the much wider family of the Household Division, whose ancestry went back to the English Civil War and the Restoration of King Charles II in 1660. The Household Division's motto, 'Septem Juncta in Uno' ('Seven Joined in One'), underlines the strong ties of kith and kin that is its hallmark.

The reigning monarch, uniquely, is Commander-in-Chief of all seven regiments of the Household Division. The Household Division enjoys a privileged position, but privilege comes with responsibility. I was determined on my appointment as Brigade Major, the Division's principal staff officer, that we should exceed the standards expected of us.

I remember saying recently to an officer who was about to take up the position of Brigade Major that it was the hardest I had ever worked in the army. He visibly blanched, remarking that surely precedent would ensure there would be few surprises in ceremonial duties.

I cast my mind back to 1977 and the firemen's strike, which had tested all our resources. I do not suppose he imagined that only a few months into the job, he would be faced with a pandemic which would see Trooping the Colour cancelled for only the second time in the Queen's reign.

The national celebrations for the Queen's Silver Jubilee in 1977 were just the tonic Britain needed. For those of us who lived through that decade, it is easy enough to be nostalgic. The reality was grim. The 1970s were desperately difficult years, politically and economically. We were seen as the sick man of Europe: power cuts, strikes, grim headlines, the financial crash after the Yom Kippur War with oil prices quadrupling from 1973 to 1974, and the IRA bombing campaign on the mainland. The British people were understandably at a very low ebb.

In times of uncertainty we all look for constants and things we know we do well. The Jubilee year was the perfect antidote for a country grown weary of apparent decline.

As Brigade Major for the Household Division, I reminded myself of the sign on President Harry Truman's desk at the White House: 'The Buck Stops Here'.

I was fortunate, as I have often been in my career, in the advice and guidance I received from some outstanding non-commissioned officers. The Garrison Sergeant Major (GSM), Tom Taylor, was such a man. The GSM London District, always a Guardsman, is one of the most senior warrant officer appointments in the British Army. It is certainly the most visible appointment.

Few people in their right mind would ever take on the GSM on matters of protocol or turnout. At the lying-in-state of Winston Churchill, the Chiefs of Staff did a vigil with reversed swords. Lord Mountbatten turned up in full fig and said to the GSM at the time, "How do I look?" The GSM replied, "Terribly sloppy, Sir." The other Chiefs of Staff were delighted with this put-down.

Tom had joined the Grenadiers in 1942. He was not only a natural warrior but he also had a great love of ceremonial and a gimlet eye for detail. Ironically, Tom told me his love of ceremonial had started during the bitter fighting of the Normandy campaign in the autumn of 1944. During a lull in the fighting, his battalion were a little worse for wear after they discovered a large cellar groaning with cider and calvados which the French had kept hidden from the Nazis. As they were due to carry on the fight in the next day or so, the Regimental Sergeant Major organised a battalion drill parade on the square at Pont-Saint-Pierre. Tom said it was the best possible tonic for the Battalion's collective hangover.

I owed him a great deal during a Jubilee year which was packed with ceremonial and the added pressures of many Guardsmen working as firemen during the protracted firemen's strike in 1977.

I was also lucky in the two major generals commanding the Household Division with whom I served. The first, Philip Ward, I knew well from my time in Aden. Commanding the Household Division was the perfect vehicle for his wonderful attributes which I have already highlighted. Philip cared deeply for the people and fabric of the Household Division. He was an exemplary ambassador for the Division and the army.

My second boss at Horse Guards was equally impressive, albeit in different ways. John Swinton was a Scots Guardsman of ancient lineage of which he was rightly proud. His ancestors had fought and died for James IV of Scotland at Flodden Field in 1513. Flodden was the last medieval battle and the bloodiest of affairs, where the English billhook under the Earl of Surrey got the better of the Scottish pike.

The Swinton warrior spirit has never left the family. John lost the lower part of his left leg in hard fighting in Nazi Germany during the last days of the Second World War. Ironically, his father had lost the same part of his leg a few days before the Armistice in 1918. John took pride in his daughter, the acclaimed actress Tilda Swinton, with her enigmatic and chilling film performances.

Given such a bloodline, it was not surprising that on first acquaintance John could appear austere and aloof. He did have the rather disconcerting habit of removing his wooden leg and polishing it in front of you. He always dismounted from his horse in great style, taking both feet out of the stirrups, swinging his good right leg over his charger's back and landing with a heavy thud on the ground. John insisted that we all wore field boots and spurs on military visits. Both he and Tom Taylor sported walrus-like moustaches and, when walking together across Horse Guards, would look as though they had both been hired by Central Casting for a film set.

John Swinton was the last of the Household Division Major Generals to have fought in the Second World War. It gave him, as it gave my first four Welsh Guards commanding officers, a generosity of spirit and a willingness to listen to and encourage young officers. The war had taught them the importance of not compromising on the highest of standards. They were angered only by the shoddy, the second-rate, or anyone showing indifference to others.

He was kind enough to grade me as outstanding in my confidential report. The Commander-in-Chief United Kingdom Land Forces wrote to him saying that he would not agree to the grade as, in his opinion, the job of organising ceremonial parades in London did not warrant it. John replied that he had already agreed the grade with the Queen, and would the General like to take it up with Her Majesty? There was no further dissent.

My two years as Brigade Major gave me time to get to know my cousins in the Household Division family. Like any family, it was full of idiosyncrasies, nicknames and a certain amount of nonsense. But we were all much the richer for it. The collective sense of pride and mutual loyalty was palpable. Some battalions were better than others, but that, as it always does, came down to leadership. Even during those two years I saw poor battalions become excellent and sometimes the other way round.

In retrospect, I do not think the 1970s and 1980s were a purple patch for the Household Division as a whole. The rest of the army caught up with us. For too long we had rested on our laurels, relying on our nuanced relationship with the establishment and popularity with the public through Trooping the Colour and other ceremonial events. Institutional arrogance had begun to creep in.

The Household Division are first and foremost operational soldiers. We had so far escaped the cuts and amalgamations that had pared the rest of the army almost to the bone. Even as I write these words, I see there are proposals to slash the army from 72,000 to 55,000 to defend Britain's interests in a world of growing uncertainty.

We never seem to learn the lesson that threats often emerge from nowhere. A balanced military capability remains indispensable to complement technological innovation to combat cyber warfare, and the need for a new generation of combat drones.

Nevertheless, I remain buoyant about the Household Division's future. It is not just the 'soft power', influence we enjoy through public duties and ceremonial; or the hard currency we generate for the country through tourism. The last 25 years have given the Household Division significant operational experience through the Balkans, both Gulf wars, Iraq and Afghanistan. We have acquitted ourselves as well as any of the regiments in the British Army.

Sir Arthur Conan Doyle wrote his poem 'The Guards Came Through' in 1917. It was his testament to his son, Arthur, killed in action in 1918. It had been written in much the same vein as Rudyard Kipling's 'My Boy Jack', a lament for the loss of his son fighting with the Irish Guards at the battle of Loos in 1915.

From time to time I like to re-read Conan Doyle's poem to remind me of the great family that is the Household Division.

> But Lord, if you'd hear the cheer,
> Irish, Welsh and Scot, Coldstream and Grenadier,
> a trifle of swank and dash, cool as a home parade,
> twinkle, glitter and flash, flinching never a shade.

Commanding the Welsh Guards in Berlin

*In the midst of the Cold War, surrounded by Soviet-
controlled East Berlin and East Germany, West Berlin,
controlled by the USA, France and Britain, had great
symbolic significance.*

BERLIN

I look back on my time commanding the Welsh Guards in
Berlin as some of the happiest days in my life. Berlin was
competitive. It was as much a diplomatic as a military posting
as we served alongside our French, German and American
allies. It was exciting living in a city which, in the 1970s, was
a lot more seductive than London.

There was also a sharpness to Berlin. Its past history was
never far away. Until the Wall came down in 1989, Berlin was
an accurate temperature gauge for world affairs.

At the Yalta conference in February 1945, Winston Churchill,
Franklin D. Roosevelt and Joseph Stalin agreed to carve up
Germany and Berlin into four zones of occupation controlled
by Britain, the USA, the Soviet Union and France. Berlin was
sliced up into 20 administrative areas. Britain looked after
Charlottenberg, Tiergarten and Spandau. The USA looked

after six areas including the famous 'Checkpoint Charlie'. France had responsibility for two areas, and the Soviets held on to eight districts in the east. The Soviets also occupied the land surrounding Berlin, leaving West Berlin encircled. On the night of 13 August 1961, the Wall went up between West and East Berlin. The Cold War had started – unrelenting, and the focus of world affairs for close to three decades.

There may have been a slight thawing in the Cold War as the Soviet Union and the West pursued a policy of Détente in the mid-1970s, but it was not noticeable to the British Army's Berlin Infantry Brigade. We were 100 miles inside East Germany and surrounded by half a million soldiers from the Warsaw Pact, the defence organisation comprising the Soviet Union and seven other Eastern Bloc countries. The Soviets admire fortitude, and I believe they respected us in our commitment to defend West Berlin.

Against that ominous political and military background, there was a strong sense of purpose and an opportunity to train the Regiment as I saw fit. I was fortunate in that I took over the Battalion from Peter Williams who had led, trained and motivated the Battalion with calm efficiency and his characteristic energy.

We were based in Wavell Barracks in Spandau, well built, austere but comfortable with a large parade square. We were close to the Grunewald forest and the Havel river, all of which we could use for imaginative training. The Grunewald and Havel were also wonderful backdrops for high-profile visitors. Everyone wanted to visit West Berlin at the height of the Cold War.

Our Colonel, The Prince of Wales, came to see us in the early summer of 1979. He had taken over from Prince Philip as our Colonel in 1975. I am not sure he took to us early on.

At his first Regimental dinner, he found himself surrounded by moustachioed badgers, some of them not unlike the *Colonel Blimp* characters portrayed by the artist Rex Whistler, who had been killed in action serving with the Regiment in 1944.

But as time moved on, The Prince of Wales has become a greatly loved and respected Colonel, steadfast in his support of the Regiment. We have been extraordinarily fortunate to have him as our Colonel.

We put on an assault river crossing of the Havel for The Prince of Wales. I asked the Regimental Sergeant Major, Emlyn Pridham, to lead the assault and keep the boats in some semblance of order. It was only afterwards that Emlyn told me he had never learnt to swim.

Fortunately, we were fully up to strength as a battalion. This was helpful as, with careful planning, it allowed me to get people away for sport, courses and adventure training, including a well-organised programme in Steibis in Bavaria to teach Guardsmen to ski. These were all the things that make a soldier's life balanced and worthwhile. For many, the opportunities for sport, travel and excitement were the reasons they joined the army.

We trained hard and we played hard. We became tough and fit. At the end of our time in Berlin, as we embarked on an operational tour in South Armagh, I said to the Battalion that we were one of the best infantry battalions in the British Army. I did not say it lightly.

My company commanders were first rate; not one dud amongst them. My principal staff officer, Christopher Drewry, was also my brother-in-law. Christopher, greatly respected and liked in the Regiment, went on to become a three-star general and probably the finest staff officer of his generation.

The Sergeants' Mess was led with style and professionalism by Regimental Sergeant Major (RSM) Glyn White and then Emlyn Pridham. Emlyn's wife, Pat, who worked in the Battalion's medical centre, had her ear to the ground and, with the Families Officer, Lewis Evans, looked after the Battalion's wives and their families. If the wives were happy, then the men were happy.

And like all good families, we had our fair share of characters. Our medical officer was a Scot called Hector MacDonald. He was a laconic Highland Scot with bushy eyebrows and an expressionless face. A good bedside manner was not his strength: "Mrs Jones, there's nothing wrong with you, except you just need to lose three stone." And to a Guardsman who complained of insomnia, "Right laddie, you won't be needing your bedding then."

The young officers were a lively bunch. Most of them pretended to be unaware that they were surrounded by the Soviet Third Shock Army. They all seemed to disappear to the French Sector in the evenings, or a club called the 1001 run by someone called Monica. I never enquired as to what went on there, but I suspect it wasn't quiet evenings playing bridge and discussing how best to handle the Soviet threat.

If I ever had cause to have my knuckles rapped by the brigade commander, it was invariably because one, or more, of the young officers had overstepped the mark. One day, I was summoned by the brigade commander, a dour Scottish Presbyterian, who said, "Charles, I'm extremely impressed by the way you're training your battalion, but I've been receiving reports that your young officers spend a lot of their time in, ahem, well, er, establishments of ill repute."

I may have misjudged his mood and replied, "As far as I know, Brigadier, this happens only on Wednesday sports afternoons." This rather flippant reply was met with a glare.

The Regiment was on show, not only to the rest of the British Army in Berlin but to our allies. I was determined that we would not be seen as stuffy, a criticism which is too easily levelled at Guards regiments. We accepted every invitation whether it was personal or regimental and I made sure my driver, Guardsman Hughes, knew every entrance and exit to every possible social or military venue in the British, French and US sectors.

If anyone came to visit the Battalion, we insisted that from the moment they entered the barrack gates, they felt that their visit was of the utmost importance to us, regardless of their position or rank.

There was, however, one incident when we were visited by a civil servant from the MOD who, on arriving in the Officers' Mess, announced his civil servant's grade, adding that it equated to the status of a major in the army. The hapless civil servant was introduced to me by a young officer as "Major Status".

On the face of things, there was not much the Berlin Infantry Brigade could do with our French, German and American allies if there was a concerted Soviet attack to wrest back control of West Berlin. What we could do effectively, however, was to delay the city being overrun, to give a breathing space for Western diplomats and the huge military and economic might of the USA to bring the Soviet Union to heel. Well, that was the theory anyway. I am glad it was not put to the test.

We did have regular crash-outs, however, called *Exercise Rocking Horse*. These were designed to test our ability to deploy at short notice, equipped and ready to fight. We also, on occasion, had to provide a quick reaction force known as the 'Alert Platoon'. Their task was simple enough: pick up the telephone within three rings, answer "Alert Platoon" with a palpable sense of urgency, and get to any part of West Berlin within 30 minutes to handle any military threat. Fortunately before my time, our first 'Alert Platoon' call-out did not go well. The platoon had been at a party the previous night and were in a poor state. On a practice crash-out, the telephone rang for three minutes rather than three rings, and a bleary-eyed, half-comatose Guardsman answered in a strong Swansea accent, "Eh, boyo, what do you want then?" Brigade Headquarters were unamused.

Nevertheless, the defence of West Berlin gave a strong focus to our training: how to fight in built-up areas; the solid infantry skills of marksmanship; using ground well; fire and manoeuvre; and building up our fitness and levels of endurance.

We knew the chokepoints where we could give the Soviets problems, and we got to know the West Berlin underground sewer system so that we could move men, ammunition and supplies to where they were needed.

Our German allies even dusted off their plans to halt the Red Army in the battle for Berlin in 1945. I considered these only partially useful, as I doubted the practicability of turning young Guardsmen into fanatics who would run up to Soviet tanks and shove anti-tank mines under their tracks.

One of the constant reminders of Berlin's Nazi past was Spandau prison. Its only prisoner during our tour of Berlin was Adolf Hitler's deputy, Rudolf Hess. Hess had been given life imprisonment at the Nuremberg War Trials in 1947 for crimes against humanity. The last war criminal to serve time there was Albert Speer, Hitler's Reichsmarschall, for armaments and slave labour. Speer had been released in 1966. But the Soviets insisted that Hess should remain in prison.

Spandau was in West Berlin and it gave the Soviets an excuse to have a presence in there. Each of the powers took it in turns to guard Hess. There was also the threat of the

'Werewolves', an underground revanchist Nazi movement, springing Hess from prison.

The Soviets were hard on Hess. They removed his books and television. We allowed him these small luxuries and gave him seeds to create a garden. He repaid our good faith by creating a flowerbed in the shape of a swastika. Hess was a wily old fox and one day, as a Welsh Guards duty officer walked past his little garden, said, "Vould you like a plum from ze tree?"

The officer politely replied, "Oh, well, er, yes, how kind, thank you."

Later that day, Hess reported that a British officer had stolen a plum. This became a major incident, stoked up by the Soviets, with diplomatic telegrams winging their way between the various foreign ministries.

A healthy competition between regiments is a good thing. It builds *esprit de corps*. The other infantry battalions in Berlin were the 1st Battalion the Green Howards, a regiment largely recruited from Yorkshire, and the 2nd Battalion of the Parachute Regiment. The Parachute Regiment and the Household Division have a close affinity born from shared adversity and a healthy regard for each other's sense of belief.

We suffered a solid defeat 7-2 at the hands of the Green Howards in the Berlin inter-regimental boxing competition. I had taken over command of the Battalion only four days before. Morale slumped and I honestly felt that the Guardsmen connected the debacle with my arrival. It's easy to forget how much soldiers attach to visible success.

The next year we found ourselves in the boxing final against the Parachute Regiment. The atmosphere with close to 800 men present was tense. We were tied at four bouts all. The final bout was light heavyweight between a tall, powerfully built Parachute Regiment officer and Guardsman Howells from No. 3 Company (known as 'The Little Iron Men').

The Parachute officer's long reach seemed to be paying dividends as he fended off Howells. As he grew in confidence, the officer let his guard down. Howells launched a terrific uppercut which lifted the officer off the ground and onto the canvas for a straight knock-out. Guardsman Howells was cheered to the echo. The unfortunate Parachute Regiment officer came to the dinner afterwards, clearly punch-drunk, reeling between tables as he apologised to his fellow officers for letting the side down.

Coincidentally, two other future heads of the British Army were serving in Berlin at the time: General Sir Richard Dannatt was then a captain in the Green Howards; and General Sir Mike Jackson was a major serving as the Berlin Infantry Brigade's Chief of Staff.

Mike Jackson devised a 'March and Shoot' competition to determine the best platoon in Berlin. It was an endurance march over 7 miles wearing day fighting equipment and carrying ammunition. This was immediately followed by a gruelling assault course. The platoons were then tested on their shooting skills at targets placed at distances between 100 and 300 metres away.

In reality, it was a hard examination in teamwork. A platoon from Prince of Wales Company led by Lieutenant Robert Mason, a former Oxford University triple rowing blue and President of the University Boat Club, won by a comfortable margin. Robert later remarked that he found the competition a good deal tougher than the Boat Race.

These successes may sound like small beer, but it had long been my experience that regiments, particularly in peacetime, reaffirm their sense of identity and belonging by achievements on the sports field and in military competitions. I do not think any of the Guardsmen had taken part in an athletics competition, and I decided we should have one in the Berlin Olympic Stadium. The stadium, designed by Hitler's architect, Albert Speer, was a magnificent setting and hosted the notorious 1936 Olympics when Hitler wanted to show off the athletic prowess of his so-called 'Master Race'. This fell apart when the remarkable American black athlete Jesse Owens ran in gold medal after gold medal.

The athletics meeting proved to be more like a circus fairground. The Guardsmen entered into events they had never done before. I overheard a couple of Guardsmen discussing their chances: "I think I'll have a crack at that pole vault, I seen it once on the TV, looks like fun. What about you, 43?"

"No, the pole vault's not for me. Mind you, the hammer looks a good laugh, and no running about needed."

Commanding officers who regard 'being extremely busy' as a measure of success are doomed to fail. I took the view that the Battalion should concentrate on a few things and do them really well. At the time, we had some excellent marksmen in the Battalion and just the right man, Colour Sergeant Frank Ward, to train, motivate and lead the team. We won the Regular Army Skill at Arms Meetings for Berlin and BAOR from 1977 to 1979.

One thing you need to master in an infantry battalion is to shoot straight and, once again, our success in this gave the men a genuine sense of pride and belonging. More importantly, the rest of the army, which often looks at Guards regiments through the prism of public duties in London and Trooping the Colour, took notice.

The Queen's Birthday Parade was also held each year in Berlin. The format was not unlike Trooping the Colour. In our first year in Berlin, 1977, this had been a bit of a disaster, as the brigade commander at the time, an Engineer, had given the wrong word of command. Fortunately, our RSM, seeing an impending fiasco about to unfold, ordered the Welsh Guards to stand firm. The Green Howards and Parachute Regiment were not quite so observant and shuffled off in every direction. Chaos ensued.

In 1978, the Queen herself attended the Berlin Parade. Her Majesty was accompanied by her Crown Equerry, Sir John Miller. John, for whom I had enormous respect, had been my first commanding officer.

John was a stickler for detail. On meeting the General Officer Commanding Berlin, Bob Richardson, a lantern-jawed lowland Scot, John told him he was wearing his sword the wrong way. Richardson looked aghast and replied he had always worn it that way. I remember John's response well: "Well, I have to point out that you must have always worn it the *wrong* away. I suggest you wear it correctly before Her Majesty spots it. She doesn't miss a thing."

The young officers were still a constant headache, but they did make up for it all by putting on my 40th birthday party in the Officers' Mess. Unbeknownst to Kate and me, they all gave the Mess staff the night off and dressed up as waiters themselves. The wife of a French colonel who was seated next to me remarked how dashing and attentive the Mess waiters were. I have never been one for marking new decades, but my 40th birthday in Berlin at the height of the Cold War was tremendous fun.

Half-way through our Berlin tour in 1978, we were warned off for an operational tour in South Armagh, Northern Ireland.

The loss of life, both civilian and military, was not as high as when we had last served there, but the dangers remained very real and the IRA in South Armagh were bitter opponents.

The topography of South Armagh bore no resemblance to Berlin, and I decided to take the Battalion to Schleswig-Holstein on the Baltic coast in November 1978 for a two-week training exercise. It had a reasonable climate in the summer months, but it could be miserably cold and wet in the winter. The biting Baltic wind and icy rain, grim though it was, was not so different from what I expected we would have to endure during a winter tour of rural South Armagh.

I doubt that anyone who came on that exercise in Schleswig-Holstein remembers it with fondness. I decided the Battalion should dig trenches and learn to live and cope in adverse conditions. As I learnt in the SAS, if you cannot manage yourself, it is pointless to imagine you can manage and lead others.

It also helped me decide how best to deploy the Battalion. I soon saw which company commander was best suited to a particular area of responsibility; who should lead the Close Observation Platoon (COP); who would be calm and efficient in headquarters; and how to get the logistics right where everything, and everyone, would have to move by helicopter.

I think I got everything about right. There was one young officer who I decided should be tucked away in South Armagh as Battalion photography officer. I had previously stood behind him on an exercise as his platoon was attacked by the enemy landing by helicopter in front of his platoon position.

He took out a cheroot, which he calmly lit, then turned around to me saying, "Oh hello, Sir. I wonder what these chaps want; they're all wearing strange uniforms with red bits." He left the army shortly after the Northern Ireland tour.

Some months later I received a letter from him thanking me for putting up with him, asking if I could give him a reference for the New York School of Dance and Ballet.

We ended the fortnight in Schleswig-Holstein with a night-time battalion attack. It was not something we would ever have to do in South Armagh unless events took a real turn for the worse, but it was an exercise in collective discipline.

I had remembered my lessons from Libya, Greece and BAOR, which was that it is extremely difficult to move a body of troops by night to the right place at the right time. I used the Battalion's Corps of Drums to drum us into battle. I was well aware that this was wholly unrealistic. It wasn't Waterloo in 1815, but on a bitterly cold, starless night it was very good for morale.

Our return by convoy from Schleswig-Holstein did not go without incident, provoking the usual 'flash' telegrams between Berlin, Moscow, London and Washington. Russia tightly controlled the corridor between the East German border (Checkpoint Alpha) and the West Berlin (Checkpoint Bravo). Cold War rules dictated that the Russians were not allowed to inspect the interiors of our vehicles, but they were allowed to check the vehicle manifest and the numbers of soldiers inside.

The last convoy comprised 19 vehicles with supposedly 53 men. The Russians, however, counted 54 men for which there was no plausible explanation. The convoy commander, Julian Peel Yates, my excellent reconnaissance platoon commander, was meticulous but perplexed. The Russians were jumping up and down.

There was an explanation but one which was straight out of the Soviet playbook on British stereotypes.

The Officers' Mess silver had been placed on one of the trucks 12 hours before the convoy was due to leave. A lance corporal from the Mess had been ordered to get on the truck and not to lose sight of the silver. However, the convoy commander had not been informed. The Soviets, having got one over us, were thrilled. It may seem trifling now but, in the Cold War frost, these little discrepancies could become international incidents.

Our time in Berlin was coming to an end. All those who served there at that time remember it with great affection. Regiments, like families, ebb and flow in their fortunes; but I like to think our time in Berlin brought the best out of people and gave them the confidence to face our forthcoming operational tour in South Armagh with calmness and composure.

Just a month before we deployed to Northern Ireland, we heard the news that the IRA had murdered Lord Mountbatten and members of his family, and our fellow regiment from Berlin, 2 Para, had lost 18 men in the Warrenpoint massacre.

Commanding the Welsh Guards
in South Armagh

A harsh, unforgiving environment which exerts a
powerful grip on all those from the British Army who
served there.

WINTER 1979–80

Early in December 1979, a Welsh Guardsman returning from patrol noticed an army water bottle close to an observation post (OP) adjacent to his base at Crossmaglen. The Guardsman, thinking a previous patrol had unwittingly dropped it, went to pick it up. An alert sergeant just managed to shout a warning. It was a lucky escape. The water bottle was booby-trapped and would almost certainly have killed the Guardsman. The incident showed that any drop in concentration, however innocent, could result in great sorrow.

South Armagh exerts a powerful grip on the memories of Welsh Guardsmen who served there during the Troubles. It was branded as 'Bandit Country', but this suggests South Armagh was a place of mere casual lawlessness. It was a great deal more murderous than that.

Over a quarter of all military casualties in Northern Ireland, killed or maimed, occurred within a 10-mile radius of the heart of South Armagh. The IRA's South Armagh Brigade were not just a bunch of criminal thugs. Many were involved in smuggling to fill the IRA's coffers to buy arms and fund their operations, but in their black hearts they were a meticulous, well-organised operation determined to "get the Brits out".

In the early autumn of 1979, shortly before the Battalion deployed to South Armagh, the British Army in Northern Ireland and the political establishment were on the back foot. The murders of Lord Mountbatten and members of his family on 27 August, and 18 soldiers from the Queen's Own Highlanders and the Parachute Regiment at Warrenpoint on the same day, shook everyone to the core.

The IRA's South Armagh Brigade had planned and carried out a highly sophisticated operation at Warrenpoint. They had studied our tactics; they knew exactly how we would respond to the first bomb going off, and in what timescale. We fell into the trap and lost another 11 soldiers, including the Queen's Own Highlanders' commanding officer, David Blair. Mrs Thatcher had been Prime Minister for just four months. She flew out to be briefed on the crisis. Our brigade commander, David Thorne, told her of his doubts that the Royal Ulster Constabulary (RUC) could continue to take the lead in South Armagh.

Things were at a low ebb as we arrived in South Armagh. I was determined, however, not to accept that the Welsh Guards were there just to hold the IRA at bay. If your strategy as a commanding officer was to play safe and keep a clean sheet, then you had no business to command.

In my career, I have often felt there was sometimes limited value in the knowledge derived from experience. It can impose on you patterns of thought. South Armagh was not Malaya or Aden or, for that matter, similar to my experience of counter-insurgency in Belfast. South Armagh was a place apart, where the IRA had many factors working for it.

First, there was the topography of the land and its proximity to the border with the Irish Republic, where we had few friends and where the terrorists could slip across with ease.

Second, the countryside, framed by blackthorn hedges, was hard going and concealment was nigh impossible. The local farmer would notice any change in vegetation; dogs would bark from a quarter of a mile away; cows would meander over to where a patrol was trying to hide up, proof enough to any farmer that soldiers were there; and you would get no succour from the local population who, if not actively supporting the IRA, would not contemplate giving you any information, save a sullen look.

The IRA's South Armagh Brigade and the 'fighting men of Crossmaglen' were steeped in rebellion that went back to the 17th century. Their blood ties of kith and kin were bound by myths and grievances handed down from generation to generation. Names such as Murphy, Caragher, McMahon, Martin, McCabe and others were known well enough to the RUC and Army Intelligence. You would have seen the same names published as outlaws and cattle-thieves in the early 18th century. Other IRA members were just referred to by their menacing nicknames, for example 'The Undertaker' or 'The Surgeon'.

If they had had iPhones or laptops in the late 1970s and 1980s, it would have made no difference to our intelligence gathering. They communicated only face to face, usually across the border in a safe house or a staunchly Republican bar in Dundalk. If they planned an operation and brought a young volunteer in for a task, then he or she would be given no detail of the operation except for the task they had to carry out.

At the centre of this murderous lot was Thomas 'Slab' Murphy. He owned and controlled the Slab Murphy farm complex straddling the border, south-east of Crossmaglen. Smuggling was an extremely serious business and inextricably linked to IRA strategy. The Murphy family made a fortune smuggling pigs, grain and cattle, though oil smuggling was the principal source of income and chief money-spinner for the IRA. Oil and petrol tanks were situated on both sides of the hedge that marked the border, and a gravity-feed system took the fuel underground from one state to the other.

It was a simple but effective criminal enterprise, exploiting price differences between Northern Ireland and the Republic. Some said at the time that Murphy was the IRA's Chief of Staff; others that he commanded the South Armagh Brigade. As a senior RUC police officer said to me on arrival, and pointing at the map of Slab Murphy's farm, "This is where everything bad stems from. If you meet Murphy driving along the road, he'll head straight for you and you'd be wise to go straight into the ditch."

People often remarked to me at the time why we didn't just "take him out". Without hesitation, I replied that we operate within the rule of law. To do otherwise would betray the values of a commission in Her Majesty's Armed Forces. I have never changed my view on this and, many years later, co-authored a book with Michael Quinlan who was Permanent Under-Secretary of State at the MOD on *Ethics in Modern Warfare*.

Army intelligence gathering was not up to much at the time. We had precious little in the form of signals or electronic intelligence. We relied almost entirely on human intelligence. Informers, or anyone suspected of passing information, even speaking out of turn, met a grisly end. They would be interrogated, tortured and shot in a 'safe house' in the Republic. The body, sometimes booby-trapped, would then be dumped on our side of the border in plain view. Any forensic evidence to mount a trial was in the Republic and out of our jurisdiction. The Irish Police, the *Garda*, were not inclined to make any evidence available.

In my experience, many commanding officers who embark on an operational tour feel they have to make an immediate impact. The more frenetic the activity, the more they feel they are making their mark. This can be a mistake and it often results in early casualties. However good and realistic the training has been beforehand, you need to (I use a cricketing analogy), 'play yourselves in'. The first few weeks are about finding your feet, being methodical and cautious. And then, of course, during the last few weeks of the tour you are tired, mentally more than physically, and you want to go home.

In 1979–80 we were on a four-month tour, so we really only had ten weeks of productive soldiering. The tours were extended to six months in the 1990s. The IRA were not bound by time. Many will recall that chilling saying made by an IRA spokesman after the Brighton bombing in 1980: "We only have to be lucky once, but you have to be lucky all the time."

I was confident from the tour's outset that we had all the right commanders in the right posts. Crossmaglen was the most dangerous place in South Armagh, and there I had placed Prince of Wales Company under Major Angus Wall. Angus, who bore more than a passing resemblance to the actor Charlton Heston, was calm and unflappable, with just the right touch with his Guardsmen and officers. In command, I have always felt that if you have the right people, you should leave them to get on with things. In that way, you instil confidence and they grow in the job.

I always asked the commanders to come to a proper Sunday lunch at our headquarters in Bessbrook where we had the chance for some useful and genial discussion and, more importantly, the exchange of intelligence information. My company commanders were all out on a limb in their respective locations in our tactical area of responsibility. There is some truth in the loneliness of command. They all looked forward to getting away from their bases and relaxing, if only for a short time.

I also made sure our relations with the RUC were as good as possible. Understandably, they felt a little under the cosh after multiple murders at Warrenpoint and of Lord Mountbatten. I met as many of them as I could, assuring them that we fully supported the primacy of the RUC in the conduct of operations.

David Thorne, a former Royal Anglian who commanded 3 Brigade, could not have been more supportive. David was an infantryman through and through, and a good friend to the Regiment.

At the Guardsmen's level, it was mostly about good infantry skills. The best way to counter the IRA was to apply the basic battlefield principles that every Guardsman learns at the Guards Depot: shape, shine, shadow, silhouette, movement, camouflage properly, move tactically, avoid crossing gates or where there is an obvious aiming mark for the IRA sniper or bomber, watch your flanks as you are moving, mutual support, and look out for changes in pattern in the way the local population behave.

With experience you get an instinct for it, but at the beginning of an operational tour, it takes time for it to become second nature.

I was sceptical about winning 'hearts and minds' in South Armagh. I knew the natural courtesy and good humour of Welsh Guardsmen could only help, but we were up against centuries of mistrust and hatred.

I was, and always have been, an advocate of working with the Press. In this, we were blessed in our PR officer and HQ company commander, Vyvyan Harmsworth. Vyvyan, whose father Peter had been killed in 1943 serving with the Regiment in North Africa, was a member of the great newspaper family who owned the *Daily Mail*. I also knew Rod Tyler, who was the *News of the World*'s features editor, from my time as Brigade Major during the Queen's Silver Jubilee celebrations.

Vyvyan Harmsworth's famous name in journalism helped us to arrange for two excellent journalists from the *News of the World* and a photographer to 'embed' themselves in Crossmaglen. We did not restrict them in any way. They lived, ate and slept as though they were soldiering themselves. There is no reason to fight shy of the Press unless you have something to hide.

It could not have been a more successful initiative. It generated a lot of positive PR for the army, and it kept the Welsh Guards very much in the public eye. And when we came to face our first reversal of fortune, the Press could not have been more sympathetic.

On 13 November, just a few weeks into our tour, we lost Paul Fryer, an 18-year-old Guardsman from Pontywaun in Gwent. Paul was murdered by an IRA booby-trap attached to a telegraph pole at Ford's Cross near Crossmaglen as he and his patrol returned to base. A second Guardsman was wounded during this incident.

Any death in action can quickly unsettle people. In a Regiment like ours, with its strong sense of family, loyalty and the obligations of friendship, Guardsman Fryer's loss was keenly felt. Once we dusted ourselves down, we pressed on, determined to honour his memory and complete a successful tour without any more casualties.

As I look back ruefully on that sad event 40 years ago, I do regret that we may not have done enough to support the young officer who led that ill-fated patrol. If we had known then what we know now about post-traumatic stress disorder (PTSD), we would have ensured he was given more support. The officer left the army shortly after the tour and led a troubled life until his premature death a few years ago. Since Iraq and Afghanistan, the army has done its utmost to address PTSD, with some success.

In an otherwise sorrowful turn of events in Crossmaglen, there was one story which boosted morale and remains in our collective memory. We had inherited in Crossmaglen a dog called 'Rats', a rescue dog and a cross-breed between a corgi and a terrier. Rats had been there for a couple of years and, apart from doing his day job of keeping the base clear of his namesake rodents, rather took to accompanying patrols and the occasional helicopter ride.

At some stage before our arrival, Rats had been caught in a car bomb and had a few tiny bits of metal in him. Dogs sense and feel human emotions acutely, and when Guardsman Fryer was murdered, Rats curled up in a ball, noticeably out of sorts.

Needless to say, the *News of the World* team witnessed this and ran a big story which even got onto the main BBC news. Rats became something of a national treasure back home. At the end of our tour, an army vet had a look at Rats and found that he had a heart murmur and, like a Second World War bomber pilot with 30 completed missions, was entitled to a safe billet and happy retirement. The safe billet was Vyvyan

Harmsworth's house in Kent, where he lived a comfortable six more years.

Now that we were midway through our tour, I was determined to take the fight to the IRA, change the pattern of operations, and do everything we could to put the terrorists off balance. The SAS had been operating for some time in Northern Ireland, with considerable success. As I had served in the SAS as a troop and squadron commander, I felt quite at ease in talking to their head of operations in Northern Ireland to win his support for a joint operation in South Armagh.

We called the initiative Operation *Voluble*. Someone who talks incessantly is seen as voluble, which is why we chose the name. The incessant patrol activity by night and day in South Armagh would create uncertainty in the minds of the IRA.

Our close-observation platoon was run by Aldwin Wight, who later went on to join the SAS and win the Military Cross in the Falklands campaign. He and his men worked side by side with the Special Forces in South Armagh. It was what the US would later call in Iraq and Afghanistan 'The Surge'.

Early one morning as I was listening to the BBC Radio 4 *Today Programme*, news came through that some British soldiers had been arrested by the *Garda* in the Irish Republic. It turned out that they were members of our close observation platoon. They had set up an OP just 200 yards over the border. One of the Guardsmen in the patrol had awoken in the small hours screaming from a nightmare. He had been injured in the Caterham pub bombing in August 1975. The screaming woke up locals, who called the *Garda*.

Aldwin came to see me to explain what had happened. It was a serious incident, but I said to Aldwin I would take the flak from the new brigade commander. I was happy that it was a genuine mistake made with the best of intentions. Aldwin deserved my loyalty.

I encouraged individual initiative from commanders on the ground within the operation's overall framework. Operation *Voluble* helped build our friendships and boost our spirits despite the miseries of a foul South Armagh winter.

Our colleagues in the 2nd Battalion of the Parachute Regiment continued to have a hard time of things. They had a company under our command at Forkhill. It was not quite as dangerous as Crossmaglen, but neither was it a place for the faint-hearted. The Paras had already had 16 murdered at Warrenpoint, and another private blown up by an IRA command-wire bomb in a milk-churn at Tullydonnel near Forkhill in December 1979; but the events of New Year's Day 1980 were especially unfortunate. An officer and a private were shot dead by fellow patrol members when an ambush set for the IRA went badly wrong.

The rest of the tour was relatively calm except for the occasional mortar attack. The South Armagh Brigade had developed an unparalleled proficiency in mortars over the years since the first one was used against Crossmaglen in 1974. One such attack took place late one afternoon towards the end of January 1980 as I was listening to opera in my room at Bessbrook Mill. The attack turned out to be a false alarm, of which we had quite a number, but you were never quite sure.

As with Berlin, every general and every politician wanted to visit South Armagh. Mrs Thatcher came to see us just before the Christmas of 1979. Her husband, Denis, accompanied her and I took them both to visit Prince of Wales Company in Crossmaglen. Denis loved talking to the Guardsmen, with whom he had an easy-going affinity. Mrs

Thatcher was equally good with the Guardsmen, motherly and very genuine in her concerns that they would be missing Christmas at home.

I remember talking to her about the threat of mortar attacks from across the border. She turned to her then Northern Ireland Secretary, Humphrey Atkins, and said, "Humphrey, can we mortar them back?"

Atkins, a former naval officer, grimaced and replied, "I'm not sure that would go down too well with our friends in the Republic, Prime Minister."

Mrs Thatcher did, however, show great foresight (and I would ask the reader to take this in the humorous spirit that is intended) when, according to an aide, she said, "That Colonel Guthrie, he's going to the very top of the army."

We also had a visit from our Colonel, the Prince of Wales. He showed characteristic courage in visiting us, having lost his beloved uncle and mentor, Lord Mountbatten, murdered in Sligo only three months before. His visit was a great tonic to the men.

Senior military officers' visits were sometimes more problematical. Vyvyan Harmsworth would come and see me when we were notified of a visit. "Sir, General 'Plunger' is coming to visit us next Monday. How do you want to play things? Perrier water and a cold cheese sandwich in the operations room, map marked up and camouflage cream on? Or silver on the table and a proper lunch with whatever good wine I can lay my hands on?"

Fortunately, by then I knew, or had come across, most generals in the British Army and could make a judgement on how best to conduct a visit. When I eventually became a general, I was pleasantly surprised never to be given just a glass of Perrier water and a cold cheese sandwich.

The end of our tour, and the end of my time in command of the Regiment, was drawing to a close. I was mindful of what had happened to a rifleman in the Royal Green Jackets a year before. On his last day of duty, he had been blown up by an IRA booby-trap bomb as he tried to tear down an Irish tricolour flag from a telegraph pole.

I stressed the need for the utmost vigilance to the end. I spent my last few days saying my farewells. I had served 20 years in the Regiment and had made many friends amongst all ranks. I didn't find it at all easy.

Postscript 1

In December 2015, Thomas 'Slab' Murphy, the IRA commander in South Armagh, was found guilty of nine charges of tax evasion after a 14-year investigation. He was tried under anti-terrorist legislation as the judge could not guarantee the safety of witnesses. At a previous trial of Murphy in 1999, a man who testified against Murphy had been bludgeoned to death.

Murphy was released in 2018 and returned to live in his farm straddling the border in South Armagh.

Postscript 2

On 13 November 2019, 40 years to the day after his death, Paul Fryer's family received the Elizabeth Cross. This award is given to the families of members of the British Armed Forces killed in action from a terrorist attack. Many former members of Prince of Wales Company attended the commemorative service at Danygraig Cemetery where Paul Fryer is buried.

12

The Coconut War

Expect the unexpected – but fighting spear-wielding rebels in the New Hebrides required a leap of the imagination.

SOUTH PACIFIC: THE NEW HEBRIDES, SUMMER 1980

I had joined the British Army in 1959 for travel and adventure. Some 20 years later, I found myself flying to the South Pacific where the turn of events became more bizarre than I could have possibly imagined.

I was just three weeks into a new job in the MOD as a colonel in the Directorate of Military Operations (DMO), responsible for our operations outside the UK and Europe. By 1980, there had been 28 British Army operations in its dependencies since 1945. No one, however, thought Britain would ever be sending troops to the New Hebrides in the South Pacific to square up to not only a spear-wielding rebel force, but also to its European ally and joint administrator in the New Hebrides, France. I am not sure anyone at the time, least of all the DMO, had heard of the New Hebrides. Of course, we all thought we knew where it was. As a colleague remarked to me, "Glorious place, terrific fishing, a flight to Glasgow and you're almost there."

What became known in the popular Press as the 'Coconut War' was one of those many hangovers that Britain had to face up to as it did its best to retreat with grace and fairness from its colonies as they won their independence.

The South Pacific is evocative. Romantic stories like *Mutiny on the Bounty*, where British sailors lost their reason to the siren call of exotic temptresses from Tahiti, and the wildly popular musical *South Pacific*, with its haunting lyrics as in the song 'Bali Ha'i', intensified the region's mystique: "Bali Ha'i may call you... Come to me, come to me."

The reality, as I came to discover, was rather different. The New Hebrides is 10,000 miles from London. It is 1,000 miles east of the top of Queensland, Australia, and west of Fiji. It comprises 82 islands, the largest of which is Espiritu Santo. The total population is the same as in Newcastle. It is a magnet for cyclones. As I write, Tropical Cyclone Harold has devastated the islands with winds of up to 160 miles an hour.

The dry months are between June and November and the sea temperature is an inviting 23 degrees Celsius all year round. It is poor and rugged, with most inhabitants living a hand-to-mouth existence in small bamboo-hut villages where they often speak their own language.

That whole part of the South Pacific is known as Melanesia. Its peoples have a distinctive ancestry, aboriginal and some African, with a few white settlers thrown into the cooking pot. I could not help but notice that, through some random genetic mutation, there was a high incidence of blond hair.

In the 1880s, in their headlong rush to expand and colonise large parts of the globe, Britain and France claimed parts of the New Hebrides archipelago. In 1906, it agreed on a framework for managing its respective affairs there which was portentously referred to as 'The Anglo-French Condominium'.

Joint administrations rarely work. By the late 1970s, there were in effect four administrations – British, French, a joint administration and an embryonic administration. Independence Day loomed, and the condominium had become pandemonium. In a vacuum with competing interests, mischief-makers foment mayhem. Unrest had been smouldering in the New Hebrides for some time as it approached its Independence Day, set for 30 July 1980.

At that time Britain had a much larger hangover to cope with in southern Africa. Rhodesia, a much more politically and emotionally charged British colony because of its large population of white settler farmers, was making its tortuous and often bloody way to independence. Rhodesia eventually became the Republic of Zimbabwe. Against this backdrop, the New Hebrides was small beer. Political, diplomatic and military minds were focused elsewhere.

In the run-up to Independence, the relationship between the Foreign Office and its French counterpart, the *Quai d'Orsay*, was pretty tetchy. Britain and France have always had different philosophies, a distinctive view of the world and a disparate way of doing things. After France's gruelling experiences when they were pushed out of Algeria and Indochina, they were determined not to let another of their interests slip through their hands.

The preposterously pompous and Anglophobic French president, Giscard d'Estaing, said at the time, "To be French is the highest state of civilization. Independence is illogical."

Doubtless Giscard and the French wanted the New Hebrides to remain a French colony, like its neighbours, Tahiti, New Caledonia and Moruroa (its nuclear testing ground); but that was a wholly unrealistic scenario. It was obvious that many of the French population living on Santo were supporting the rebels.

The rebellion kicked off with the shooting of a prominent opposition deputy on 11 June. The rebel opposition were a minority group that had lost the regional elections in the main island of Santo. They were led by Jimmy Stevens, a local firebrand of Scottish highlander and Melanesian descent. It was said that he was descended from one of Captain Bligh's crew who had been set adrift after the mutiny on the *Bounty* to begin their momentous open-boat voyage to the Dutch East Indies.

Stevens declared independence in Santo, referring to himself as Prime Minister. I only caught a brief glimpse of Stevens when he was clapped in irons at the rebellion's end. He had a commanding presence. Noticeably taller than his fellow islanders, he had a thick white beard and deep-set eyes. He wore a beret embroidered with a gold snake. To his followers, he was known as 'Moses'. Like so many self-proclaimed evangelists, Stevens liked waving his wand: he enjoyed the company of 23 wives and had sired more than 50 children.

We arrived at a consensus with the French and we both agreed to send troops, acting together to put an end to things. In a signal to the MOD, I recommended that we should send Britain's spearhead or quick-reaction regiment, 42 Commando Royal Marines, under Lieutenant Colonel Colin Howgill. The French sent their colonial police force. Eyebrows were raised at the *Quai d'Orsay* as the Royal Marines cut a rather different dash to their colonial police force who were dressed almost identically to their *Gendarmerie*. It was a simple enough quandary: the French found it difficult to crush Jimmy Stevens and his rebels because they were French citizens, and we couldn't do much except confiscate a large number of weapons held by French residents.

As I watched events unfold from my drab office on the fifth floor of the MOD, I decided I had better get out there and see things for myself before wheels came off the British wagon and the whole enterprise began to look like a Gilbert and Sullivan comic opera. My boss, Major General Derek Boorman, readily agreed and told the powers that be that he was sending out a military advisor to the Governor of the New Hebrides.

Before I left the MOD, I was called upon to brief the generals, civil servants and relevant politicians on our prospects. They seemed a little tense. There's a time and a place for humour. "Gentlemen," I began, "We have two options." They all nodded in anticipation. "We have a plane that can get us there; but it cannot land. And we have a plane that can land – but it cannot get us there."

I overheard Barney Hayhoe, the Army Minister, making the remark, "Well, I know one should always expect the unexpected, but I never thought we'd been sending troops to the New Hebrides."

I went home to our new house in Vauxhall to find my wife, Kate, painting a radiator, rather startled to see me at midday. "Have you been sacked already, Charles?" she asked.

I grimaced, muttering that I was flying out to the New Hebrides later that day. Kate missed the 'New' in Hebrides. She put down her paintbrush and went off to find my uniform, woolly jumpers and my Barbour jacket. As we said our farewells, I remarked that I would be back within a fortnight.

It was to be another two months before I saw her and our sons, Andrew and David, again. To Kate's amazement, she received a telephone call from the MOD a few days after I left, saying if she wished to write to me, the letter should be addressed to the "British Commander, South Pacific".

As I touched down in the New Hebrides capital city, Port Vila, I saw a light aeroplane taxiing on the runway. After I had waved the pilot down, clambered in and shouted in his ear above the din of the aircraft engine, he quickly agreed to fly me around the archipelago. I now saw why the area was in the Pacific's 'Ring of Fire', with nine active volcanoes, including the highly temperamental Mount Yasur. The terrain looked inhospitable. Small villages of bamboo huts were dotted around, with no obvious means of travel between them, except by foot.

It was an invaluable reconnaissance. I had learnt by then in my military career that it is only too easy to get side-tracked by tactics – vital when you are outwitting the enemy in battle – but of little consequence when trying to build relationships and ensure co-operation between the people who mattered. I needed to go and see the key people managing the joint administration the next day.

The British Governor, Andrew Stuart, was 6 feet 7 inches tall. He appeared even loftier in his red and white cockatoo-plumed governor's solar topi hat. His father had been the Anglican Bishop of Uganda. Andrew had spent much of his career in the Colonial Service as a district officer in Uganda.

The Colonial Office had come to an end in 1965 and Andrew transferred to what became known as the Foreign and Colonial Office (FCO). He was still a little touchy about this and felt that his colleagues in King Charles Street, the FCO's rather grand headquarters, were a touch condescending towards him. We got on well, and in his memoirs, *Of Cargoes, Colonies and Kings*, he wrote that I was "A thinking soldier who knew his own mind and was not afraid to speak it; Charles knew about soldiering, politicians and human nature." Praise indeed, but I like to think that my military career to date, particularly my SAS service and period commanding the Regiment in South Armagh, had prepared me well.

Nevertheless, I had to write up my military appraisal and determine if the spearhead battalion, 42 Commando, Royal Marines, could land in Vila. Fortunately, I had brought with me an RAF officer, the excellent Wing Commander Henry Holt. Henry was equipped with a piece of kit which measured landing weights and concrete strengths. He told me our Hercules C130 cargo planes could land there, and so could the VC10 passenger aircraft. It was just left to me in my appraisal to demonstrate that a good infantry battalion could make short work of Jimmy Stevens and his rebels.

For his part, Andrew gave me an accurate summary of the situation and the French approach to colonial rule. "Charles, what you need to remember about our French friends is that they have an overriding sense of the grandeur of France. They're much more *dirigiste* than we are. Our trump card here in the New Hebrides," he said, "is our education system. We provide excellent primary education. The French only bother to educate their *élite*. The people here also prefer the rule of common law rather than French Napoleonic law." He paused, then summed up: "The point is that there are a lot more British than French supporters here. School teachers, nurses, doctors, shopkeepers – they're all with us."

That was reassuring news, though I smiled when I found out later that those convicted of crimes were happy to be tried under our rule of law but preferred the French prison in

Port Vila, because prisoners there were given wine and cheese with their meals at the weekend.

I also learnt from Andrew Stuart that he had received an intelligence report saying that Jimmy Stevens and his supporters had received $250,000 from the American-based Phoenix Foundation. Apparently, this was a group of real estate millionaires from Nevada who had previously attempted to set up an independent tax-haven on the island of Abaco in the Bahamas. That piece of information played right into my hands as I arranged the next day to meet the French Governor and his military advisor.

It was plain to see that Andrew Stuart did not rub along with the French Governor, Jean-Jacques Robert. I made it my business to get on with him, knowing well enough by then that it is only misplaced ego that gets in the way of building rapport with people. In one of those happy strokes of luck, Jean-Jacques and I realised we had met before. We had played rugby against each other. I remembered he was a rather fizzy scrum-half and had also played for the great French rugby club, Toulouse. Needless to say, our common love of rugby meant we got on very well. His military advisor was Colonel Vidal from the Deuxième REP, the airborne regiment of the French Foreign Legion. He saw my SAS wings and, in the spirit of solidarity with those who jump out of aeroplanes, he could not have been more friendly.

It would not have been appropriate for me to mention the Phoenix Foundation to the French Governor (Phoenix did sound rather like *Spectre* in the Bond films) nor their $250,000 bung to Jimmy Stevens. Instead, I had a quiet word with the French Colonel. Given the French dislike of sinister American millionaires muscling in on their interests, I helped Jean-Jacques Robert influence the French Foreign Ministry.

We had now established common ground and a shared understanding of what needed to be done. Anglo-French collaboration was now working well, and both countries agreed that French and British troops should come to the New Hebrides to restore the authority of the new government.

That evening I was invited to dinner at the French Governor's residence. It was the first of many occasions. Jean-Jacques and his wife gave wonderful parties. The Melanesian waiters wore tailcoats and crisp white shirts. The food, a mixture of French and Asian cuisine, was memorable. The wine, always French, was equally impressive. Andrew Stuart was certainly right about one thing: the French look after their *élites* well. It was all in stark contrast to the suppers of shepherd's pie around the kitchen table with Andrew and his wife at his residence.

Nevertheless, I think we had got it right. Despite the glories of French culture, we had established a far stronger level of support amongst the New Hebridean people.

The insurrection drifted on for a few weeks. The Royal Marines operated with great professionalism in intelligence gathering, and they got on well with the locals. One rebel was shot dead by the *Gendarmerie*, and what French support there was for Jimmy Stevens ebbed away. He was eventually captured and sentenced to 14 years in prison. He chose the French prison (of course) with its wine and cheese at the weekends and occasional conjugal visits from one or more of his 23 wives.

On 30 July 1980, the newly named Republic of Vanuatu celebrated its independence from British and French colonial rule. It joined the Commonwealth the same year. The celebrations marking its 40th anniversary took place on 30 July 2020. It has done extremely well over the last four decades. The wonderful scuba-diving attracts people from all around the world, particularly Australia. The only concerns are of frequently destructive cyclones and (more recently) Chinese expansionism in the region.

I look back on those two months with affection. Despite the rather surreal turn of events, it reminded me of the importance of getting on with people, whatever their background or culture.

I do not think the international community took much notice of the 'Coconut War'. It attracted a certain amount of mocking press coverage and cartoons back home.

The Argentine Junta, however, would have done well to pay attention. Mrs Thatcher clearly wasn't one to tolerate being pushed around by Jimmy Stevens, nor for that matter anyone else. They should have thought about that before invading the Falklands two years later.

For my troubles, the MOD scoured its records for a suitable medal. I was awarded 'The Queen's Certificate and Badge of Honour'. The citation read, "For meritorious services to the local community in overseas territories of an exceptional nature". It was a commonplace award in Victorian Britain at the empire's height as portraits of generals in the Army Museum confirm.

The medal's ribbon is Day-Glo yellow. It always attracts comments and beady looks when I wear it. I see people muttering, "Mmm, how on earth did he get that medal?" At one stage, it ended up in my sons' dressing up box.

Sometimes I have to pinch myself that the whole episode wasn't just a dream.

13

Commander, 4th Armoured Brigade

BAOR shakes off its complacency in the ritual dance of deterrence.

They say timing is everything. Ability is nothing without opportunity. My appointment as Commander of 4th Armoured Brigade in Münster could not have been at a more fortuitous time. Changes were beginning to sweep through the British Army of the Rhine, which had become hidebound and defensive. The architect of this change was a remarkable soldier, Nigel Bagnall, who had taken over command of 1st British Corps in 1980.

Commanding a brigade is the highest level of operational command over which you can truly get to know your officers and soldiers. You can use your personal influence and presence to help people grow. It was also a wonderful time to be in Germany as the sorrows of the Second World War faded away and our relationship with the German people became more than just *"Ein Bier, bitte."*

I had been in command less than a month when I was called upon in my office by the *Oberbürgermeister* of Münster, Dr Werner Pierchalla. I had no inkling of the purpose of his visit and was a little anxious that some grave misdemeanour had been committed by soldiers under my command.

I should not have concerned myself. Dr Pierchalla announced that 4th Armoured Brigade were to be honoured with the Freedom of the City of Münster. It was a singular honour and a happy reflection of how Anglo-German relations had progressed.

Dr Pierchalla, whom I began to know well, had been caught by the Soviet Red Army outside Smolensk in 1943. He had been taken away to be shot, but for reasons he never understood, a Russian female doctor asked for his life to be spared. He remained a prisoner of war with hard labour until 1949. His wartime experience and five years in hard labour had not embittered him; instead, it had given him a strong desire that the years left to him should be full of optimism and reconciliation.

The Freedom of the City was something we all looked forward to, though the cavalry regiments under my command, the 17th/21st Lancers and the Queen's Royal Irish Hussars, viewed with some dismay the prospect of having to get out of their chariots to perfect their foot drill.

Meanwhile, there were more pressing issues to deal with. The arrival of Lieutenant General Sir Nigel Bagnall as Commander of 1st British Corps was just the shake-up BAOR needed. Any institution can become moribund after time. People can become complacent and lethargic, content with a routine and a way of doing things that does not stretch them. An example of this torpor was the 'BAOR warrior' type, who had served in Germany for too long, knew every training area backwards, and had become accustomed to exercises that were predictable and unimaginative. Under Bagnall, a gifted thinker, BAOR became fresh, fun and exciting.

Bagnall not only knew his trade but took the trouble – and this is a rare quality – of throwing himself in the deep end if he felt inertia was creeping into his own personal development. It was this quality that I most admired.

He had joined an infantry regiment, the Green Howards, at the age of 18 and won the MC and Bar in the Malayan Emergency; the citation noted his "Gallantry, coolness and ruthless energy".

He was ambitious and, like many officers at the time, he recognised that Northern Ireland was a respectable career path but also an operational area over which you had little influence. BAOR was the place to be. Bagnall transferred to the Royal Armoured Corps, mastered tank warfare and learnt fluent German.

His appearance and almost medieval look helped him in his endeavour to shake things up. He had a shock of ginger hair with unruly tufts over which he had little control, a strong angular face, an aquiline nose and blue-grey eyes. If you spoke to him, he would look at you without expression. Many people found that unnerving.

It is no bad thing for generals to have idiosyncrasies. It pays to be recognised or known for something quirky, such as Monty's Australian bush hat. Bagnall was tone deaf and had to be prompted to stand to attention if the National Anthem was sounded. He was a proven warrior, but he had a habit of shuffling along with nothing resembling a soldierly gait. He also had a novel way of wrapping up dinner parties at his formal residence, the aptly named Spearhead House. He instructed his staff that, at 11pm sharp, they should open the French windows to let the air in and clear the fug. As Spearhead House was on top of a hill, this had the desired effect of prompting the guests to be on their way.

Bagnall made the study of war respectable. To be known as a 'thruster', or worse still a 'military shit', was to run contrary to the ethos of the gentleman amateur who only showed his true worth when battle was joined. By then it would be too late. Bagnall, who had personally shot dead a communist branch committee member and whose platoon had dispatched 18 terrorists in the Malayan Emergency, had no time for glorious defeats.

If war came about, it seemed natural that we should study the German Army's experience in Russia during the Second World War. The German Army had been invited to join NATO in 1955 to help combat the common threat of communism. The old war horses, the former panzer generals, had much to teach us. I remember meeting General Ferdinand von Senger und Etterlin who was Commander-in-Chief Allied Forces Central Europe. Von Senger had struck up a friendship with Bagnall as they wrestled with how to contain and defeat the Russians if they invaded the West. Von Senger's father, Frido, had commanded the German forces at Monte Cassino. It was Frido who said to the great military historian, Sir Michael Howard, "May I give you a word of advice? If you are going to invade Italy, do not start at the bottom."

Von Senger had fought at Stalingrad aged 19. By the end of the war, he had been wounded 13 times, including the loss of one arm. Needless to say, he was a tough old bird. He had no small talk and was very much in the "*Jawohl Herr General*" school of panzer generals. His favourite saying was, "*Ordnung aus dem Chaos*". He was an admirable man, if perhaps a little too demanding of his staff, who sometimes thought they were refighting the battle of Stalingrad. It was Von Senger and Bagnall who persuaded the German Government to agree that, if the Soviets invaded, forward defence at the West German border would be doomed to failure.

It was against this background that 4th Armoured Brigade found itself at the heart of Bagnall's new operational doctrine and its flagship, the Corps *Counter-stroke*. In essence, this meant allowing the Soviet Third Shock Army to run its course, run out of fuel and supplies as its logistical tail sought to catch up, and then we would catch them on the hop with bold and aggressive armoured thrusts from their flanks.

At a Corps Study Day, Bagnall summarised this as "Shock action along the line of least expectation", to which one humorous cavalry commanding officer piped up, "Very good, Sir! May I suggest that we now retire to the Mess and enjoy some Hock action?" Bagnall had a dry sense of humour and he allowed himself a faint smile.

It was all exciting stuff, particularly for the squadron commanders and company commanders of the Brigade, on whose shoulders the success or failure of such an operation would fall. The Royal Armoured Corps had rather lost their dash and verve in the inertia of BAOR in the 1970s. I did not share the great Duke's views on cavalry: "They cannot manoeuvre, excepting on Wimbledon Common; and when they use their arm as it ought, offensively, they charge too far and too fast and, dammit, never keep a reserve." But I did feel the *Counter-stroke* was just the tonic they needed to shrug off their lethargy and regain their natural *élan*. We were also helped by the arrival of the Challenger MK1 tank and the Warrior infantry fighting vehicle.

It may seem obvious now, but the concept of building a team around a common endeavour was, to some senior officers at that time, an alien concept. They relied too much on their rank to get their message across, and would brook little opposition to their views. I used to have regular study days where all the key players in the Brigade would meet and we would debate how best to execute *Counter-stroke* quickly and emphatically. I would select a clear aim for the day and made sure we kept to it; but apart from that I would allow free rein to our discussions. Shared ownership of a challenge is a great boost to morale and motivation.

The *Counter-stroke* operation was a special role for 4th Armoured Brigade, the jewel in the Corps' crown, and made life for us all a lot more worthwhile and enjoyable than that experienced by others in BAOR. We even began to look forward to the ritual dance of BAOR autumn exercises, usually heavily choreographed, where we would execute the *Counter-stroke* operation in the glorious landscape of North-Rhein-Westphalia (*Nordrhein-Westfalen*). We practised and rehearsed until we were close to pitch perfect. The sense of renewal began to spread through the whole of BAOR.

Even my House Sergeant, Sergeant Carl Kefer, who also looked after me in the field, got into the swing of things, though sometimes to my dismay. Early one morning, as I was collecting my thoughts ready to brief the Brigade's commanding officers waiting outside, I overheard Sergeant Kefer outside my Land Rover-adapted caravan say, "Good morning, gentlemen. I'm pleased to say that the Brigadier has had a good night's rest and has breakfasted well. He is much looking forward to you giving your all in today's operation."

Such was the tempo of operations on exercise that one commanding officer fell asleep during my Orders Group (briefing on how I wanted things done). My new Chief of Staff, the excellent Robert Gordon, was horrified but I knew the commanding officer had been flat out for 36 hours. I told Robert to allow him to carry on his snooze but to brief him later when he was a little more refreshed. Nothing further was said.

Sergeant Kefer was with Kate and me for a number of years as our House Sergeant. I frequently seemed to succeed a certain officer in my appointments, whose wife was well-upholstered. Kefer's first duty when we took over my predecessor's army quarters was to find out which side of the bed she slept on as the mattress stuffing was invariably flat.

There was an extra benefit to all this, albeit a personal one, and to young army officers reading these memoirs, or indeed anyone wishing to progress in life, an educative one. If you aspire to high command, you must build your own constituency. You need to be both seen and heard. The *Counter-stroke* operation allowed me to talk to the rest of the army about BAOR's revised strategy.

A bit of showmanship is no bad thing in senior officers and, if coupled with an idiosyncratic speech defect, can add to the occasion's theatre. In my case, I can't pronounce my 'th's. Instead, they come out as 'f's or 'v's, in such ways as "What do you fink about vat?"

I have no record of my presentations on *Counter-stroke*, but I do recall my closing words: "Gentlemen, *Counter-stroke* is a bold operation. The army has plenty of soft-skinned vehicles, but this is not an operation for soft-skinned men." I paused at that point for a few seconds to fix the room with a stern look. "It is an operation which requires great fortitude and steely commanders at every level."

It was not all about the serious business of soldiering. As I have mentioned, one of the Brigade's happiest memories was the granting of the Freedom of the City of Münster. Perhaps it is because I am a Guardsman that I have an enduring affection for ceremonial. But I also believe that the British Army derives much of its strength from its shared sense of history and institutional memory passed down from generation to generation. Ceremonial, army music, the Regimental marches, trumpets, bugles, pipes and drums: all of these things help to build pride and create a strong sense of belonging.

I was glad we had a dress rehearsal for the parade. The Household Cavalry in Knightsbridge lent me one of their horses, as I had decided to lead the parade mounted. Someone there must have had a warped sense of humour as the horse might as well have been an untamed stallion from Wyoming. At an unearthly hour, the autumnal sun hinting at an appearance, I made my way to the front of the parade with some 1,500 men behind me on my charger to await the Bandmaster to lift our spirits with some gentle music.

The Bandmaster waved his baton and the two bands erupted into a rousing rendition of the *Star Wars* theme. For a few seconds all seemed well before my charger did indeed charge off at the gallop, sparks flying off Münster's cobbled streets, with me rocking from side to side on its back until I could regain control. I gingerly made my way back, noting the barely concealed grins of the 17/21st Lancers, the Queen's Royal Irish Hussars and the Irish Guards. I turned to the Bandmaster, mustering all my dignity and quietly remarked to him, "I don't think we will have that particular piece of music on the day."

The *Bundeswehr* kindly provided me with a replacement horse which was as tranquil as the first horse had been flighty.

The granting of the Freedom of the City of Münster marked an important moment in the lived experience that BAOR had become. Throughout my tour of duty there, Kate and I had made it our business to get to know, and get on with, all the people that made up the family that was 4th Armoured Brigade.

We made many good friends with local German families, many of whom we have kept in touch with. They were cultured, civilised and gracious. The aberration of the Nazi era was rarely mentioned. The Germans are great royalists and were much in thrall to the visits of our Royal Family who were Colonels-in-Chief to the regiments in the Brigade.

One such visit by Queen Elizabeth The Queen Mother to the Irish Guards on St Patrick's Day in 1984 caused some merriment, as I also invited the nuns from the local convent to the drinks party in the Queen Mother's honour. The convent turned down my offer of a couple of minibuses to get them to the party, proudly announcing they would arrive and return under their own steam. Their own steam turned out to be a raft with which, under the grip of a formidable Mother Superior, they expertly negotiated their way down the River Aa. The nuns got on famously with their hosts, the Irish Guards, their shared Catholicism more than just a point of interest. Their return journey to the convent was less well navigated.

Less entertaining was the temporary loss of our army residence, Cambrai House, to a fire. These things happen, but it brought home to me the pettifogging nature of the jobsworths who ran the Service Family Accommodation through the MOD. I had always been sensitive to the needs of service families and the strains placed on them through constant moves. The handing over of an army quarter, or unintended mishap, played to the worst instincts of army bureaucracy.

Fortunately, I had an outstanding Deputy Chief of Staff, Ian Durie, who was anything but a blockhead. He saw off the jobsworths and got things done. It helped that Princess

Alexandra, Colonel-in-Chief of the 17th/21st Lancers, was due to make a formal visit to her Regiment and would be staying at Cambrai House. My experience at the time came back to haunt me when, many years later, the future of the MOD's housing estate became a controversial subject.

Nothing matters more than people. You cannot spend enough time on them. Loyalty and judicious praise to deserving people pay dividends. It helps them to grow in confidence. My predecessor at 4th Armoured Brigade, an outstanding soldier in his own way, put the fear of God into people. It is a style of command that delivers results, but it does little to engender loyalty.

When I arrived at Brigade HQ, people were edgy and lacking in confidence. I always regarded people who served with me as the future of the army. I spent a particular amount of time on my immediate staff at Brigade HQ, and the company commanders and squadron leaders of the regiments under my command. All that mattered to me was they should fulfil their potential to the best of their ability. Andrew Cumming, Robert Gordon, Ian Durie, Robert Corbett and Charlie Fattorini all became generals.

I always made a point of taking great care with the assessments of officers in their annual confidential reports. A man's career could be made or broken with a good or adverse report, and I hated to see people being treated unfairly.

At the time, a pompous and sub-standard commanding officer submitted glowing reports on two mediocre officers who happened to be, like himself, Old Etonians. At the same time, he wrote disparaging reports on two officers who had impressed me but who were from less illustrious schools.

I overruled all four of these reports. As a result, the two Etonians were downgraded. The other two were upgraded and both, quite rightly, went on to become two-star generals. The commanding officer's career went no further.

I always gave people a second chance to prove their worth unless they were palpably useless. One officer of great promise had come unstuck on a drink-driving charge. His commanding officer wanted to bring his career to an end. I had seen the officer's potential and overruled his commanding officer. Drink-driving is not something I take at all lightly, but a first offence did not warrant ruining a career.

My time commanding 4th Armoured Brigade was a defining period in my military career. It was also an extraordinarily happy time for us as a family, and I began to feel that I had developed all the right attributes and experience to rise to higher command. My subsequent appointments as Chief of Staff at 1st British Corps Headquarters, GOC 2nd Infantry Division and Corps Commander followed on from that.

It was my job to keep a firm hand on the tiller and ensure that the renewed sense of vigour and fighting spirit in BAOR was not lost. The end of the Cold War and the so-called peace dividend brought with it a markedly different set of challenges which fell on my lap when I assumed command of BAOR and the Northern Army Group in 1992.

My only regret was much later, when Nigel Bagnall was not made Chief of Defence Staff. He had become very outspoken, and Mrs Thatcher did not take to him at all. He failed her "Is he one of us?" test.

Later on, when I became CDS under Tony Blair, I fell out with Bagnall. I was not sure whether it was professional jealousy, or because he thought Blair and Brown did not have the interests of the army at heart. He was wrong about Tony Blair; but in my view he was dead right about Gordon Brown.

14

Sport

The tennis ball never knew how old I was or the
stresses of my working week.

TENNIS

It was early evening in June 1998, but the heat and humidity in Dhaka, the capital of Bangladesh, was draining. I had asked my ADC, Guy Bartle-Jones, to see if he could arrange a doubles match at the High Commissioner's residence. The British Defence Attaché volunteered to play against us and asked if a friend of his, a wing commander from the Bangladesh Air Force, could make up the foursome. Guy and I won the first set, but we soon began to wilt in the enervating heat. Before long I was beginning to see stars rather than tennis balls dancing in front of me. I came off the court feeling like a limp rag.

There was a sharp exchange of words between Kate and Guy as she reminded him that we were due to attend a formal dinner hosted by Bangladesh's Chief of Army Staff in an hour's time.

My SAS and rugby days were long gone, and I had never considered jogging or bicycling enjoyable or dignified ways of keeping fit. After I had reached my mid-40s, my options were becoming limited. Golf was too time-consuming, and I could not see myself observing the stuffy rituals of the club house. Squash was heart-attack material, given the change from gentle warm-up to violent acceleration. I enjoyed playing ping-pong, but I was not sure "The general would love a game of ping-pong before dinner" would have been quite the right image. A game of snooker or billiards with a glass of *Kümmel* or port to hand might be acceptable at a country house weekend after retirement, but it would do nothing at all for me in terms of fitness. I loved skiing but that was limited, at most, to ten days a year.

Tennis is as much a mental as a physical game. Every time the ball comes to you, you have to make a decision. Every time you hit the ball, you live with the result. It is that much better playing with a partner, as his or her strengths can make up for your limitations; and after a certain age, playing with a partner is less tiring.

In tennis you have to be alert and think the whole time. Perhaps it is a little too far-fetched to draw an analogy, but I like to think the mixture of intuition, exploiting the weaknesses of your opponents, footwork, hair-trigger reflexes and mastering the basics, drew parallels with the profession of arms.

As a leader you must always be prepared to adapt your style when circumstances change. I preferred playing on grass because it was fast and unpredictable. The different conditions you find on clay or hard courts require a different style of play. Every sportsman or sportswoman says of their particular sport that it is a metaphor for life, or that you can tell a lot about a person on the rugby field or golf course (or even potholing). I would not indulge myself to that extent, but I joined the army for sport, travel and friendship. Rugby in my early career, and tennis later on, gave me all of these and taught me quite a bit about myself.

Only one of the Iron Duke's ADCs survived the battle of Waterloo. Henry Percy, fortunate though he was, had three horses shot from under him. My ADCs had less onerous responsibilities. They had to be companionable, be able to read a map and get me from A to B wearing the right kit; but I also insisted that they should be able to play tennis to a reasonable level. I sometimes think they spent more time organising my tennis matches than they did on my military programme. I always kept a tennis racket and a clean pair of whites in the office.

I became a member of the All England Lawn Tennis Club (AELTC). People often remark they do business playing golf or shooting. I rather suspected they spent more time rummaging around for lost balls, or trying to keep warm in the dead of winter as a few wily pheasants flew overhead. Watching tennis at Wimbledon on a summer's evening was a much better way of getting things done.

I used to play with a delightful New Zealander, John McDonald, who had played for New Zealand in the Davis Cup. He had also played at Wimbledon and managed to fix up a doubles match on Wimbledon's Centre Court. What John could not arrange was ball boys and ball girls, so we spent a good deal of time clambering over seats to pick up shots that had gone astray. On that first occasion on the Centre Court, I remember playing well above myself. I put it down to the grandeur of the setting and its history. It was not the time for an indifferent performance.

John was good at arranging a weekly doubles match through my ADCs during the seven years I spent as CGS and CDS. I was often out of the UK; if I was in London I always looked forward to our weekly matches with an eclectic mix of partners from business and political life. The Kuwaiti ambassador, Khaled Al-Duwaisan, was a regular. He was a lithe left-hander and swooped like a hawk at the net.

Tennis gave me balance in a working life that had little let-up. It also gave me friendship from many walks of life. When I commanded the 2nd Infantry Division in York and my sons were at Ampleforth College, I played once a week with Father Edward Corbould, a Benedictine monk, who was their housemaster. Father Edward was an outstanding man, and a tennis player of guile. He also trained and ran Ampleforth's cross-country team, and though he had quite a few years over me, I always seemed to be catching my breath. After yet another defeat, he would say, "Well, that was a good match, but I don't think the Holy Spirit was with you today."

I admired Father Edward's spirituality and plain goodness. He had little influence over my decision to convert to Catholicism, although that had been in my mind for some time. It just seemed to be the natural thing for me to do.

Fortunately, I have never been drawn to try to make a connection between faith and tennis, though watching Roger Federer at his best was quite close to a religious experience.

15

Reflections on Command

Soldiering is a noble profession; study your chosen calling, study the great commanders and learn to read other people.

The commanding officer of a distinguished Highland battalion narrowly escaped capture by the Japanese after conducting a gallant rear-guard action at the fall of Singapore in 1942.

He was later was summoned to a Study Day at GHQ in India. The day was attended by every senior commander in India, including the Commander-in-Chief. The commanding officer was asked to give a presentation on his experiences. He began by saying, "The reasons for the recent disaster are many – and they are all sitting in the front row."

Ironically, our disastrous defeat at the hands of the Japanese was best summarised some 40 years after the fall of Singapore in Nigel Bagnall's phrase "Shock action along the line of least expectation". This was the essence of the *Counter-stroke* plan to defeat the Russians if they invaded the West.

There was no better example of this than the Japanese victory at Singapore where the line of least expectation was to invade Singapore from the North through the supposedly impenetrable jungle of Malaya. The 'shock action' was the use of massed Japanese infantry on bicycles.

I have perhaps been a little harsh on myself in writing that I had little enthusiasm for academic study. This chapter has a different pace and tone to previous and subsequent chapters. I merely wish to share some common-sense advice to those aspiring to high command on the pitfalls to avoid when leading and managing the business of war.

History, particularly military history, has always gripped me. We have been extraordinarily fortunate in Britain to have had, since the Second World War, some outstanding military historians: Michael Howard, Max Hastings, Anthony Beevor, Hew Strachan and Andrew Roberts. As a commander you cannot study it enough, not least because it is a reminder that the human condition has changed very little in two thousand years. Failures on the battlefield, as well as successes, often stem from the same reasons, though they may be cloaked under different guises. But you have to be cautious, as there is no surer road to disaster than trying to apply too rigorously the lessons of past campaigns to a current operation. Churchill understood this when he said, "No battle repeats itself."

I often envied the US Pentagon, which had a budget sufficient to send their most promising officers in their early or mid-forties to prestigious US universities to complete a PhD in a topic relevant to the profession of arms or public affairs. It is rare that their British counterparts are given either the time, resources or support to develop their professional knowledge in such a way.

As you grow older, irrespective of profession, you become more set in your ways. When I was a supposedly up-and-coming divisional commander, I was asked to give a number of lectures at the Staff College in Camberley and to the army's future leaders at the commanding officers' designate course in Larkhill. I enjoyed these opportunities, as I felt it was at this stage of an officer's career that I could make the most impact.

Thirty years have passed since I gave these talks. As I reviewed the lecture notes I kept, and my experience of command at every operational level, I still believe the attributes that commanders need remain applicable.

No two commanders are the same, and there is no such thing as a command formula. What is successful in one set of circumstances may not work in another. What was right for the British Army in Northern Ireland was wrong for Basra in the 2003 invasion of Iraq. I am pretty certain General Montgomery would not have risen above the rank of Brigadier in peacetime – his style of command did not sit easily with the complacent culture of the British Army at the time – but he was certainly the right man for the Eighth Army in North Africa in 1942.

Like Monty in 1942, a new commander can engender a new spirit within days of their arrival. The reverse is also true. Previously good regiments can wither away if the wrong person is placed in command.

Shortly after I finished my time as CDS, a promising officer who was at the time attending the Advanced Command and Staff Course wrote a widely circulated defence research paper entitled 'The Shaping of a General'. He analysed seven four-star generals, of whom I was one.

He asked for my opinion. I identified two fundamental qualities required for high command: credibility, and what would be described now as networking. Few would disagree with the first quality; the second attribute, networking, is a good deal more nuanced.

By credibility, I would stress the importance of a broad and mixed career. Operational experience is important, and the lack of it must be a disadvantage. I am not a great admirer of Napoleon, but I agree with his dictum that he would not promote an officer to high command "who was for ten years not under fire".

I have always been suspicious of commanders who say they spend most of their time on administration. They need to remind themselves what the army is for, though I accept that peacetime soldiering does need a different emphasis, particularly in regard to keeping soldiers motivated and the importance of imaginative training.

If you study the great military commanders – and the more you do so the better – you will not be surprised to see they share the similar attributes of physical and moral courage, integrity and fortitude. But different levels of command require different qualities. There are more than a few officers who have been brilliant platoon commanders, fine company commanders and good enough battalion commanders, only to find themselves out of their depth as brigade and divisional commanders.

You cannot command a brigade like a battalion. Basil Liddell Hart, the military historian, wrote of Monty, "As a young officer, he did not show the natural signs of leadership, or a knack of handling men. Indeed, when he was given command of a battalion, he brought it to the verge of mutiny by misjudged handling." Monty's brilliant Chief of Staff in the Eighth Army, General Freddie de Guingand, when asked what Monty was really like said, "Actually he was a bastard, but unquestionably the man for the moment."

Ambition and energy feed off each other. You need energy to satisfy the demands of ambition. Energy diminishes as you get older, and I agree with Field Marshal Wavell that a good young general will usually beat a good old general. It is harder to accept casualties as you get older. As the years go by, I have found myself increasingly prone to tears of emotion. It is not a sign of weakness, merely the normal wear and tear of any human heart.

One of the attributes often missing from an analysis of a commander's qualities is confidence. In the Second World War, Patton and Monty had this in spades. They also knew how to speak to the troops under their command in plain language, instilling confidence in the prospect of final victory.

As a battalion commander, I would address the Battalion two or three times a year to tell them how well we were doing and what there was to look forward to. I am not a natural speaker, but perhaps a little better than one Guards commanding officer who, on telling his battalion they were to be posted to the Cameroons, opened with the words, "Gentlemen, Africa is an anathema, the Cameroons an idiosyncrasy."

Confidence comes from operational success. In the British Army we are keen to train, but reluctant to test. Careers should not be ruined in a simulated exercise, but I am all for putting people under pressure. They always emerge better for it, and more confident. Command Post Exercises (CPXs) are there to test communications rather than tactics. Unlikely scenarios get thrown at you.

I remember my Chief of Staff at 4th Armoured Brigade, on one such simulated exercise, getting a bit hot under the collar as it appeared that a squadron of Soviet T72 tanks were about to break through. I told him not to concern himself as they would have run out of fuel by the time they reached us.

Selection and maintenance of the aim is drummed into one as the master principle of war. During my career, I saw that most commanders found it easy to select the aim but were easily deflected from maintaining it. Siren voices got to them and plans were nibbled at, all couched in courteous terms and British understatement: "Wouldn't it be a good idea if we...?" or "Shouldn't we also consider the sensitivities of...?" and similar diversions.

It was essential for the Northern Army Group to bring in greater mobility and offensive action at group and operational level. Some of the corps from other NATO countries were concerned that their roles would be diminished, and that they would be weaker in some respects. Their egos, both personal and national, were threatening to derail the aim, and the result was a great deal of futile squabbling amongst them. Eventually, our determined strategy of mobile defence was adopted.

I have always been pro-European, but it partly was the memory of these national rivalries that convinced me that a European Army was not viable.

———

Almost the first piece of advice I would give a commander is to get themselves a good Chief of Staff. They are your alter ego, and you must tell them everything. As a commander you are solely responsible for the plan, but you must allow the Chief of Staff and staff to get on with the detail.

Ensure your staff do not 'staff things to death', passing drafts amongst themselves, commenting here and there until the whole thing looks like, as Monty used to say of an over-staffed plan, "a dog's breakfast".

As a commander, you may not have too much choice over your staff or junior commanders. I took a dim view of commanders who said they didn't have a good team; worse still were commanders who blamed their predecessors or claimed they had been dealt a poor hand.

Monty said he spent a third of his time on people, and that has to be right. As a commander you should get to know the strengths and limitations of all your key people. Change or move them to where they are suited best, and take an active interest in their personal development. Don't hang on to people you like too much just because you enjoy their company. They often become stale or tired of their job. Move them sideways or upwards, or arrange for a posting that you know will suit their talents or re-energise them.

The term 'soft power' is a fashionable currency today. Senior commanders rely too much on coercive or 'hard power' to get things done. They ignore the importance of building relationships through being personable, culturally aware and showing a genuine interest in others.

Towards the end of a gruelling tour of Northern Ireland in February 1980, I visited one of our patrols, which was commanded by a platoon commander, Simon Rhodes, who had not been with us for long. As I approached him, he looked terribly anxious, as if I was going to challenge him on his tactical deployment. I knew he was a keen skier and we spoke for about ten minutes about skiing and what his plans were for his leave. Simon went on to build a successful career in executive search and not long ago, at a Regimental dinner, he reminded me of our conversation and what an impression it had made on him.

I have met and known countless talented officers who have not reached their potential because they believe their work speaks for itself. It rarely does. To be influential, you need to be both seen and heard.

I have always taken time to develop a wide circle of friends, acquaintances and contacts both inside and outside defence. If you always choose to have a sandwich at your desk, you are missing an opportunity to be an ambassador for the army.

As CDS, I achieved more over lunch with Michael Portillo, the Conservative Defence Secretary, and Lord Robertson, the Labour Defence Secretary, than any number of meetings surrounded by civil servants.

The army downhill skiing championships were held each year in Sonthofen in Bavaria. I had long been an advocate of skiing as a way of developing strength of mind amongst soldiers and young officers. When I became Commander-in-Chief, Kate and I would invite as many key army commanders as possible to watch the championships. It was also a wonderful opportunity to find out what their thoughts and concerns were, and to get to know them and their wives better. Cynics may describe this as networking. Those aspiring to high command, however, need to understand its benefits. It allows you to help others and build good working relationships with people.

Allan Mallinson, a former Brigadier who has achieved fame as a writer of military history and novels, asked to come and see me when I was CDS. He was about to take up a posting as Military Attaché in Rome, and sought my advice.

I think Allan was expecting me to say that he should get a thorough grasp on Italian security and defence strategy. He looked startled when I told him that all he really needed to do was to entertain well.

Philip Ward, under whom I served as Adjutant when he commanded the Welsh Guards, taught me the importance of keeping a notebook and writing down the names of people you have met, and something about them. When you next meet someone and you ask, for example, if their son or daughter got into the university of their choice, or if their wife has recovered from an illness, this small gesture of interest will reap its own reward.

It was another Labour Defence Secretary, and a fine one at that, Denis Healey, who wrote and spoke about the importance of developing a hinterland, the place to which a well-rounded person travels to give balance to their life. You do not want to earn the reputation of being a 'military shit'. Bird-watching, bee-keeping, opera, reading poetry and numerous other pastimes have all been the interests of successful commanders.

It pays to be able to read other people and find out what is important to them. When I commanded the Welsh Guards, I had four different brigadiers, and they all varied in attitudes and interests.

One of them was puritanical and spent his time reading Military Police reports on soldiers' misdemeanours. There will always be incidents with soldiers which bring discredit on a period of command. All you can do is be broad-shouldered and robust, and make it clear that you also feel even more strongly than they do about the incident. Bullying and abuse are different matters. If it is an isolated case, you deal with it severely. If it is widespread, then it is a failure of leadership – your leadership. Do not expect any leniency.

Between 1995 and 2002, during my time as CGS and CDS, four young army recruits died from gunshot wounds at Deepcut barracks in Surrey. Allegations of bullying and harassment were widespread. Despite a government review, no conclusions were drawn as to the cause of death. It was heart-breaking for the families involved and an enduring stain on the army's reputation. I made it clear to all senior officers that instances of bullying or discrimination in their commands would exact a severe response.

It is not a sign of weakness to ask advice. It is human nature to like being asked to give advice. It helps build trust, but don't write endless missives setting out misgivings and disagreements. If you do disagree with a senior commander, make sure you are on firm ground and have done your homework, and only when you have established a dialogue of mutual respect. Don't make a habit of it.

Another of the brigadiers was a Royal Engineer who knew precious little about infantry soldiering. He knew that, but he didn't need reminding of his shortcomings. He positively beamed when I congratulated him on the handling of his reserve troops during an exercise.

Any profession which is witness to the extremes of human behaviour requires leaders with a good sense of humour. The absurd and the bizarre are never too far away in the profession of arms.

Von Moltke, the great German commander, once said, "In war, even the mediocre is quite an achievement." Von Moltke was said to have smiled only twice in his life. The first time was when he heard his mother-in-law had died; and the second was when he was told that a 'town' defending Stockholm was in fact a fortress.

Soldiering is a serious business, but there is always a lot to laugh about even if the humour may seem a little dark. As the American poet Ella Wheeler Wilcox wrote, "Laugh and the world laughs with you; be glad and your friends will be many."

––––––

As I reviewed my lectures to the Staff College all those years ago, I saw that I ended them by talking about the mechanics of command on operations. Routine does matter, and it is important to establish one as far as you can. I liked to spend as much time as I could visiting my command during the day. I spent the hours of darkness in bed, to be updated at first light by my Chief of Staff. I ensured my staff got adequate rest, ate well and sensibly and had time for exercise, even if it was just a walk in the gift of nature.

Clausewitz once said, "A great part of information is contradictory, a still greater part is false, and by far the greatest part is uncertain."

I am completely persuaded that technology has a hugely important part to play on the battlefield, but I am not persuaded that it will make command that much easier. Photographs from recent conflicts in Afghanistan often show senior commanders staring into laptops or gathered around screens as drone or satellite images pour through. As the poet and writer T.S. Eliot said, "Where is the information we have lost in data? Where is the knowledge we have lost in information? Where is the wisdom we have lost in knowledge?"

Background noise or pressing concern? The important or the trivial? The reliable or the fake? Only an experienced operational commander will know the difference. Will video-conferencing ever satisfactorily replace a person-to-person conversation? I doubt it.

The atmosphere of a headquarters, the tone of voice, fear masquerading as confidence, the look on a person's face when they are off guard: all these are hard to gauge remotely.

One of the flipsides of simulated training and CPXs is that commanders on operations and staff in HQs over-communicate. Commanders and staff can sometimes babble too much, asking for more and more updates which actually add nothing.

You must train your staff to tell you when there is a change you need to know about. If you are commanding effectively and not allowing yourself to be swamped with detail, that means a change that will materially affect a level of command under you.

When Montgomery was Army Group Commander in Normandy, he gave strict instructions to his staff that he was only to be woken if a corps was under serious threat. I accept that peacetime soldiering and an understandable concern about casualties has meant this is unrealistic nowadays, but commanders must guard against immersing themselves in a level of detail that obscures the wider and more important picture.

The officer who wrote the defence research paper on 'The Shaping of a General' drew no definitive conclusion as to the attributes needed for high command. However, he did acknowledge in his analysis of the seven generals that the first signs of a gladiatorial spark were seen at school. All had been at public or grammar school; all had been Head of School or prefects; all had been prominent on the sports field or an extra-curricular activity. The services have always been a wonderful vehicle for social mobility, if less so in its higher reaches. That has changed over the last two decades.

One of my former ADCs, with whom I have kept in touch, has a daughter who wants to join the Welsh Guards after Sandhurst. A generation ago that would have been unthinkable. There is no reason at all why a woman should not one day be CDS, although it probably won't happen in the few years left to me. She would need operational experience at every level of command, and by that I mean leading men and women into battle.

My only hesitation would be the physical hardship that combat entails, but that becomes less important at higher levels of command and, frankly, is only tricky if you are serving in the infantry.

———

Humility becomes us all. Senior commanders often become too accustomed to the ornaments of their position and rank. I reminded myself of this when I gave up divisional command in York with all its trappings, including a large Ford Granada with a driver and telephone. I drove myself to London in a small Datsun Cherry for my next posting as

ACGS in the MOD, to which I travelled every day on the number 88 bus.

A few years later, I was given just a few days' notice on my appointment as CGS. The pack had to be shuffled pretty quickly after the then Chief of Defence Staff's indiscretions with the exotic and heroically named Bienvenida Buck.

In 1997, Kate and I found ourselves moving from the grand Flagstaff House in Rheindalen to a small flat in Kingston House, while most of our possessions remained in Germany.

As to the challenges of command as we approach the mid-21st century, I allowed myself a wry smile when I read that a US four-star general recently described the future battlefield as "Algorithms vs Algorithms, with the best Algorithm victorious".

We can only hope it does not come to that.

16

Kate

*It was a partnership: she raised our two sons, moved
house 23 times in 31 years, and her support was a
priceless asset throughout my career.*

Kate has always been assiduous in keeping photograph
albums. They are wonderful (sometimes hilarious) memories
of our lives together. In one album there is a picture of me
'duty-dancing' with the pear-shaped and none too easy-on-
the-eye wife of a foreign dignitary. Kate captured the look of
alarm on my face as I was thrown around the dance floor in
the UK's national interest. Over the years we have worked
out a code together: a raised eyebrow, a slight shrug or an
imperceptible nod to say, "time to leave".

I was best man at the wedding of Kate's sister, Sue. Sue was
marrying my closest friend from the Regiment, David Lewis.
Mutual friends had tried to match-make us for some time,
but with little success. Kate was not much inclined to follow
the flag as her mother had done, and as Sue was about to do.
Kate remembers my first words to her: "You're the one who's
been avoiding me." She chuckled and replied that I did seem
vaguely familiar, but she couldn't remember where we had
first met.

After a few dates and a few overnight dashes from Münster to catch the early morning ferry to Dover and then up to London to see Kate, the Regiment was warned off for an emergency tour in Northern Ireland. This was a four-month tour with just one short break for leave. Four months is quite a long time, and I was well aware that there were one or two competitors who had to be seen off. I used to call Kate from the welfare phone in Belfast and was surprised, on one occasion, to be thanked for the flowers she had received. As I had not sent any flowers, I knew that I had little time to waste.

On my one leave from Belfast, I had asked Kate to pick me up from the Belfast early morning express. We went to Kew Gardens on our way from the airport. The conversation was a little stilted on the way to Kew. Kate had more than an inkling of my intentions and I was fidgeting in the car as I played around in my mind how to get the moment and the words just right.

In the end, I proposed to her on a bench overlooking the Thames and Syon House. In the meantime, I had telephoned her father, Colonel Claude Worrall, to ask him for Kate's hand. I remember his words to me: "I've spoken to my friends, and by all accounts you have a promising and respectable career ahead of you. You have my blessing."

Kate and I moved 23 times during my military career. Our first home was a cold, damp, mildewed married quarter, near the Staff College at Camberley. We bought paraffin heaters to keep the place warm. No one seemed to want to sit next to me at the Staff College as I stank of paraffin. Kate knew then what she had let herself in for. As our two sons, Andrew and David, grew older and came home for the holidays from school, it would often be to a new place where they had to start making friends from scratch again.

When I became head of the army, I made it my business to go and listen to the Federation of Army Wives. We changed the name in 1996 to the Army Families Federation to reflect its inclusive nature. The army is a mirror of society, and has done its best to adapt to a world of changing values. I remember with dismay a letter I received from a serving officer who was married to an officer in the Royal Army Medical Corps (RAMC). They were expecting their first child but, at the time, there was no in-service maternity leave and pregnancy meant an automatic discharge from the army. This was madness. The officer and his wife found themselves bogged down in bureaucracy with lily-livered responses from the RAMC and the army's Adjutant General: "bigger issues to deal with, we'll do our best." I wrote to Archie Hamilton, the Armed Forces Minister, who responded with his characteristic good sense. The rules were changed; and in good time, as most RAMC doctors were now deployed in Iraq and, later on, in Afghanistan. We needed every doctor.

No one is born with prejudice. Sadly, many people learn it from others. The army is no different and I was often horrified to witness injustice. I had a talented Military Assistant when I was CDS from the Gurkha Regiment who had fallen in love and wanted to marry a Nepalese air hostess. He was told, and this was in the year 2001 as I finished as CDS, that he could no longer expect to command his Regiment. We lost a talented officer who went on to build a successful life in Hong Kong with his Nepalese wife.

The army is now a better place, a much more equal place, where army wives can pursue successful careers of their own, both in the army or in civilian life. Still, the challenges of married life for servicemen and women remain formidable. In 2019, the Army Board took the decision to move the Household Cavalry Regiment from its barracks in Windsor where it had been for 200 years to Bulford in Wiltshire. On the face of things, this was a sound operational move, as it gave the Household Cavalry a key role as an armoured reconnaissance regiment in 1st Armoured Infantry Brigade. But there were mixed feelings amongst the families, many of whom had bought houses in Windsor, their children settled in good schools, and many of the wives with good careers established nearby.

For my own part, someone once said that behind every successful man is a woman. Kate was never behind me. She was beside me, often in front of me, but never behind me.

I have been a lucky man.

17

Commander-in-Chief, British Army of the Rhine

"Prediction is easy, as long as you keep clear of the future."

MARK TWAIN

John Keegan, a fine military historian, once gave me some sound advice. "Charles," he said, "you will do well to remember the opportunity costs of defence. If there is a peace dividend, it will not be reinvested in defence."

When the Berlin Wall came down in 1989 and the Warsaw Pact started to fall apart, it was clear that politicians in the West would seek to make the most of the end of the Cold War. But as the old certainties began to unravel, past grievances began to re-emerge.

Just a year after that the Conservative government introduced *Options for Change*, a restructuring of the British armed forces in summer 1990 resulting from the end of the Cold War. That same year, Saddam Hussein invaded Kuwait, and the former Yugoslavia began to disintegrate into savage internecine warfare.

It was into this 'peace dividend' in 1992 that I was appointed as Commander-in-Chief of the British Army on the Rhine (BAOR) and Northern Army Group. At a stroke I became a diplomat first and a soldier second. I was glad Kate was at my side.

Unlike my subsequent appointment as CGS, for which I had just a few days' notice, I had time to make up my mind about what I intended to do in the following two or so years at Flagstaff House.

Much of my thinking was shaped by geopolitical considerations. It was not the time for the United States to ease up on their commitment to European security now that the Cold War was seemingly at an end. They were our closest ally, and our sole guarantor of peace. As I said on more than one occasion, "If the EU does not do more, the US will do less."

We also had to do quite a bit of handholding in Germany and the former Warsaw Pact countries, particularly Czechoslovakia and Poland.

Czechoslovakia had divided into the two independent states of the Czech Republic and Slovakia on 1 January 1993. The Prague Spring in 1968, when the Soviet Union invaded Czechoslovakia with 650,000 troops, was in living memory; and the Soviet massacre of 22,000 Polish officers at Katyn in 1940 was indelibly printed in the Polish consciousness.

There had been clear political and strategic direction from both the US and the UK in the First Gulf War in 1991, but in the matter of Yugoslavia there was nothing but incoherence from the UK, which had just tipped Mrs Thatcher overboard.

The US and its allies found themselves at sixes and sevens over Yugoslavia's disintegration. Selection and maintenance of the aim, that all-important military principle, was hard to identify (let alone agree upon) in what the EU and the UN now saw as 'a partnership of equals'.

Options for Change in 1990 had left the British Army in a vacuum, with no clear focus. The Royal Armoured Corps was halved in strength; ancient regiments with distinguished records disappeared overnight; BAOR was reduced from four armoured divisions to just one.

Somehow, I would have to keep the army motivated and trained. Into this mix and period of rapid change, I now assumed command of 1st Netherland Corps, 1st Belgian Corps and 1st German Corps. I also had 3rd US Corps – known as 'America's Hammer' – in reserve and based in Fort Hood, Texas.

Fate and world events intervened as they always do. Despite *Options for Change*, the British Army was able to play a major role as we navigated the new world disorder that followed the collapse of communism.

My first trip to the US to visit the army group's reserve, the US 3rd Corps in Texas, began comically. My Military Assistant (MA), Richard Shirreff, an outstanding officer and cavalryman who went on to be Deputy Supreme Allied Commander Europe, arranged that we should go riding on arrival at Fort Hood. Richard rightly felt that, after a wearisome flight, we should shake off our torpor with a cross-country ride with the US 1st Cavalry.

Fort Hood is on a magnificent scale, equidistant between Dallas and Houston and covering some 340 square miles. Our largest UK garrison at Catterick covers 3.75 square miles – not much more than 1 per cent of the size of Fort Hood.

The 1st US Cavalry was exactly as you would expect from a division on which Francis Ford Coppola based his air cavalry attack to the music of the 'Ride of the Valkyries' in his film *Apocalypse Now*. We were met by their senior commanders, who all wore Stetson hats bearing the division's insignia of the gold-coloured Norman shield with a black horse's head.

Our riding master was a first sergeant, thick-set and with close-cropped hair and crow's feet underneath his pale blue eyes. He did not waver from the traditional Texan script and drawled, "Howdy, General. Now, I expect y'all will need fixin' with some boots before we go ridin' out yonder."

To my dismay, although my ADC had given the correct size of boot to Fort Hood, I found I couldn't get them on. The problem was a recurring one of gout. That was not something I could own up to, as it would fall straight into the US playbook of a typical British general.

"You okay there, General?" asked the First Sergeant.

"Yes," I smiled, "It's just an old parachute injury which flares up from time to time."

My American colleagues looked suitably impressed as Richard, my MA, turned away, stifling his mirth.

The US 3rd Corps had an important role to play if the former Soviet Union, still smarting from the collapse of communism, decided to wrest back its lost territories in Eastern Europe. A wounded beast is at its most dangerous in its death throes.

As Lenin once said, "Quantity has a quality of its own", and the US 3rd Corps, though stationed in Fort Hood, had a formidable armoury pre-positioned in Germany. Apart from the US 1st Cavalry, it had also had the US 1st Infantry Division, 'The Big Red One', immortalised by its performance on Omaha beach on D-Day and its glorious motto, 'No mission too difficult, no sacrifice too great — duty first.'

I spent a good deal of time nurturing our relationship with the US 3rd Corps and the wider US Army, particularly NATO's Central Army Group (CENTAG), commanded by US General 'Butch' Saint. I had enormous respect and admiration for them, and just as importantly, I felt it would be too easy for us to drift apart, there being no obvious remaining threat to unify our thinking and efforts.

In the light of this, I think we were all relieved to see in the First Gulf War in 1991 that a British Division, under the redoubtable Rupert Smith, was closely integrated and under command of an American corps. This made the best possible start in facing the challenges of the period after the Cold War.

I have never had much time for politicians who bang on about the 'Special Relationship'. I have always believed in political pragmatism and our social and cultural ties. I wholeheartedly agreed with the US ambassador to Britain, Raymond Seitz, who said to me, "The shape of our relationship is fashioned by international realities, not by flickering images or happy reminiscences."

In March 1993, I was asked to deliver the Roosevelt Lecture at the US Army War College in Carlisle, Pennsylvania. My talk was entitled, 'Managing the Post-Cold War Watershed – An Ally's View'.

A talk of this nature has to appeal to both the emotional and the rational. The emotional is an easier tone to get right because it often has a true historical resonance: "We have died together for the principles of democracy and decency… Eisenhower, a great President, was the 20th century's greatest master of coalition warfare."

The rational part of my talk looked at the challenges of coalition warfare and the detail of bringing together people who had different training standards, terms of service and operating procedures.

Curiously, at the end of my lecture the first question I was asked was what it was like to be gay in the British Army. I replied that I would not like to be gay in the British Army at that time. I am glad to say, 25 years on from then, it does not matter a jot what one's sexual orientation is. Still, at the time, it was an issue that exercised the minds of the US Joint Chiefs of Staff. President Clinton, who had come to power in January 1993, announced that he would immediately allow gay people to serve in the US Armed Services. I received a telephone call from US General Hugh Shelton, a good friend and ally, to ask my advice. I said to take the President to visit a nuclear submarine as soon as possible and show him the 'hot bunking' arrangements for all personnel. Soon after, Clinton announced, "Don't ask, Don't tell" as the official US policy on military service by gay personnel.

Berlin was the city that most keenly felt the collapse of communism. It was now the capital of the reunified Germany, and *de facto* the European capital with the most political and diplomatic importance.

Mindful of my belief that any commander should go and see for himself what was going on, I set up my forward or Tac HQ in Berlin. Rheindahlen, 375 miles to the west, would remain my main HQ. We retained a garrison in Berlin at the request of the Germans – there were still 380,000 Russian soldiers in Germany in 1990 – and it was not until 1994 that the last British soldiers, the Queen's Lancashire Regiment, left Berlin.

My Tac HQ in Berlin was the former residence of the British Commander-in-Chief's Mission to the Soviet Forces in Germany (BRIXMIS). We were fortunate in that the last commander of the Berlin Infantry Brigade was David Bromhead. David was the great-great nephew of the Rorke's Drift hero, Lieutenant Gonville Bromhead VC. David and his wife, Susan, were a wonderful team.

My Tac HQ bore little resemblance to Montgomery's caravan at El Alamein in 1942, but diplomacy, entertaining and making people feel welcome were uppermost in my mind. I would instruct my staff that work would finish at noon on Friday. They could then make the most of their weekends in Berlin, and Kate and I could prepare for the arrival of our weekend guests.

My first visit to one of the Eastern European countries formerly under the Soviet yoke was to Poland. I had long admired Poland, a country weighed down by the sadness of its history but implacable in its optimism.

It is easy to overlook that Poland has seven countries that border on its territory, including three that remain within the Russian sphere of influence: Ukraine, Belarus and the Russian province of Kaliningrad. Feelings of deep-rooted insecurity are never far away.

My meeting with the Polish Defence Minister, General Tadeusz Wilecki, did not get off to the best of starts, as my staff car was stolen outside my hotel in Warsaw. A taxi was found, a Polski Fiat, and my staff and I crammed our way into it to get to the Polish Defence Ministry.

We arrived feeling slightly stupid and on the back foot; however, once the obligatory toasts with *Zubrowka* bison-grass Vodka got underway, all went swimmingly. The toasts, as the meeting progressed, became increasingly raucous, "*Za nas*" (to us); "*Za piekne panie*" (for beautiful women); and "*Za tych co nie moga*", a solemn toast to those friends who were not present.

It was the first of my many trips to Poland, and I always went away with my admiration enhanced for a country that has made a significant contribution to Western security and United Nations peacekeeping.

Berlin had always retained its cultural power during the Cold War. After the *Bundestag* (German Parliament) voted in 1991 to move the seat of the German capital from Bonn to Berlin, the city's flair for the arts and culture became even more intoxicating. Everyone wanted to visit Berlin, and Kate and I invited and entertained as many of our friends as we could from every walk of political, diplomatic and military life. A visit to see a performance of Mozart's *Die Zauberflöte* at the magnificent Deutsche Oper in what was formerly East Berlin, or a picnic on the River Havel, did a great deal more for the New World Order than any number of NATO conferences. We may have been about to lose our military presence in Berlin, but I was determined that we should not lose our influence.

One of my regular guests was my old sparring partner for tennis, Father Edward Corbould. Edward did not need much persuading to slip away from his monastic duties at Ampleforth Abbey. He would ask permission from the Abbot on the grounds that he was required in Berlin to look after the pastoral needs of a high-profile recent convert.

Edward was often accompanied by Major General Chris Tyler and his wife Suzanne. Chris had been my maintenance commander when I was GOC 1st British Corps. He had become a good friend and was my godfather when I became a Catholic convert. Amusingly, he was turned down by the Irish Guards, who were alarmed because he had a handful of A-levels. The Irish Guards suggested he might try the Royal Mechanical and Electrical Engineers instead. After he retired from the army, he became the first Catholic Governor and Keeper of the Jewel House at the Tower of London since the Reformation.

Given my travel itinerary – I was away a great deal – I only wished my RAF Andover carried an air miles bonus. I had a German Chief of Staff at my main HQ who was highly efficient, but straight out of central casting. The only thing he was missing was a monocle and a *Schläger* cut across the cheek as a duelling scar. I had to rein him in tactfully from time to time, as he was a martinet with junior staff.

NATO conferences were regular; they were a good opportunity to catch up with the key commanders in the Northern Army Group from Belgium, the Netherlands and Germany. The only point of contention was from the Belgians who complained that, at these conferences, it was always they who organised the food. I tried to end this national stereotyping but without success.

The NORTHAG annual dinner was always fun, particularly one year when I had a chance to turn the tables on my companionable ADC, Mark Carr, after he had beaten me soundly at tennis. Just before we sat down for dinner, I noticed Mark was chatting up an attractive *Fräulein*, blind to his duties to chat up those guests who seemed to be on their own. Once we had sat down, and spotting that Mark was still in deep conversation, I announced to everyone that my ADC would now say grace.

ADCs have to learn the job quickly, as Mark discovered on one of his first trips with me. We had returned to RAF Northolt for a meeting of the Executive Committee of the Army Board. Mark was responsible for ensuring all suitcases and briefcases were checked on and off the flight. On arrival at home, I discovered my briefcase was missing. After muttering "highly confidential documents" and giving Mark the darkest of looks, he was sent back to Northolt to recover my briefcase. He arrived back in a muck sweat as I told him that it was only my wash bag.

The collapse into civil war of the former Republic of Yugoslavia in 1991–92 was a murderous and complex affair, and it was to exercise my mind and those of many others throughout the 1990s. In writing these memoirs, I have had to remind myself of the bloody train of events by re-reading Misha Glenny's superb book *The Balkans, 1804–2012*.

President Tito of Yugoslavia died in May 1980, aged 87. Yugoslavs of all nationalities went into mourning, unable to contemplate how the country would govern itself without Tito's iron grip at the helm.

They were right to worry. Yugoslavia only came into existence after the Great War following the disintegration of the Austro-Hungarian Empire. Yugoslavia comprised six constituent republics: Slovenia, Croatia, Serbia, Macedonia, Montenegro and Bosnia-Herzegovina. There were two autonomous provinces: Kosovo, with a significant Albanian and Muslim population; and Vojvodina in the north, with strong ties to Serbia. Tito, during his presidency, had suppressed all ethnic and religious tensions.

After Tito's death, it was inevitable that these ethnic and religious tensions would resurface and grow until 'Kill before you are killed' became the guiding principle for survival.

In 1991, two powerful and vociferous republics, Croatia and Slovenia, declared independence. Shortly afterwards, Bosnia-Herzegovina followed in declaring independence after the Bosnian Serbs held a referendum. The referendum ignored the Bosnian Muslims, who constituted about half of the population.

War between the various irreconcilable factions was only a matter of time. It did not help that European sympathies ran along ancient alliances. The sympathies of Austria and Germany inclined towards Slovenia and Croatia, whereas France, Britain and Russia were more sympathetic to the cause of Serbia.

In November 1991, a United Nations Security Council Resolution paved the way for peacekeeping operations, a term that was replete with incongruity as there was no peace to keep. The various factions were intent on genocide. That repellent phrase 'ethnic cleansing' soon enough became common currency.

The hastily formed UN Protection Force (UNPROFOR) drew heavily on regiments based in Germany but, unlike in the First Gulf War, the US was reluctant to get overtly involved. Without their leadership, there was little consensus as to how to contain the violence.

For the West to intervene, I felt that four conditions had to be met: (1) it must be a moral cause; (2) it must be in our national interest; (3) we must be certain of success; and (4) we must have public opinion behind us. In the Gulf War we had all four. However, in Bosnia-Herzegovina, nothing except (3) was certain.

For historical and religious reasons, most European countries had a dog in the fight. Outside Europe, Pakistan and Saudi Arabia were providing arms to the Bosnian Muslims. To complicate matters further, although BAOR was providing a lot of the manpower, operational control switched to the Commander of the Field Army in the UK. It was all becoming an unholy mess. UNPROFOR was soon in trouble, and it was clear that I should get out there and see for myself what was going on.

The main headquarters was in Sarajevo, the capital of Bosnia-Herzegovina, commanded by a French general, Philippe Morillon. He was not a fighting soldier. He had spent much of his career in the French National Assembly as a military expert, and the remainder in the French Ministry of Defence.

Despite all that, he was a master of his craft as a political soldier and the right man for an unenviable job. He conformed to a certain stereotypical view of French generals and had two ADCs: one for his military programme, and one for his private life. The latter, white-faced, jumpy and juggling telephones, seemed a great deal busier than the former.

Sarajevo, Bosnia-Herzegovina's capital, was bleak, freezing and under siege by the Bosnian Serbs and the old Yugoslav People's Army, largely made up of Serbs. It was a siege which lasted longer than those of Stalingrad in 1941–42 or Leningrad in 1943. The death toll may not have been as high, but the conditions were just as grim.

Outside Sarajevo, things were equally bloody. Three hundred UN troops were killed in Bosnia, a higher casualty rate than in the Gulf War. UNPROFOR was badly in need of a Land Operations HQ outside Sarajevo.

I was able to provide one of my ablest BAOR commanders, Roddy Cordy-Simpson, as an additional Chief of Staff to Morillon with the task of setting up a field HQ at Kiseljak, north-west of Sarajevo. We also had a brigade HQ under Andrew Cumming in Divulje, near the city of Split. I knew Andrew well from my time in 4th Armoured Brigade. He was a talented cavalryman, and had an infantry battle group with him commanded by Bob Stewart, who later became an MP.

My visit to Andrew's HQ was not without incident. We would have been quite happy to be billeted in a UN transit camp, but Andrew's Chief of Staff decided that because I was a four-star general, we should be staying at a hotel.

I could not have cared less, and actually I would have preferred a UN transit camp with a French cookhouse. The hotel, hours away from Andrew's brigade headquarters, turned out to have a dual-purpose role: it soon became apparent that it also served as a brothel for the French Foreign Legion.

Any chance of a good night's sleep was lost in a cacophony of noise: boots crashing, doors banging, groans and cries, and mattresses squeaking. I didn't sleep a wink. Andrew's Chief of Staff, the next morning, chirpily asked me if I had slept well. I rarely, if ever, lose my temper but my response was unprintable. It didn't seem to do his career any harm; he went on to be a four-star general himself.

My mood was further worsened during my visit when I asked the HQ Signals Squadron what they hoped to achieve during what was becoming a demanding and sensitive tour of operations. Their sergeant major, quite straight-faced, replied he wanted to set up a Hawaiian bar in the Sergeants' Mess.

Fortunately, my irritation at his ill-considered and unprofessional response was offset by a visit to a specialist UK Signals attachment of brilliant linguists who were listening in to the Serbian radio nets. I congratulated them on their success and professionalism but undermined any impact I might have had by breaking into French for some reason and saying, "*Au revoir, et bon chance.*"

The threat of the Soviet Union and the Warsaw Pact that had defined BAOR for half a century was now gone.

With it went a whole way of life. We had also lost what I would describe as the friction of war, or at least the possibility of war. There were periods of demanding training: six-week deployments to the British Army Training Unit Suffield (BATUS) in Canada and large, carefully choreographed exercises in Germany.

But BAOR had been a comfortable existence and a settled pattern of life. The Rhine Army Summer Show was not unlike the great Durbars of the Indian Army in the Victorian era. Change, when it comes, can be quick and lasting; but once you come to terms with the initial shock of it, change (if it is well managed) can be a good thing. Complacency usually leads to risk-aversion and stagnation.

I was troubled by the challenge of keeping what was left of BAOR motivated and trained after *Options for Change*. We had been reduced from 55,000 to 23,000 men and women. We were now only able to field one armoured division instead of four. Tactical airpower was reduced by half by the closure of the RAF bases at Wildenrath and Gütersloh.

Luckily, Britain was able to rise to the level of events as policymakers were caught off balance, distracted by the seemingly interminable problems in the Middle East.

The revival of an obscure Balkan squabble seemed trivial set against the rising tensions after Iraq had invaded Kuwait in August 1990; but as we were to discover during the 1990s, the Balkan crisis became far from trivial.

Germany once again became a base for us; we could launch back into expeditionary warfare and move directly to the trouble spots after the old certainties of the Cold War had been swept away. However, we needed an organisation that could implement this, a coherent structure to replace what was left of BAOR that was credible in the eyes of our friends and foes.

With the Speaker of the House of Commons, Betty Boothroyd, and Edward Garnier, Shadow Attorney General, in 1999. (Crown Copyright)

The traditional Maori welcome on a visit to the Royal New Zealand Army, 2000. (Crown Copyright)

The magnificent Black Watch at the parade marking the transfer of sovereignty of Hong Kong to China, July 1997.

After Michael Portillo, I was equally fortunate in working with George Robertson, Tony Blair's Minister of Defence. In this 1998 photograph George is flanked by two other outstanding Ministers of Defence, Lord Carrington and Denis Healey. (Crown Copyright)

A midsummer visit to NATO's most northern flank, the Norwegian archipelago of Svalbard, 1999.

Above With Tony Blair and George Robertson, both decisive and supportive, in 1998. (Crown Copyright)

Left The special relationship. Kate and I with the US Chairman of the Joint Chiefs of Staff, General Hugh Shelton, and his wife Carolyn, in 1999. (Crown Copyright)

'Was there a man dismayed?' A visit in 2000 to the valley of death in the Crimea, the scene of the Charge of the Light Brigade in 1854.

A visit to the Black, Asian and Minority Ethnic (BAME) recruiting team, 1999. (Crown Copyright)

Reconciliation: a warm welcome from President Menem of Argentina, 1998. (Crown Copyright)

A heartfelt salute at the Monument to the Fallen of the Falklands War in the Plaza San Martin in Buenos Aires, 1998. (Crown Copyright)

Speaking at a leadership conference sponsored
by the *Guardian* newspaper, 1999.
(Crown Copyright)

Shaking hands in 1997 with a splendid veteran
from the Crete campaign of 1941.

A good listener and decisive in action: Tony Blair and I thrashing things out
during the crisis in Kosovo, 1999. (Crown Copyright)

A Royal Navy Lieutenant Commander bringing me up to speed on the events in Kosovo, late May 1999. (Crown Copyright)

A couple of weeks later at Trooping the Colour as Gold Stick and Colonel of The Life Guards, 1999. (Crown Copyright).

Above One for the ladies, 1999. (Crown Copyright)

Above Two impressive Israelis, not to be trifled with: Ehud Barak, Prime Minister of Israel, and General Shaul Mofaz, Chief of the Israeli General Staff in 1999. (Crown Copyright)

Below A briefing by Israeli senior officers, 1999. (Crown Copyright)

Above 'Let 'em have it!' Firing the Israeli light machine gun, 1999. (Crown Copyright)

Clambering aboard the formidable Israeli main battle tank, the Merkava in 1999. (Crown Copyright)

The view from the Golan Heights in 1999, a commanding position? (Crown Copyright)

A friendly welcome from the Commander of the People's Liberation Army (PLA). The PLA budget was $14.6bn in the year of my visit, 2000. In 2021, it is $209.4bn. (Crown Copyright)

Outside the 'Forbidden City', Beijing, 2000.

No sinister sect, just a visit to Chateau Pomerol with Hugh Shelton, US Chairman of the Joint Chiefs of Staff, and General Jean-Pierre Kelche, Chief of the French Defence Staff, in 2000.

President Musharraf of Pakistan, an astute ally in the fight against those elements who wished to do serious harm to the West, 2000. (Crown Copyright)

Admiral Boyce, my successor as Chief of the Defence Staff, on my right in 2000. (Crown Copyright)

Concurrent activity: training for Trooping the Colour, wearing only my helmet as Colonel of The Life Guards, whilst talking to General Hugh Shelton at the Pentagon in 2000.

Sierra Leone civil war, 2000 – a potentially nasty outcome but with the right people in place: Brigadier David Richards on my right (later Chief of the Defence Staff 2010–13) and Peter Westmacott, Foreign and Commonwealth Under-Secretary of State (later our ambassador to Turkey, France and the United States). (Crown Copyright)

Always a magnificent sight, horses of The Life Guards kicking up dust at Trooping the Colour in 2000. (Crown Copyright)

A visit to Georgia in 2000, greeted by President Eduard Shevardnadze, a former Minister of Foreign Affairs for the Soviet Union before communism's collapse in 1989. (Crown Copyright)

Forty years on: inspecting the Passing out Parade at Sandhurst, August 1999. (Crown Copyright)

With my ADC, Harry Legge-Bourke, at the Welsh Guards Memorial in the Falklands in 2000. (Crown Copyright)

My farewell to the Pentagon. General Hugh Shelton presents me with the award of an Officer of the Legion of Merit in 2001. (Crown Copyright)

Left A Farewell to Arms.

Below 'Civvy Street' beckons.

"CDS Retirement Cocktail Party after 44 years"
Thursday 15th February 2001
Commencing 1830hrs
South Concourse Hall, Ministry of Defence, Whitehall.
RSVP Tel: 020 72186031 Chots: CDS/ADC E Mail: CDSMODUK@AOL.COM

"CDS Retirement Cocktail Party after 43 years".

Thurs 15th Feb 2001
Commencing 1830hrs
South Concourse Hall

Lord Robertson and Lord Carrington and the author at the House of Lords in September 2001.

Playing tennis in 1996; a perfect antidote to the stresses of a busy working life.

The Gold Sticks in full fig, 2009. (Crown Copyright)

Welsh Guards on the Queen's Birthday Parade in 2008. (Crown Copyright)

With the Prince of Wales in 2013 during the Walk on Wales to support Welsh Guards charities.

Enjoying a happy retirement with Kate after... 23 moves, 2014.

On 2 October 1992, 1st British Corps was disbanded and became the Allied Rapid Reaction Corps (ARRC). The ARRC, first commanded by Lieutenant General Sir Jeremy Mackenzie, remains an enduring success to this day as NATO's high readiness force for deployment worldwide. In 2017, some 23 NATO countries provided servicemen and women for the force, which is now headquartered in Gloucestershire.

In a period of profound change, everyone fights for influence and resources. RAF Germany was commanded by an air marshal who, frankly in my view, was a menace and whose common sense and strategic understanding came second to his personal ego. On receiving his knighthood, he became impossibly grand – and his wife even grander. He would keep his ADC up all hours, instructing him to hover in the background until all the guests at his dinner parties were ready to leave. The harassed ADC was under strict instructions to help the guests with their coats, to which the Air Marshal would then say to his ADC something to the effect of, "Oh, are you still here? How good of you, I thought you were taking the evening off."

I was determined that the superb US Apache helicopter AH-64D should remain under British Army control, and be flown by Army Air Corps pilots, who understood army requirements far better than did the Royal Air Force.

RAF Germany, officially disbanded in April 1993, were equally determined that they should fly the Apaches, thereby retaining some influence and prestige. In this they were strongly supported by RAF officers who had served their entire careers in the MOD.

A conference was held at my main HQ in Rheindahlen to discuss the matter which, fortuitously, coincided with a visit by the Higher Command and Staff Course.

I asked my ADC, Mark Carr, to ask all the army brigadiers on the course to come and see me so I could brief them on my plan to out-manoeuvre the RAF. They were all up for it.

I briefed them carefully, telling one of them to ask a question on how the RAF saw the Apache helicopter operating in the attack and armoured reconnaissance role after the RAF had put forward their case. "After that, let someone else at the conference speak, and then another one of you needs to ask this secondary question." I then told him what to ask. "That should settle it."

They soon caught on that I was pushing the RAF into a cul-de-sac where they would have no case to answer.

We won the day, and the Apache still remains under army control, a formidable platform to hunt and destroy tanks, and immeasurably enhancing the army's offensive capability.

The Air Marshal retired prematurely from the RAF after he was accused of using £387,000 in government funds to refurbish his official residence. He argued that the funds had been approved, but this was not supported by the MOD.

I have always been a great advocate of imaginative training, including a surprise element that is tough but memorable. As we entered a new phase in our relations with the German people, we had to give up a few jewels in the crown. One of these was the Soltau-Lüneburg training area, although I don't suppose any British soldier who trained there in mid-winter will remember it with much affection.

One jewel we did retain, however, was the British Army Training Unit in Canada. This was in the prairie land of Alberta, between Medicine Hat and Calgary to the north-west. It covered some 2,700 square kilometres, with 400 permanent staff and 1,000 vehicles. It was as fine a place as any for live firing and manoeuvre, and for smoking out those who could not read a map.

The tactical training looked after itself under the professional eye of BATUS, but I made it my business on my many visits to anchor our relations with the Albertan community. In the summer of 1993, I went out to BATUS with my MA, Richard Shirreff.

I also persuaded Robert Cranborne to accompany us. He was then Minister of Defence and a friend from the Beefsteak Club. It was important to show our politicians how lucky we were to have such a superb training facility. Robert was the head of one of England's most historic and distinguished families, and he had strong military links. Three of his brothers had served with the Grenadiers, and he was just the right man to bring along. He observed a live-firing exercise at battle group level and I was confident that he would return to the MOD convinced that BATUS was a priceless asset for the British Army.

The accommodation at BATUS was basic – we all shared a dormitory – but Robert took it in his stride. The Regimental Sergeant Major at BATUS would wake us at first light with the words, "Gentlemen: stand by! In ten minutes' time I shall return and switch all the lights on."

Robert was a friend of Fred Mannix, a Canadian billionaire from Calgary with interests in real estate, ranching, coal, oil and gas. Fred invited us all for a weekend at his ranch. The ranch was a paean to the old West, stretching for miles and miles, with 10,000 head of cattle. Fred was an old-style frontiersman, urbane and savvy but conscious of his obligations to society. His eyes were those of a man who, from an early age, were used to weighing up both people and his surroundings in an instant. He told me that his sole aim was to "reinforce the success of my grandfather and father who started and built up our family's business".

Fred was a generous host. He arranged for us to have a crack at his cross-country course. Richard, Robert and I were all experienced horsemen, but the horses were pretty lively as you would expect from Calgary, a city famous for its stampede rodeos and chuck-wagon races. Robert was unhorsed at one of the ditch obstacles, which remains to this day known as 'Cranborne's Crash'.

It was during a visit to the US Army that I realised that I had become far too large. I remember looking up at a somewhat obnoxious mirrored ceiling in the vast hotel suite in which I had been put up, and thinking, "That can't be me."

As soon as I returned to London I went to a bookshop and bought Michel Montagnac's book on dieting. I followed it mercilessly and also took Kate to *ein Kurort* (health farm) in Bavaria to accelerate the process of looking as a British general should.

While I was there, I received a telephone call from Richard Shirreff to say that the CDS, Air Chief Marshal Sir Peter Harding, already flying by the seat of his pants, had been caught with his pants actually down. The lady in question, Bienvenida Buck, was married to a Tory MP, Sir Anthony Buck. Harding's position was untenable, particularly as it coincided with Prime Minister John Major's *Back to Basics* initiative.

Richard told me we should prepare to pack our bags at once, as there was a good chance that, after shuffling the pack, I would become the next CGS.

18

Chief of the General Staff

*"I began to wonder whether I was Alice
in Wonderland, or whether I was fit
for a lunatic asylum."*

GENERAL SIR ALAN BROOKE, CGS 1942

As I was about to take up my appointment as CGS in 1994, an old friend of mine said to me that he did not envy me my new position in having to manage the army's decline. I remember being slightly aggrieved by his remark, pointing out that the army had never been busier.

The Balkan conflict was far from over and many countries, particularly in Eastern Europe, were pretty nervous as to what the new world order would look like after the collapse of communism.

I also told him that the peace process in Northern Ireland would need to be handled with great care. We all wanted peace, but it was the process that would be regarded with suspicion on all sides of the political divide. I was determined to ensure the army did not make any unforced errors.

But I did wonder, as I walked along the long corridor on the sixth floor of the MOD towards my new office, what the next few years would bring. I glanced at the photographs of my predecessors as CGS dotted along the walls: 'Wully' Robertson who rose from footman to field marshal; Alan Brooke, the brilliant strategist who kept Churchill's more questionable schemes at bay; Montgomery, the outstanding battlefield commander; Bill Slim, the victorious commander of the 14th Army in Burma; and Gerald Templer, the architect of the 'hearts and minds' strategy which allowed for the skilful withdrawal from our colonies. They were men of the front rank who had formidable challenges to overcome. I was always mindful of their legacy.

On the face of things, my friend had a point about managing decline. The army was a third of its size from when I joined in 1959, and it was shrinking year by year. John Keegan's comment about the "opportunity costs of defence" never rang more true. The percentage of the country's GDP spent on defence was as low as it had ever been, and the trend was downwards.

I knew I would have to strike a balance between acquiescence with government decisions, retaining a strong independent view and ensuring that the spirit of Waterloo, D-Day and the Falklands campaign was not lost.

Given the short notice of my appointment, I inherited some of my predecessor's commitments, which included an early trip to visit the Swedish Army Board. The MOD worked closely with the Foreign and Colonial Office (FCO) in organising overseas visits, which were a mixture of high-level defence sales, diplomacy and operations. A visit to Sweden, apparently, was long overdue. If I had known that I would be required to strip naked for my country and discuss reducing tensions in the Baltic in a sauna with the rest of the Swedish Army Board, I might have decided to postpone or cancel the visit.

Sweden, like Switzerland, is a country with a proud history of neutrality. It was on the cusp of joining the EU; it had a strong defence industry, and it enjoyed close ties in defence cooperation with EU countries. It also had a maritime border with Russia, whose submarines would stealthily slide their way through the Baltic Straits to the North Atlantic.

The FCO thought I should also gauge their appetite for joining NATO. The meetings were constructive and far-reaching. A similar trip to Finland in 1972 when I was MA to the then CGS, Michael Carver, had also ended in a sauna with me birching Carver.

As I entered the sauna with my Swedish Army Board colleagues to sweat away life's problems and discuss hunting Russian submarines, I noticed my ADC, Richard Stanford, hanging about outside and still fully clothed. Plates of *Surströmming* (fermented fish), smoked herring, salmon and trays of ice-cold aquavit and schnapps lay on a trestle table to the side. I said, "Richard, why don't you join us and hand out some of those delicious-looking local delicacies which our hosts have laid down? I'm afraid you'll have to strip off as well."

Richard, who had only been with me a couple of months, visibly blanched. He was with me for two years, and despite that minor baptism of fire, he became an effective, level-headed and well-liked ADC. He became a major general and is still serving at the time of writing.

Another early commitment I needed to honour was a trip to South Africa. The long-awaited end of apartheid (institutionalised racial segregation) and South Africa's first multi-racial election resulted in the creation of the new South Africa National Defence Force (SANDF).

SANDF had to integrate the African People's Liberation Army (APLA), the military wing of the African National Congress Party headed by Nelson Mandela. Black soldiers would now comprise 75% of the force. I was there with my team to advise on the structure, training and equipment the new SANDF would need.

It immediately struck me how tough and battle-hardened the APLA men looked, while by comparison the white South African colonel who hosted our visit was the fattest and most unfit officer I had ever set eyes on.

———

Much of the 1990s was dominated by the peace process in Northern Ireland. The commitment to lasting peace was not controversial, but the process of achieving it was regarded with suspicion by almost everyone.

Op *Banner*, the name given to the army's deployment in Northern Ireland, was to take up an increasing amount of my time. I had not been there since the autumn and winter of 1979–80, when I relinquished command of my battalion in South Armagh. The spiral of violence which accounted for 500 deaths in 1972, of which 108 were soldiers, had fallen to 69 deaths in 1994; only one of those was a soldier.

The British Army was not going to win the war against the IRA in any recognisable way. Instead, we allowed a political process to be established towards the goal of lasting peace without unacceptable levels of intimidation.

We should always be proud of this. As far as the army was concerned, the process of gradual demilitarisation started just after I became CGS in 1997, when the IRA announced its first ceasefire. Much of the groundwork for this was done by John Wilsey, the GOC Northern Ireland.

John was a close friend from Sandhurst, where he had tried to persuade me to be his wingman in the *Daily Mail* London to Paris air-race and return to Sandhurst in the sidecar of his Norton 500 cc motorcycle. John had a great feel for operations in Northern Ireland and the demands made on the soldiers involved. We reduced our presence there by three battalions and stopped daytime army patrols in Belfast.

We were at the fag-end of the Conservative government which had started in 1979, and which was to splutter on in an ugly display of infighting and open disloyalty. The petulance displayed by John Major, the Prime Minister, over the Exchange Rate Mechanism, Maastricht and Europe, and his Back to Basics campaign did nothing to help. It was not an edifying spectacle.

Despite that, I respected Major for his strenuous efforts to get the peace process off the ground. Like so many seemingly insurmountable problems, it often gets down to the right people with a shared determination to sort things out. Unfortunately, he was not the right man.

The peace process was blessed with having the remarkable John Hume as its principal architect. John was the most influential Irish Nationalist politician of his generation, and the first politician to challenge the assertion that the root cause of the Troubles was the British presence in Northern Ireland.

A durable peace settlement was still a few years away. Desperate acts of violence continued on both sides of the sectarian divide. The Unionist marching season at Drumcree, always provocative to Republicans, exposed huge divisions.

President Clinton indulged in unhelpful political gestures. He shamelessly played to the Irish American lobby, led by Senator Edward Kennedy. Like his father Joe, who was ambassador to the UK during the period of appeasement, Edward Kennedy was anti-British and a scoundrel. At one time, he had pretensions to the presidency. These came to an end when an interviewer asked him, "What right have you to be president when you were expelled from Harvard for cheating and left a woman to drown in your car?" Kennedy arranged for a US visa to be issued to the hard-line Republican Gerry Adams, thereby undermining the trust of Unionist politicians.

In 2009, Gordon Brown announced an honorary knighthood for Edward Kennedy. It was, to say the least, a controversial and dubious award.

The stipulation that IRA weapons should be decommissioned as a precondition for a peace settlement was politically naïve. The IRA comprised a mixture of gangsters, criminals and terrorists fighting for a united Ireland, but decommissioning was an admittance of defeat they could not accept.

Whatever confidence-building measures the army could enact in Northern Ireland to run in parallel with the peace process were lost on 9 February 1996. The IRA detonated a powerful truck bomb in Canary Wharf at the heart of the City of London, killing two people and devastating a wide area. The peace process came to a standstill.

I agree with George Bernard Shaw's maxim: "I dislike feeling at home when I'm abroad", but I might have drawn a line on this adage during my next overseas visit as CGS to Bulgaria.

Bulgaria had been an important member of the Warsaw Pact. When communism collapsed in 1990, it had 2,400 tanks and 2,500 artillery pieces. NATO needed to cultivate a relationship with Bulgaria and bring the country into NATO's Partnership for Peace initiative.

I was sent to persuade Bulgaria that its long-term interests were best served within the NATO Alliance.

The usual visit programme was laid on after several meetings with General Tsvetan Totomirov, the Bulgarian Chief of Defence. I was taken to a Bulgarian orthodox monastery where they distilled their own liqueur, a fruit brandy which was a near-lethal 80 per cent alcohol proof.

The British Defence Attaché warned me that one glass was sufficient; two glasses and I would be on the floor, and any more than that might end up with me being severely compromised.

I downed three without too much bother, only then to be taken off to a formal dinner where I was seated next to Totomirov's wife. She was colossal. She looked as if she had been in the Bulgarian shot-put team, and she threw me around the dance floor like a rag doll.

This 'duty dancing' was not in vain. Bulgaria joined the NATO Partnership for Peace in 1994, and formally joined the alliance in 2002. Bulgaria has been a stalwart member of NATO ever since.

I always took great pains to get to know and get along with the civil servants in the MOD. Michael Quinlan, with whom I co-wrote *Just War: Ethics in Modern Warfare*, Christopher France, Richard Mottram and Kevin Tebbit were all towering figures, with intellects to match.

Civil servants are easy targets when things go awry, invariably at the hands of politicians. Christopher France spent most of his time when he was at the Department of

Health coping with Edwina Currie's mishaps where she declared that 'most of the egg production in this country, sadly, is now affected with salmonella', sparking outrage among farmers and egg producers; and Richard Mottram had just as miserable a time after the MOD when, after a communiqué went badly wrong, he announced, "I'm fucked, you're fucked, the whole department is fucked, it's the biggest cock-up ever, we're all completely fucked."

I was fortunate in the appointment of Michael Portillo as Secretary for Defence in June 1995 after his predecessor was sent to the Foreign Office. Michael was a good listener, unlike many Conservative politicians in the MOD who felt that their time in the school CCF had made them masters of the battlefield.

Portillo was clever and read his briefs punctiliously. Of Spanish descent, he was *simpático*, that lovely Spanish word which has no single translation in English but conveys so much more than 'sympathetic' or 'nice'. He was good with everyone, whether they were a young soldier serving in Northern Ireland or an experienced senior officer.

He was, however, in thrall to an advisor, the eccentric figure of David Hart. Hart provoked him into his ill-judged 'Who Dares Wins' speech at the 1995 Conservative Conference. It was the only time he misfired during his time as Minister of Defence.

It was the measure of Portillo that he was man enough to telephone me after his speech to apologise for an uncharacteristic lapse of judgement.

The Minister of Defence had its own lavatory on the sixth floor, but I was obliged to share one with Nicholas Soames, the Minister of State for the Armed Forces. Like his grandfather Winston Churchill, Nicholas was a trencherman and raconteur. Whenever I bumped into him in the loo, I always found it tricky to get on with the business of the day while he regaled me with gossip.

As one might expect, Nicholas Soames had a great sense of history, and an innate feeling for the ordinary soldier. Our visit to Gallipoli in Turkey together for the 80th anniversary of the campaign was memorable, but only partly because Soames's grandfather Winston had attracted great criticism for the campaign's failure. I still chortle when I recall that the Turkish took the visits of NATO generals very seriously; but those of Western politicians rather less so. Nicholas Soames, who was then generously proportioned, was placed at the back of the military cavalcade on the back seat of a Fiat Punto as we made our way around the battlefield. Nicholas took it all his stride and with his singular sense of humour.

I also remember the visit well because my ADC, Richard Stanford, found the grave of his great-uncle who had been killed in action serving with the Lancashire Fusiliers, a heroic regiment which won 12 VCs before breakfast.

As CGS and as a former SAS officer, I had become increasingly concerned about the number of SAS books being published. Many people agreed with me. It led me to having a tricky telephone conversation with the man who started the rot, General Sir Peter de la Billière.

Peter was a distinguished and courageous former SAS officer and the Commander British Forces during the First Gulf War in 1990–91. But he had lost a good deal of money in Lloyd's of London. After the Gulf War, he had become a well-known public figure and publishing houses were only too willing to sell his exploits. Peter had retired and there was a valid autobiographical theme in both his books, *Storm Command* and *Looking for Trouble*. There were, however, unfortunate revelations about SAS operations which were unacceptable. They betrayed confidences and undermined the Regiment's mystique.

I had to ask Peter to resign from the SAS Regimental Association and tell him he would not be welcome in any SAS Mess. I still have mixed feelings about this. Peter had been a towering figure in the history of the SAS.

———————

In the words of a former Chief of Defence Staff, the Balkans remained "a hotbed of cold feet". Even after Sarajevo's destruction by Serbian artillery bombardments, and the appalling suffering of its population, the international community was at a loss to know how to respond to the utter senselessness and misery of the entire conflict.

The UNPROFOR ground operation continued to bumble along, wearing their blue berets and driving their white-painted vehicles. As Michael Rose, a fine soldier and colleague from my SAS days and by that stage UNPROFOR commander, remarked to me, "You can't make war in white-painted vehicles."

I could see that the Balkan conflict was likely to dominate British Army operations for the foreseeable future; the Balkans were susceptible to received wisdom from people who knew little of the region's complexities and tangled history. Politicians of all parties in the UK and in Europe thought they understood the situation. But as a US State Department office remarked in 1995 'the only thing the Balkans exports is history'.

Fitzroy Maclean was one of the few people who understood the region well, so I invited him to come and talk to the Army Board over dinner at the Royal Hospital. Educated at Eton and King's College Cambridge, Maclean was one of just two men who rose from Private to Brigadier in the Second World War; the other was Enoch Powell.

He was allegedly one of the inspirations for Ian Fleming's *James Bond*. In the Second World War he specialised in commando raids behind enemy lines. David Stirling, who founded the SAS, said of him, "Don't be put off by his ponderous manner and slow delivery. After all, he is a Scottish baronet; but he's all right."

Churchill pounced on Fitzroy Maclean to fight alongside Tito and his partisans against the Germans in Yugoslavia. Churchill's brief to Maclean was unequivocal: "Don't concern yourself with what happens to Yugoslavia after the war. Simply find out who is killing the most Germans and suggest means by which we could help them to kill more."

Maclean's book *Eastern Approaches* taught me a good deal about the Balkans and its record of savage internecine warfare. His talk at the Royal Hospital dinner held us all spellbound. His final words, "Frankly, you'd be better off invading Russia in mid-winter", did little for my composure over our involvement in the region.

I made frequent visits to Bosnia to see for myself what was happening and what we could do to help. I was proud of the British willingness to step outside the limp UN mandate and take the fight to the Bosnian Serbs and the Croats.

The Croats had the tacit support of the US but were guilty of equal atrocities towards the Bosnian Muslims. The Duke of Wellington's Regiment did the British Army's reputation proud when it entered the UN 'safe haven' of Goradze and saved the Bosnian Muslim enclave from being overrun, and probably much worse, by Bosnian Serbs.

Other nations did not have our operational doctrine learned over years in Northern Ireland and BAOR, and were far less inclined to get stuck in to defend, with force if necessary, the lives of unarmed men, women and children.

However, it would be wrong to lay blame at the feet of the UN troops in Bosnia. The lack of political will and the Clinton administration's reluctance to consider any plan that might involve US ground troops meant that the UNPROFOR became badly demoralised and a convenient scapegoat.

Real responsibility lay with the governments of the great powers, the five permanent members of the UN Security Council: France, China, Russia, the UK and the US. They were unable to agree on a feasible peacekeeping mandate for UNPROFOR.

In the light of this, it was more important than ever to keep a weather eye on our relationship with the US Pentagon. The Chairman of the US Joint Chiefs of Staff was John Shalikashvili. John, born in Warsaw in 1936, was the son of an *émigré* Georgian officer and Polish mother. He was the first foreign-born officer to be Chairman of the US Joint Chiefs. In that sense he was the epitome of the American belief that regardless of birth or background, you could achieve anything.

I first met John when he asked me to attend a memorial service for those British and American servicemen killed in a 'blue-on-blue' incident in northern Iraq in April 1994, when a Blackhawk helicopter with 26 people on board was mistakenly shot down by US fighter aircraft. One of those killed, Harry Shapland of the Irish Guards, was a good friend of my ADC, Richard Stanford. The service was held in a chapel next to the Pentagon. I arrived to find the bereaved families, some 200 in all, assembled in a large hall outside the chapel. John turned to me and wholly unexpectedly asked if I would say a few words.

I did my best, and I hope that what I said was reassuring to the bereaved families. The palpable sense of sadness in the hall has never left me. As I began my few words, President Clinton arrived, and that just heightened the level of expectation. I was introduced to him at the end and saw at first hand his personal magnetism. He had an ability to make you feel you were the only person who mattered; but I sensed it was artificial.

The murder of 8,000 unarmed Muslim men and boys in the UN safe haven of Srebrenica by Serbs on 11 July 1995 was a sickening stain on the conscience of the international community and the UN.

A Dutch UN battalion was tasked to protect Srebrenica, but the Dutch troops were rooted in the UN's fatal philosophy of impartiality and did nothing to prevent the massacre.

I have never attached blame to the Dutch troops. They were ill-served by their government and defence ministry. They were also badly equipped and ill-trained to carry out such a task. I felt much sympathy and sorrow for them. Many of them remain haunted by the shame of Srebrenica.

The massacre at Srebrenica was a catalyst for action by the international community, particularly the United States. In late 1995 a political settlement was brokered at Dayton, Ohio; it brought a fragile ceasefire between the Bosnian Serbs and the Bosnian Muslims.

More importantly, the responsibility for the ceasefire now lay with the new NATO Allied Rapid Reaction Force (ARRC), led by Michael Walker. The staff were also largely British and many of its key fighting elements were also ours.

It was not to be my last encounter with the Balkans. The entire region, much like the Middle East, was – and remains – unfinished business. When I became CDS in 1997, the Balkans were once again to exercise my mind.

During my time as CGS, I found I spent around five months each year abroad. The day-to-day running of the trainset was left largely to the ACGS, a job I had done myself between 1987 and 1989.

My ACGS, Tim Granville Chapman, fell neatly into Von Moltke's description of officers who were best suited to high-level staff rank, in that they should be clever and industrious. In Von Moltke's view, officers who were clever and lazy were better suited to high command because their temperament would allow them to see the wider picture and not get bogged down in unnecessary detail. Tim once took umbrage when I asked him why, if he was so terribly clever, did he have to work so late.

The opportunity costs of defence were a constant headache as the government sought to find savings wherever they could. But opportunities to generate cash savings for the MOD in the short term will often prove a waste of taxpayers' money in the long run.

Nevertheless, Michael Portillo was right to point out there were far too many establishments and expensive buildings to keep up in the education of servicemen and women. There were, for example, four separate staff colleges. There were also obvious savings to be made in the MOD's landholdings and its huge housing estate.

Home ownership was becoming increasingly within the grasp of service families, where both parents were working and wanted stability for their children, particularly their education. These were complex projects, ideal for my ACGS to work on late into the night. Tim Granville Chapman's reward for his fine work on this was to become the first Commandant of the Joint Services Command and Staff College (JSCSC).

Less successful, however, and a good deal more controversial, was the MOD's decision to sell off 55,000 homes in 1996 to a private equity fund run by an ex-Nomura banker, Guy Hands. They paid £1.66bn cash up front, valuing each home at £30,000 when the average house price in the UK was £103,000. The MOD then rented them back from the private equity fund.

As the National Audit Office wrote, "This has cost the public sector a great deal in capital growth, and it has been a great deal for the landlord."

The 55,000 homes are now valued at £7.3bn.

A country may have shared interests and shared values with another country, but it is relationships that matter. There was no more important relationship in the Middle East than our friendship with the Omani people.

The Sultanate of Oman had been a loyal friend to Britain ever since we helped Sultan Qaboos bin Said overthrow his father in 1970. I first came to know the Sultan as CGS when I was introduced to him by Air Vice Marshal Sir Erik Bennett. Erik had been the air advisor to King Hussein of Jordan and then helped to create the Sultan of Oman's Air Force (SOAF) in 1974.

I struck up a lasting friendship with HM Sultan Qaboos. It helped that two of my officers in the Welsh Guards, David Mason and Romilly David, had distinguished themselves in battle in the Sultan's army.

Sultan Qaboos was an absolute monarch, but he was extraordinarily enlightened. He used his country's growing oil revenues to improve the infrastructure, healthcare and education of the Omani people. A devout Muslim, he nevertheless allowed complete religious freedom.

I visited the Sultan every year, and he invited me to stay in the Al Alam Palace in the old part of Muscat, Oman's capital. I would advise the Sultan on defence matters and how Britain viewed his neighbours in the Middle East. In return, he would allow the British Army to train in Oman and use various launchpads for our ordeals in Iraq and Afghanistan.

The friendship between our two countries was cemented in the 2019 Joint Defence Agreement and the creation of a new British military base.

Sultan Qaboos's death in early 2020 left the wonderful Omani people bereft of a remarkable human being, but the succession looks secure under his protégé, HM Sultan Haitham bin Tarik.

Too much travel, too many official dinners and not enough exercise (despite a weekly game of tennis) had taken its toll. It was after I returned from a trip to Oman that I began to feel unwell. I took myself off to the Woolwich Military Hospital where the army doctor diagnosed a deep vein thrombosis – a typical symptom of heavy air travel. A charming nurse from the Queen Alexandra's Royal Army Nursing Corps gave me a bed bath and giggled when I said to her, "There are not many nurses who can say they have the undivided attention of the CGS by holding his balls in her hand."

On my return to the office, I found that I had a computer on my desk. I asked my ADC, Richard Stanford, to show me the 'on' button and what a 'mouse' did. I then gave him strict instructions to keep the thing turned on during working hours to convey the right impression. This was just before a massive MOD upgrade to Windows, a debate to which I found it hard to contribute.

I suspect that now I would be called an analogue general for a digital age, but I have always reassured myself with the Iron Duke's words when presented with information he wasn't too sure about: "Is that so? Bring me my horse. I shall go and see for myself."

Towards the end of my time as CGS, I began to turn my thoughts to who the next government might be. The Conservatives had been in power for 18 years and were a busted flush. The country showed every sign of wanting things to change and I was pretty clear that, if I was to be the next CDS, I needed to build trust with Tony Blair and the key individuals who were likely to form his first administration. My broad operational experience counted in my favour, as did my strong relationship with senior civil servants, and politicians on both sides of the House.

A month after I had taken over as CDS, Labour under Tony Blair won the election with a resounding majority. Michael Portillo, who had been an outstanding Defence Secretary, lost his seat. Perhaps for the first time in my life I realised how brutal politics could be. At a stroke, Michael lost everything: his ministerial position, his seat as an MP, and his livelihood. He was clever enough to realise it was probably coming, but it must nevertheless have been a bad shock.

As Michael was clearing his desk to face an uncertain future, I asked Richard Mottram, the MOD's Permanent Under-Secretary, to call the whole building together and clap Michael Portillo out of the building. Michael was cheered to the rafters. He looked visibly moved by our small but heartfelt gesture.

19

Gold Stick, Colonel of The Life Guards

A singular honour as Colonel of the senior regiment of the British Army, though after the 2018 Trooping the Colour, I'm not sure I agree with Winston Churchill's dictum that, "no hour of life is wasted that is spent in the saddle".

When I joined the army in 1960, The Life Guards Officers' Mess car park looked like the Jack Barclay Bentley showroom in London's Berkeley Square.

The Life Guards were a natural haven for the sons and scions of Britain's grandest families. The future 11th Duke of Marlborough, known as 'Sunny', took his own pack of hounds when the Regiment was serving in Germany in the 1950s, only to describe the posting as "far too provincial".

One of their officers, finding himself unable to pay his Mess bill, held up a provincial bank wearing a quilted Barbour jacket and armed with a sawn-off shotgun. The irony was that the money he robbed was worth a good deal less than the value of his handmade Purdey shotgun, which was now worthless in its sawn-off state. I am not sure The Life Guards were taken very seriously at that time as a military force.

This was in sharp contrast to the Second World War, when as part of the Household Cavalry Regiment, they distinguished themselves with 30 Corps in the breakneck dash to liberate Brussels. But peacetime soldiering and the salons of Mayfair had dulled their appetite for serious soldiering.

Thirty years or so later in 1990, while I was serving as the Corps Commander in Germany, I received a telephone call from James Ellery, who was at that time Commanding Officer of The Life Guards. James wanted my advice on who should be the next Colonel of The Life Guards. He suggested we have dinner.

We met at a restaurant called 'Zum Treuen Husaren' (The Loyal Hussar) in Sennelager. If the Regiment was underpowered in the 1960s and early 1970s, it had transformed itself as part of 5th Airborne Brigade to become an armoured reconnaissance regiment. It was now a worthy heir to its illustrious history and hard-fought battle honours from Dettingen to Waterloo to El Alamein.

I had known James on and off for some time. I knew him to be a fine commanding officer and I admired him for passing 'P' Company, the Parachute Regiment's arduous selection test week, at the age of 38.

James was perhaps somewhat Prussian in his views. He would not allow anyone to wear jeans leaving barracks, so you would find the lay-bys nearest to the barracks taken up by both officers and troopers changing into or out of jeans, depending on whether they were leaving or coming back from a night out.

It was clear from our dinner, however, that rather like a head-hunter who asks a businessman who they know might suit a particular role, James was sounding me out for the position as their next Colonel.

The British Army is full of idiosyncrasies and traditions which may seem archaic to the lay person. But if things are going badly, as they often do in the profession of arms, it is tradition and the sense of shared history and sacrifice that holds everyone together.

The Colonel of the Regiment is not the same as a colonel serving in the army. It is an honorary position, usually a distinguished former or serving officer, and is not unlike the non-executive chairman of an established company.

The Colonel of The Life Guards also carries with it the title of 'Gold Stick-in-Waiting to the Monarch'. This tradition stems from the Tudor era, when two officers were placed close to the monarch to protect them against would-be assailants. Their staff of office was a stick with a gold head. A gold stick was considered more magisterial and less provocative than the drawing of a sword.

It was a singular honour, but one about which I had some reservations.

First, my predecessors as Colonel had been very grand and well connected: Prince Alexander of Teck; Prince Augustus of Saxe-Weimar; a flank of field marshals; and Earl Mountbatten of Burma, known affectionately by The Life Guards as 'Colonel Dickie' and who had been murdered by the IRA in 1979.

Second, the current Colonel was Major General Lord Michael Fitzalan-Howard, a wartime Scots Guardsman, whom I knew well but who was becoming increasingly frail. Michael, the younger brother of the Duke of Norfolk, was a previous Major General commanding the Household Division; he had always taken enormous pride in The Life Guards. His retirement from such a prestigious position had to be handled sensitively.

My third reservation was that as an infantryman and former SAS officer, I was reluctant to change horses and be seen as a cavalryman in a Regiment whose nicknames, admittedly given by envious foot-soldiers, were the 'Cheesemongers', the 'Donkey-Wallopers' and the 'Tinned Fruit'.

In truth, I did not need much persuading from James that I should throw my hat into the ring. As a serving officer in the higher reaches of the army, I knew that I could do much to contribute to the professionalism and the good name of the Regiment.

James also assured me that he had canvassed the opinions of the Regiment's up-and-coming officers and senior non-commissioned officers, who wanted a senior serving officer who could fight their corner. That was going to be important in the years to come as the defence budget was pared to the bone, and more and more regiments were forced to amalgamate or disappear altogether.

The appointment would be made by the Queen on the advice of Michael Fitzalan-Howard. James felt that my recent conversion to Catholicism (Michael belonged to Britain's leading Catholic family) might help matters in Michael's mind at least. As things turned out, Michael soldiered on as Colonel for a few more years, and I became Colonel of The Life Guards in 1999.

Few regiments were to escape *Options for Change* and the false promise of a 'peace dividend' after communism's collapse. In my experience it is much better to come up with a plan before a disagreeable solution is forced upon you.

The Life Guards and The Blues and Royals decided to form a union; in 1992 they became the Household Cavalry Regiment. The beauty of this accord, unlike an amalgamation, was that it allowed both regiments to retain their distinctive uniforms and traditions – and their own Colonel.

As well as James Ellery, the union between The Life Guards and The Blues and Royals was blessed in its other senior officers at the time. Andrew Parker Bowles, as Commander of the Household Cavalry and Silver Stick-in-Waiting (another Royal Household position and attendant to the Sovereign) was responsible for officer selection. Andrew could see that too many lounge-lizards and *boulevardiers* were of no use in the long run.

Andrew's connections ran far and wide. Andrew, like Michael Fitzalan-Howard and me, was a Roman Catholic. Perhaps some people became concerned about the long reach of the Vatican creeping into the Household Cavalry, but it was no more than conjecture. He saw that the cachet of the Household Cavalry would allow him to recruit officers from Oxbridge, many of whom had blues (sporting colours). This investment paid off, particularly in The Life Guards, who produced many officers who won their parachute wings and went on to serve in the SAS.

The Life Guards were never dull. They may have had more than their fair share of fraudsters, jail-birds, bounders and drug-chauffeurs before my time as their Colonel, but you could not find a more eclectic and professional mix in the British Army. James Blunt, the successful pop star and heart-throb, had learnt his trade in Kosovo where he had his guitar strapped to the side of his armoured reconnaissance vehicle.

It would be unfair and an injustice if I were to attribute The Life Guards' current success, and the esteem in which they are held, to my time as their Colonel. The signs of renewal were there to be seen in the 1970s and 1980s under the leadership of Desmond Langley and Simon Cooper, both of whom went on to command the Household Division. Arthur Gooch and James Emson proved equally robust.

Any regiment needs a sense of purpose if it is to flourish. The Life Guards' role as an armoured reconnaissance regiment aligned to the Airborne and Commando brigades gave them focus and motivation. It had moulded them into seriously professional soldiers.

I served as Colonel of The Life Guards for 20 years. Their distinguished service in the Balkans, Iraq and Afghanistan spoke for itself. I trust that in some small way, I was able to impart to the Regiment some of the experience and wisdom I had acquired in my 40 years' service. I took the time to mentor their officers and senior ranks, conscious that I owed a great deal in my career to those who had spent time helping me as a young officer.

One of the unsung joys of life is riding out in Hyde Park in the early morning. When I was CDS, I would ask for an experienced Life Guards trooper to accompany me. I would often learn more about how everything was going in the Regiment than in any formal briefing. I would not betray any confidences but, when I next saw the commanding officer, I might say "I hear X is an interesting officer." Action, if warranted, would then be taken.

I handed over the Colonelcy of The Life Guards to Edward Smyth-Osbourne. Edward is the first born-and-bred Life Guards officer to accede to the Colonelcy. I believe Edward, currently commanding the Allied Rapid Reaction Corps, is a product of The Life Guards' transformation since the early '90s into a Regiment worthy of its glorious heritage.

After the 2019 Windsor Horse Show, I gave my final address to the Regiment and The Life Guards Association. It had been a great privilege to be their Colonel for 20 years. In return, they gave me the reward of witnessing their rightful return to being one of the army's finest regiments.

I had made many friends there and, as a gesture of the Regiment's friendship, I was presented with a sword stick that could also be used as a hip flask.

It was filled with Welsh whisky from Penderyn. Beneath the handle, there is a silver band with the initials FMCRLG. (Field Marshal Charles Ronald Llewelyn Guthrie)

I would have preferred my time as Colonel not to have been marked by being thrown from my horse in my 80th year at the Trooping the Colour ceremony in 2018. It was not helped by Prince Philip reminding me that he had ridden until his 90th year.

If I walk down Whitehall, I look to see the two sentries of The Queen's Life Guard in full dress, on horseback, outside Headquarters London District. I always experience great pride to know those immaculate ceremonial soldiers are also proven operational warriors.

20

Chief of the Defence Staff

*Every prime minister expresses surprise as to how
much time he or she has to spend on security issues.
I was now the principal advisor to the government
on all defence matters.*

"Prime Minister," I said, "if we don't take action in Sierra
Leone, there's a good chance our hostages will be skinned
alive by the West Side Boys."

Tony Blair looked aghast. It was now early September 2000,
and he was well over three years into his premiership. I had
been his CDS from his first day in office. I had grown to like,
admire and respect him. We had probably been suspicious of
each other at the outset; his new Labour government was an
unknown quantity. He would have said the same about the
armed services.

Like many other prime ministers, he was surprised by how
much time he would have to spend on defence and security
issues. The kidnapping of a group of soldiers from the Royal
Irish Regiment by a murderous bunch of renegade soldiers high
on heroin and homemade hooch was typical of the random
and unpredictable problems any Prime Minister has to face.

Blair would have been quite within his rights to ask for a detailed plan of how the SAS would rescue the kidnapped soldiers from a brutal end. He looked at me and in that disarming way of his simply said, "OK, let's do it."

It was a measure of how, after three years, we had learnt to work together. It was also a measure of one aspect of Blair's doctrine of humanitarian intervention in that he would take a stance and, as others around him scurried for cover, he would hold to it. It was a great strength of his; but this particular strength became a weakness in time, as he was to find out in Iraq in the invasion of 2003.

Conservative politicians never like to hear this, but it is a false assumption to think they are the natural party of defence. I can think of just two Conservative ministers of defence since the Second World War – Peter Carrington and Michael Portillo – who took the interests of servicemen and women to heart and looked at the country's defence strategy in detail. Most saw the MOD as a tiresome stepping-stone to one of the great offices of state.

It is also a myth to suggest that servicemen and women naturally vote Conservative. It was servicemen and women who swept Clement Attlee's Labour government into power in 1945 with their catchy slogan, 'And Now Win the Peace – Vote Labour'. And it was that amiable old bruiser, Denis Healey, the Labour Secretary of State for Defence from 1964 to 1970 who, for the first time since the war, got a proper grip of Britain's defence strategy so that it reflected political and economic reality.

An old friend and one of the outstanding diplomats of his generation, Robin Renwick, arranged for me to meet Tony Blair before he came to power. This was at Blair's request and had the blessing of the Conservative Defence Secretary, Michael

Portillo. I remember we met at Claridge's for breakfast. The only thing I can recall from the meeting was Blair saying that he thought the strength of the SAS was around 40,000. When I said it was around 400, he looked bemused.

It never concerned me that he didn't know too much about defence issues. After all, Blair stated in 1996 that his three top priorities on coming to office were "education, education, and education". If he had said, "defence, defence, and defence", people would have thought he was bonkers.

My only other disquiet was about who he might appoint as Secretary of State for Defence. I should not have been concerned. The appointment of George Robertson was an inspired choice. I made a point of meeting Robertson on the steps of the MOD on his first day in office. He took his job seriously but never himself. On his third day in office, when all the lights went out on the sixth floor of the MOD, I gently ribbed him by saying, "This would never have happened under the previous Conservative administration." He grinned. We had broken the ice.

From the outset, I was determined that Blair should see the advice I gave him was non-political but based on things as they were. As the CGS, I had been the professional head of the army, but as CDS, I was the government's principal advisor on all defence matters.

It is a position that demands a high degree of political awareness, sound geostrategic knowledge and an ability to get on with people. I was confident that my career to date had prepared me for the role. It was an important distinction and I made sure Blair knew that I was his single point of contact. Subsequent administrations made the mistake of appointing middle-ranking officers to 10 Downing Street as personal military advisors. That just muddied the waters.

As luck would have it, I got off to a good start with the Blair administration. Saddam Hussein was running rings around the Western Alliance. One moment Saddam was throwing out the UN weapons inspectors looking for the now infamous Weapons of Mass Destruction (WMD); the next moment he was declaring he would re-admit the inspectors. His murderous persecution of the Marsh Arabs and the Kurdish people continued unchecked.

We contemplated a joint US/UK military strike to concentrate Saddam's mind. I took Tony Blair through the options. Clinton agreed then wavered. Tony didn't have much luck steeling Clinton to the task. The President had other more pressing questions on his mind with the Monica Lewinsky affair.

I telephoned Hugh Shelton, Chairman of the US Joint Chiefs of Staff. Hugh, like me, was the first head of his country's armed services with a special forces background. We got on well and I knew he had the ear and respect of Clinton. It was clear enough to Hugh Shelton that Saddam was playing for time. We launched four days of aerial strikes in Operation *Desert Fox* just before Christmas 1998.

———

"Good Lord, General," my ADC, Guy Bartle-Jones said. "The Chinese Guard of Honour are all wearing powder-blue uniforms made by Giorgio Armani." It was July 1997, just four months after I had taken over as CDS. I was about to take to the podium alongside the Prince of Wales, Tony Blair, Robin Cook, Labour's Foreign Secretary, and Chris Patten, the last Governor of Hong Kong, for the formal handover of Hong Kong from Britain to China. I had no idea if their uniforms were Giorgio Armani, but they certainly looked smart. They were also all well over 6 feet tall and seemingly identical, not unlike the female dancers at Paris's Folies Bergère.

After 156 years of British governance in Hong Kong, it was an emotional moment and marked the end of our last substantial overseas territory. For the Chinese, it was a coming of age on the world stage. The handover had enormous worldwide press and television coverage. The Chinese Guard of Honour and the coldly choreographed pageantry was more than a fashion statement and a display of organisational prowess. It was all in stark contrast to the quiet dignity, good humour and old-world courtesy of the farewell cocktail party hosted by the Prince of Wales on the Royal Yacht *Britannia* later that evening.

The handover was a signal of China's intent: that they were now a power to be reckoned with. I am not sure we were as alert as we should have been to what this might herald for the West in the decades to follow. We were too ready to embrace China's economic power. We failed to see that their inherent lack of scruples and their preening ambition would result in the threat they have now become. Their ruthless policy of co-option, coercion, concealment and mendacity poses the single greatest threat to world peace.

As we prepared to leave the Governor's residence for our return to the UK, I asked my ADC for my cash float which was used for tipping servants or others who had been of help. Guy looked distinctly sheepish and admitted that he had had a bad run on the roulette tables the night before. I have always seen my ADCs as surrogate sons and, providing they were good company, got on with Kate, and were not too inefficient, I would allow them a good deal of slack. Guy had a bad day of it – we had enormous difficulty getting through security at Hong Kong's airport. Chinese security could not get to grips with our ceremonial swords which we had to carry with us.

It was in late 2000 that I found myself invited on a formal visit to China at the invitation of their Chief of Defence Staff, Senior General Tang Yao-Ming. I remember the visit for two reasons. First, the Chinese interpreter who was assigned to me kept dropping his bugging device; and second, General Tang Yao-Ming spent most of the trip telling me his forces were ready to attack Taiwan at a moment's notice.

I was taken to observe their military manoeuvres which, similar to their Guard of Honour in the Hong Kong handover, were carefully staged. It was interesting to observe nearly 100,000 men and women on exercise; but it was just artificial choreography, albeit on a large scale.

On my return to the UK, I received a telephone call from my US counterpart, Hugh Shelton, who asked me for my views on the experience. The US, understandably, was becoming a great deal more concerned with the Far East than Europe. I'm not sure I put his mind at rest, but I did make the point that huge numbers and infinite resources – the People's Liberation Army could call on 2 million men and women – were little match for operational experience.

That may have been true back then, but China has now had plenty of time to observe the successes and failures of the West in Iraq and Afghanistan, and has switched its focus to local conflicts under high-tech conditions with quality resources.

I was now spending two weeks per month abroad as a soldier-diplomat. Nearer to home, however, there was unfinished business. The new Labour government after 18 years out of power had unsurprisingly called for a strategic defence review. In the Balkans, the war in Kosovo had begun. In Northern Ireland, Tony Blair was determined to bring the peace process to a head. And then, of course, there were all the other problems in Africa, the Middle East and Eastern Europe that were to exercise the minds of politicians and the service chiefs alike.

There is just one line in Tony Blair's autobiography of 691 pages which refers to the strategic defence review: "At the end of May 1997, Defence Secretary George Robertson set up the strategic defence review." I think this cursory reference was a reflection of what the Prime Minister saw as more important priorities in the first 100 days of his new administration. I think he also trusted George Robertson to conduct the review in a balanced way.

Robertson was a first-rate minister, a good listener, and he had no preconceived ideas. He deserved great credit, especially as his first experience of the military was not a happy one. In 1977, a navy Land Rover containing 100 pounds of gelignite and a box of detonators had driven into him, resulting in quite severe injuries.

The strategic defence review could have been a lot worse. I could not remember a review having been carried out in such a good atmosphere, but I kept an eye out for any crocodiles circling the canoe. I also valued the experience of the defence review as it encouraged me to study the other services' problems and aspirations.

I had one regret which, I believe, was shared by the general public. In the greater scheme of things, the cancellation of the Royal Tournament – we no longer had the spare manpower – was not going to affect our ability to take the fight to the enemy. But it was a much-loved institution enjoyed by generations of all ages since 1880. The field gun competition was always a highlight, a memorable test of toughness, courage and teamwork. I took the Salute 14 times and was never bored. I have a feeling that the Royal Tournament may return one day, but that may be just wishful thinking on my behalf and that of the public.

In truth, I do not think I am being cynical in saying that in effect such reviews are all savings exercises. We accepted £500m of savings in return for the establishment of a Joint Rapid Reaction Force, and 16th Air Assault Brigade equipped with the Apache attack helicopter. MOD procurement has always been notoriously wasteful, but that was one of their better decisions.

One of the very worst procurement decisions, taken in 1998, was to build two new aircraft carriers. In fairness to the MOD, that decision was ultimately made by Gordon Brown when he had supplanted Blair as Prime Minister.

Brown's decision damaged the Royal Navy's long-term interests. At the time of the 1998 strategic defence review, the navy had 35 frigates and 25 minehunters. In 2020 it has 20 frigates and 13 minehunters.

The navy has any number of cheerleaders in the MOD, and their slogans at that time were such things as 'Power projection', 'Maritime and trading nation', 'Sea lanes must be kept open', 'Forceful presence', 'Reaffirming our status', etc.

But the cost overruns, the manning of such behemoths, the protection they need from a much-reduced navy, all point to an unaffordable mistake. Thirty years before, the outstanding

Labour Defence Secretary, Denis Healey, referred to aircraft carriers as "Floating slums, and far too vulnerable".

I am sure the two new aircraft carriers are a good deal more comfortable than the old ones were, but Healey was right even then. They are sitting ducks in the face of our enemies' growing technological advances, and in any case we don't have enough other ships to protect even one of them, let alone two.

The strategic defence review was not the first time (nor was it the last) that I had to cross swords with the Chancellor, Gordon Brown. We got off to a poor start. His hand was all over the defence review and it had not escaped anyone's notice that the two aircraft carriers were to be assembled in Rosyth, right by Brown's parliamentary seat in Dunfermline East – an example of what is known in America as 'Pork-barrel politics'.

It was clear soon enough that Brown would not fund what had been previously agreed. When I went to see him in No. 11 Downing Street to discuss the review, he paid no attention to what I told him. It was not long before he interrupted and said with a smirk, "General, I do know a bit about defence, you know."

I gave him a hard look and replied, "Chancellor, you know fuck all about defence."

His face turned red and his jaw slackened. The meeting was at an end.

The Treasury's malign influence was to hamper the services throughout. In Kosovo, Blair had been supportive, whereas Brown had been a baleful obstacle. I genuinely felt that the Armed Forces, and the army in particular, suffered because of the damaging clashes between Blair and Brown at the time. If I raised the topic of funding with Blair, he would look distinctly uneasy and just say, "Well, you need to take that up with Gordon."

British forces were poorly provided for later on in Afghanistan and Iraq. In my view the Treasury's penny-pinching unquestionably led to unnecessary loss of life where the continued use of lightly armoured Snatch Land Rovers was pitifully inadequate in face of powerful Improvised Explosive Devices (IEDs).

I have often been asked why I didn't resign as a matter of principle. I did not give that idea a moment's thought. What would it have achieved? A few shots in the air? The headlines for a day or two? And then someone else thrown into the deep end to bash their head against a hard-nosed Treasury?

It is always better to try to work with people, build your constituency and influence events as best you can. A successor of mine as CGS, Richard Dannatt, ambushed the Labour government in 2006 through the pages of the *Daily Mail* on the deployment of British forces in Iraq. I didn't really agree with that as it hardly assisted the army's cause. In my view Richard further undermined his position in accepting a peerage from David Cameron, to whom he served as his defence advisor after he retired from the army. We should be politically neutral servants of the Crown.

In February 1997, just a month before I became CDS, an IRA sniper shot dead Bombardier Stephen Restorick. He was the last soldier to die before the Good Friday Peace Agreement was signed on 10 April 1998. In 1999, Bernard McGinn was convicted of his killing and sentenced to a total of 490 years in prison for 34 separate offences including the murder of two other soldiers. He was released 16 months later under the terms of the Good Friday Agreement. Referring to the agreement, Stephen's mother said that all she wanted was, "No more mothers, no matter on what side, having to face the death of a son."

The terms of the Good Friday Agreement stuck in the craw of many people. Nearly 40 years after the beginning of the Troubles, which had cost so many soldiers' and civilian lives, I nevertheless believe the agreement was a crowning achievement for the politicians involved.

Blair's energy and his down-to-earth Northern Ireland Secretary, Mo Mowlam, the first woman to hold the post, were an energetic and winning combination. Blair enjoyed taking a gamble. His insistence that the IRA decommissioning of weapons was not a precondition for Sinn Fein entry to talks was a brave but necessary decision.

Four months after the Good Friday Agreement, a 'Real IRA' car bomb in Omagh killed 29 people, the single most murderous attack of the Troubles. It became evident within days that this ghastly incident had made most people more determined than ever to make a success of the agreement.

For the next few years it was touch and go. I was determined as CDS that the British Army should gradually reduce its security profile to help build confidence amongst Republicans. An IRA statement, which said it had ended its armed campaign, allowed the army to begin dismantling a number of security posts and the army base at Forkhill.

As CDS, I took pride in the fact that Op *Banner* had given three generations of officers and NCOs a remarkable training in leadership, resilience and tactical decision-making. It certainly helped the army operate with striking success in the chaotic disintegration of the Balkans in the 1990s.

However, like many others in the army, I was glad to be shot of Op *Banner*. It had cost the lives of 763 soldiers and 6,116 wounded. It had drawn in huge resources over the years and had placed considerable strain on the rhythm of family life for servicemen and women. More importantly, I had been concerned for some time that peacekeeping and a stated strategy of no casualties had dampened the army's warrior spirit.

The army's performance in Basra in 2007 would bear this out. A more recent comment in *The Times* that the army, as result of Basra, had become "a self-basting mediocrity" was hard for me to read, even though it was wide of the mark. There is little doubt that the army redeemed itself, and with great courage, in Afghanistan.

I don't think anyone who served in Northern Ireland, myself included, will ever quite comprehend the decision to release 500 loyalist and Republican prisoners as part of the Good Friday Agreement. It was particularly difficult for the families of those who had been murdered. On the day that Patrick Magee, the man convicted of the 1984 Brighton bombing, was released, Tony Blair said the decision was, "very hard to stomach".

If there was any comfort to be drawn, it is that the Good Friday Agreement did lead to peace. It remains a blueprint for international conflict resolution.

"What a ridiculous question," I said to an ill-prepared journalist at the daily press conference hosted by George Robertson and me at the beginning of the Kosovo air campaign in late March 1999. I cannot even recall what the question was now, but I remember things getting a trifle tetchy as the air campaign began to attract some criticism.

As it was initially an air campaign, I could have left the briefing to Richard Johns, Chief of the Air Staff. I think Richard's nose was put out of joint, but I felt strongly that as head of the armed services, I should be seen as the single point of contact. After all, it was the undertaking I had given to Tony Blair.

Five months after the Dayton Accords and the framework for peace in Bosnia and Herzegovina had been signed in December 1995, the newly formed Kosovo Liberation Army (KLA) murdered three Serbs who were enjoying a drink at a cafe in western Kosovo. The Kosovo Albanians saw that their Serb oppressors had been defeated in Croatia and Bosnia with the help of NATO. Bosnia had also received $5bn in aid. Albania had received nothing at all, and the Serbs under Milosevic continued to deny them rights in a regime of constant repression.

True to form, the international community turned a blind eye to the murders, hoping the whole thing would quietly go away. The West had become tired of the Balkan tragedy.

Just as I took over as CDS in the spring of 1997, neighbouring Albania had descended into chaos. To add to the turmoil, Serbia's tiny sister republic, Montenegro, turned against Milosevic, and the death toll in the region began to mount.

It was becoming clear to the EU and the US that a full-blown war was about to break out in Kosovo, where the ethnicity was 95 per cent Albanian. A war in Kosovo was also likely to draw in Macedonia, which had a large Albanian minority. If Kosovo was to win its independence, then Macedonia might be drawn towards a Greater Albania.

If that happened, Greece, which insisted Macedonia had a Hellenic pedigree stretching back to Alexander the Great, was also likely to get involved. I make these points, leaden as they may seem, as they illustrate the complexity of the whole Balkans crisis. No wonder we have the term 'the fog of war'.

Milosevic, the ruthless leader of the Serbs, refused to accept a NATO peacekeeping force in Kosovo to guarantee autonomy for the Kosovars. To back down on this guarantee would fatally undermine the credibility of NATO.

The turning point was the massacre of Kosovan Albanian farmers in January 1999. NATO agreed to 30,000 troops in a peacekeeping role. After the failure of peace talks to bring Milosevic to heel with the Rambouillet Accords, NATO started bombing the Serbs on 24 March 1999.

Just four months before, it had become clear to me that the line between being a soldier and a diplomat was becoming increasingly fine. Operation *Desert Fox*, the bombing campaign to bring Saddam to heel, had had military success; but it was less of a success in diplomatic terms.

Its justification had been Iraq's failure to comply with UN resolutions on disarmament. It attracted criticism from Saudi Arabia and many Gulf states, as well as the usual suspects in the Russian sphere of influence. Ironically, I had just returned from Saudi Arabia and the Gulf States, where I had been asked to stiffen them up in preparation for the likely air campaign. It was rather a roundabout trip and I had returned via Kenya to visit the British Army Training Unit, a jewel in the army's ability to conduct live-firing exercises.

I thought I had earned a little rest and recuperation in Kenya's Masai Mara before I returned to the MOD. As the light began to fade over that heroic landscape, Kate and I were watching a pride of lions meander in the marsh close to our campsite.

The silence was broken by the sound of a satellite telephone ringing. It belonged to my Personal Staff Officer (PSO), John Ponsonby. The message, terse and to the point, said that the air campaign against Iraq was about to start. John, an RAF group captain and brilliant organiser, knew me well enough not to ask what he needed to do. We were back in London before breakfast.

In Kosovo, the Serbian air defences were no match for our air power; but the UN's naïve admission that we would not use ground troops except in a peacekeeping role gave the Serbs an enormous tactical advantage. President Clinton, mindful of the humiliations US forces had suffered in Somalia and Mogadishu, refused to commit ground troops. In an operation commonly referred to now as Black Hawk Down in early October 1993, the US forces lost 19 killed, 73 wounded, one captured and two helicopters lost.

Blair agreed with me that air power on its own would achieve little other than to unite Serbian support for Milosevic. The Serbs were also masters of deception, a doctrine they had learnt from their Russian allies, known as *Maskirovka*. Our air force and forward air controllers on the ground (spotters) were often led astray by dummy tanks and artillery positions.

The inadvertent bombing of the Chinese Embassy in May 1999 killed three diplomats. Once again, it gave the lie to the belief that precision bombing is always precise. Unease grew amongst NATO members, particularly Germany, whose limp foreign policy, which continues to this day, was essentially *Heimat Zuerst* (Homeland First).

Despite that, Blair held his nerve. It was something for which I always admired him. He demanded ground troops be sent in, which strained his relationship with Clinton to breaking point. After just 18 months in power, Blair could have become badly unstuck, but he had discovered an arena outside domestic politics where he could act confidently and decisively.

Blair loathed ogres such as Milosevic and Saddam Hussein. It gave him his doctrine of humanitarian intervention if he saw that there was the threat of violent suppression to a state's people.

He came to see me and asked if we could commit 50,000 troops. This was not feasible, as it amounted to almost the entire available British Army. He thought he could persuade Clinton to stump up 100,000 to 150,000. I remember raising my eyebrows at this, knowing that few other European countries would join in.

Still, I took the view that this was a 'just war'. It was to stop Milosevic's brutal and murderous actions to expel Kosovo's Albanians, and his use of terror and intimidation. It was also to halt what the UN Secretary-General described as a "grave threat to international peace and security".

The armed services exist to defend the country and, within reason, serve the political will of the government of the time. The request to commit as many troops as we could muster was reasonable given the mayhem, massacres and human rights violations taking place in Kosovo.

At the back of my mind, I also had a strong sense that Iraq was unfinished business. And it would be business on a much greater scale than Kosovo. The armed services could not afford to lose the friction of combat.

People join the services, as I did, for travel, adventure and excitement, and to go to war to defend our national interests and lay down their lives if needs be. It was the profession we all signed up to. Nobody flourishes just sitting around in barracks, in a naval base or on an RAF runway. It is like asking a teacher not to enter a classroom, or a lawyer to keep away from a courtroom.

By early June, a NATO-led Kosovo Force, KFOR, based on the Allied Rapid Reaction Force (ARRC) and commanded by General Mike Jackson, entered Kosovo to bring matters to a close. Under Mike's command, KFOR was in safe hands. I had known Mike since my time in Berlin. He was a formidable operator and looked like a warrior. He would take no truck from anyone, friend or foe, who he thought had not risen to the level of events.

I remember visiting my old command, 4th Armoured Brigade, then commanded by Bill Rollo, who hosted a lunch for other NATO brigade commanders from Italy, France, Germany and the US. After exchanging the usual small talk over the first course, I fixed them with a stern look and said, "Will you fight if it comes to that?"

The French Brigadier responded with a typical piece of Gallic cod-philosophy: "Until you spread your wings, you will never learn to fly."

The Italian pretended not to understand the question, and the German said, "No."

The US Brigadier looked at me and said, "You can count on us. We're part of the Old Ironsides, sir." That was the divisional motto of the US 1st Armoured Division.

Bill Rollo, wise man that he was in front of his CDS, gave an unequivocal "Yes!" The lunch was a perfect illustration of the challenges of building multi-national alliances.

In the end we did not have to fight and we would suffer no casualties. Milosevic's resolve collapsed, and on 10 June the unconditional withdrawal of Serbian forces from Kosovo was completed.

There remained one scene of almost tragicomedy. Up until then, the Russians, despite their close historical ties with the Serbs, were not doing much to interfere through the fumes of vodka that surrounded their president, Boris Yeltsin.

In the early hours of 11 June , I was awakened with the news that the Russians, in a deft sleight of hand, had occupied the airport at Pristina, Kosovo's capital. General Wesley Clark, the US Supreme Commander in Europe, ordered Mike Jackson to take them on.

Clark had overstepped the mark. He had reached his high rank through his intellectual and classroom ability; but his interference was not what was needed in such a tense situation.

Jackson famously replied to Clark, "I am not going to start World War 3 on your say-so."

The Russians calmed down. They had made their point, and the matter was settled. Clark was retired early.

The worst of the Kosovo campaign was now at an end. It had cost the lives of 15,000 civilians and fighters, mostly Albanians and Serbs. Ninety per cent of Kosovar Albanians were displaced. As far as the British Army was concerned, we learnt to operate flexibly and pragmatically where there is not only a powerful enemy threat, but also a battle for the support of the civil community.

We had become a master of operations other than war. We had learnt what kit worked well and what was a waste of money. Our new rifle, the SA80, and the recently introduced personal radios, fell way short of the mark and were far too expensive.

As a former UN Secretary-General said, "Peacekeeping is not a job for soldiers, but only soldiers can do it."

Tony Blair was right to stand up to Milosevic and to fight for justice and the interests of European civilisation. In the Kosovo crisis he showed himself to be a man of courage and principle. Once he had been convinced that a course was right, his attitude was, "OK, we'll do it."

Tony Blair's commitment to justice became his undoing in the Iraq invasion in 2003. He made the wrong decision then, but I have always given him the benefit of the doubt. The atrocity of 9/11 and the haunting images of the twin towers massacre had changed everyone's psychology. I sometimes think it led to a sense of collective PTSD in the West. It was difficult for anyone to think straight.

In between managing the business of the day as CDS, my role as a travelling soldier-diplomat took up a good deal of time. I had no reservations about the amount of travel. First, I have always enjoyed the rich experience of another culture and its people. But as I have always found throughout my career, getting things done is invariably down to getting on with people.

Two countries, however, and for differing reasons, took up a good deal of my time: the US and France.

I had always liked the US for the big-heartedness of its people. Our alliance with the US, the strong ties of kith and kin, the shared values and cultural ties, gave us immediate clout in the world. We were never rich or powerful enough to be a mirror-image, but we needed to keep close to them. If we did not, we would lose influence. There are any number of nay-sayers who say our closeness to the US is a problem with the rest of the world. There was an element of truth in this after the second Iraq War, but it does not bear much scrutiny.

Curiously, discussions between a Prime Minister and a President were not particularly effective in getting things done. I would not say that Clinton would ignore Blair's views – far from it – but it was nevertheless relationships at different government and military levels that would help swing things.

There was no better example of this than Caspar Weinberger, the US Secretary of Defence under Ronald Reagan. Caspar was of English descent on his mother's side, and he had helped us win vital US support during the Falklands campaign.

I lost count of how many times I crossed the Atlantic to further our aims. My ADCs totted it up to around 37 trips, which sounds about right. President Clinton remained in serious trouble with his impending impeachment. A rudderless US was not good for global security. My strong relationships with the US Pentagon, particularly Hugh Shelton, the Chairman of the US Joint Chiefs of Staff, helped to calm nerves.

Quite often on these visits, there was some mishap to keep my US colleagues and staff amused. On one occasion the US Pentagon had laid on a demonstration of US military prowess for all 19 NATO chiefs of defence. We were all staying at the Mirage Hotel in Las Vegas where we were to be presented with a Stetson hat to mark our visit.

Something was lost in translation between my MA, the outstanding Paul Gibson from the Parachute Regiment, and my orderly from the Welsh Guards, Guardsman Williams 001 (known as 'Fuck all' Williams because of his last three army numbers).

Williams gave my waist size instead of my hat size. As we all assembled in the foyer of the Mirage Hotel, I was presented with my Stetson which, much to the hilarity of my fellow CDSs, looked double the size of an El Paso 10-gallon hat.

There is no better illustration of the sheer power of the US military than the Cheyenne Mountain complex near Colorado Springs. At the time of my visit, it was the headquarters of US Space Command, US Defence Command and US Northern Command. I was taken down 30 levels to be met by a Canadian three-star general who was on duty.

There were at least two dozen screens showing every single military activity going on in the world. On one screen, I watched with gruesome fascination Russians mortaring Chechen rebel positions. The Canadian was less than forthcoming: "I can't answer that question, General" and "I'm afraid I can't answer that either, General."

I became rather exasperated and glared at him: "Well, is there any question you *can* answer?"

France was beginning to take up quite a bit of time, as we were determined to get them back into NATO. I have always admired the French way of life and the French military's *élan* and *panache*. I had first worked alongside them in Berlin in 1978–79, and later in the New Hebrides in 1980. I was also impressed by their warrior spirit during the Balkans where, in 1995, they took on the Bosnian Serbs at the battle of Vrbanja Bridge with the last French bayonet charge. The young French captain who led the assault, François Lecointre, is currently their Chief of Defence Staff. They have always observed their obligations to *la Gloire de France*, and the best of French military tradition. But they have always been hidebound by the machinations of the Elysée and the *Quai d'Orsay*, their foreign affairs ministry.

France was one the founding members of NATO in 1949. Militarily, it has always pulled its weight, but in 1966 President de Gaulle, in a fit of pique about the US dominance of NATO and the special relationship with the UK, removed all French forces from NATO. All non-French soldiers were asked to leave French soil. This provoked the immortal response of Dean Rusk, the US Secretary of State, to de Gaulle: "Does your order include the bodies of American soldiers in France's cemeteries?"

We all recognised France's worth as a proven military power. We were determined that France should, once again, become a full member of NATO. The French military were all for it, but politically it was a slow business. It was the French politicians' obsession with their idea of the grandeur of France and its independence that held everything up.

On a personal level, my relationship with my French counterpart, General Jean-Pierre Kelche, could not have been better, despite suffering a slight hiccup at our first bilateral conference.

I had so much reading to do that it was my habit on any overseas trip to read the visit brief on the plane. On boarding the flight to Paris, I turned to my MA, Paul Gibson, and asked for the brief. Paul looked embarrassed and said, "I'm so sorry, General, it appears I have left it in the office."

I smiled and said, "Well, not to worry, it's a working lunch, if that's not a contradiction in French terms. I'm sure we will all muddle through." In the end, it was not until 2009 that France, under the irrepressible President Sarkozy, became a fully participating NATO member.

I was delighted to visit Argentina in 1999. It was the first official visit by a CDS since the Falklands campaign. I was particularly pleased to do so because the visit allowed me to place a wreath on the Welsh Guards Memorial at Fitzroy overlooking Bluff Cove in the Falklands where the Regiment had suffered grievous losses in 1982. As I laid the wreath with my ADC Harry Legge-Bourke at my side, I felt a great sense of sadness at the loss of so many Welsh Guardsmen, many of whom I knew well from my time commanding the Regiment. I took solace at the time of the Falklands that my oldest and closest friend, David Lewis, was the Welsh Guards Regimental Lieutenant Colonel. David visited every Welsh Guards family who had lost a loved one. His innate humanity and natural empathy made a great difference to families at a difficult time.

The Argentinians could not have been more hospitable, with the exception of the Chief of the Naval Staff. I was shown brusquely to a seat in his office where, to my surprise, I saw that his walls were festooned with photographs of British ships being sunk. I was then harangued for a further 15 minutes on how the Argentine Air Force and Army had lost the campaign. On the reciprocal visit, I made sure my staff removed the china model from the coffee desk in my office of the Royal Marines raising the Union Jack in Port Stanley after the Argentine surrender.

The advice I received from our Foreign Office about where I should visit and with whom I should build a dialogue was invariably sound. I can only recall one disagreeable visit and that was to Spain, a country for which I have a strong affection.

It was clear from the outset that Gibraltar, the constant pebble in Spain's shoe, would overshadow my visit. In 2000 a UK proposal to share sovereignty over Gibraltar with Spain was vehemently opposed by the Gibraltar government who wanted it put to a referendum. The frostiness from Spanish officials and senior military figures was palpable.

The Foreign Office officials with whom I worked most closely, Peter Westmacott, Elisabeth Symons (a Labour foreign office and defence minister 1997–2001) and Robin Renwick, were exemplary. I was never convinced, however, that we should be making too many overtures to countries which were historically in the Russian sphere of influence. Russia is a proud country which has made an immense contribution to world affairs, music, literature and the arts. We humiliated them after the collapse of communism. A wounded Russian bear should never be taken lightly.

One Labour minister who was good value and with whom I got on well was Clare Short. She was not 'New Labour', more the old-style Labour patriot who understood that Labour's core voters had a strong sense of justice and a love of their country. She proved to be an outstanding Minister for International Development and she was a good support to me over Kosovo, Zimbabwe and the banning of anti-personnel mines. Her personality was too strong for some; her smoky voice and the 'I can smell a crap-artist a mile away' look on her face could be intimidating. But she had courage, and she stood by her promises.

I had learnt early on in my career, particularly during my time commanding the Welsh Guards at the height of the Troubles in Northern Ireland, the importance of the Press. Too many senior officers are sniffy about the Press. It doesn't do them or the services any good. You learn quickly enough those you can trust. Charles Moore and Max Hastings were confidants, and both were forthright if they thought we were getting things wrong. I also made the effort to talk to excellent journalists like Alan Rusbridger of the *Guardian*. The *Guardian* is not a natural ally of the services, but Alan was always open to talk about things that were important to his readership.

In the summer of 2000 I visited Georgia, the home country of Stalin. Georgia seceded from the Soviet Union in 1991 and was then encouraged, quite wrongly in my view, to join NATO and the European Union. The push to expand NATO eastwards was a grave strategic error on behalf of Western politicians. I had cause once to discuss this with the Russian ambassador to the UK. He expressed his grave concerns about NATO. Rather flippantly, I replied that there was little to worry about and that, when you have a country like Luxembourg with 450 soldiers having as much say over military matters as France or the UK, there was precious little chance of NATO agreeing on anything.

The Russian ambassador was unconvinced. We are paying the price today as Putin continues to assert Russia's hegemony and her pride over the former countries of the Soviet Union. Georgia's ambitions came to an end in the brief Russo-Georgian War in 2008.

The military aspects of the visit played second fiddle to the Georgians' legendary hospitality. The visit culminated in a dinner in a forest outside the capital of Tbilisi. I have had enough experience to pace myself and hold my drink with the best of trenchermen, but the dinner, which started at 6pm and ran through to the early hours, was a true test of my mettle. Toast after toast, each with a glass of *Chacha*, a national drink made of grape pomace, got the better of most of us, including my ADC, Harry Legge-Bourke. I was still just about standing as we made our farewells in the early hours. I remember thinking to myself how lucky we are in our country to have just the one toast: "Ladies and gentlemen: the Queen."

There was one notable exception to avoiding stepping on Russia's toes: the Baltic States of Lithuania, Latvia and Estonia. They won back their independence from Russia in 1991 after the fall of communism. They remain subject, however, to what can only be described as intense political warfare from Russia, particularly cyber and disinformation attacks. I made a number of visits there during my time as CDS to put an arm around them and set out the benefits of NATO membership. It was a worthwhile investment. The Baltic States became members of NATO on 29 March 2004. The Estonians, in particular, were as brave as lions fighting alongside us in Afghanistan.

"If Iran develops nuclear weapons, we will crush her like a beetle under our feet." Thus spoke Shaul Mofaz, the Israeli CGS to me on my first and only military visit to Israel, in the autumn of 2000.

Over the years I had learnt to tread carefully, particularly in the Middle East. An invitation to visit the Israeli Defence Force (IDF) on the disputed Golan Heights, where I was invited to climb into their Merkava main battle tank and fire the Israeli made Uzi sub-machine gun with cameras snapping away, was just such a fine line, so I declined.

Israel's demonstration of its military prowess in the Six-Day War in 1967 and the Yom Kippur War in 1973 confirmed its status as a strategic asset for the West. But there were other important allies in the Middle East, particularly Jordan, Saudi Arabia, Oman and other Gulf States. Despite the shared common foe, Iran, I knew my hard-won relationships with the Arab States would not take kindly to such an overt display of bravado on the Golan Heights.

Shaul Mofaz was ten years younger than me. He had fought in the Six-Day War, the Yom Kippur War, the invasion of Lebanon, and the raid on Entebbe to free Israeli hostages. He was also a former commander in the *Sayaret Matkal*, Israeli special forces. Shaul was of Jewish-Iranian ancestry; he lived in a tough neighbourhood surrounded by Israel's implacable enemies. Israel was fortunate to have Shaul for he epitomised the warrior spirit of the IDF.

Israel is unique in that it has mandatory conscription for women. Israel had its reservations about its women in a fighting role after the Yom Kippur War. Israeli soldiers had, understandably, found it difficult watching their women colleagues die or being maimed in combat. On more than one occasion, they had gone to their rescue only to get themselves killed or severely compromised in their mission. Israeli women soldiers may not have looked as fearsome as Shaul, but there was no doubting their professionalism. It helped influence my views on women in our own armed forces and that they should be given every opportunity to pursue a career in any branch of the services. Their courage and professionalism in Iraq and Afghanistan had proved me right. I was also introduced to the IDF specialist tracker unit, the Negev Bedouins, who are nomadic Arabs from Israel's Negev region. The threat to

Israel's survival is constant, but from what I saw, it would be a foolhardy nation who takes them on.

———

On the morning of Sunday, 10 September 2000, I was due to appear on the BBC show *Breakfast with Frost*. As a rule, the CDS appears on the show once a year on Remembrance Sunday, but the nation was gripped by events in Sierra Leone, a former British colony in West Africa.

I was a little wary of putting myself in front of David Frost. I had watched the now legendary Frost/Nixon interview and had witnessed Frost's disarming manner in luring Nixon into saying things that he had no intention of revealing.

Not that I had anything to hide at 9.30 that morning. The British Army operation to rescue our hostages in Sierra Leone was well underway and the first signs were that it was a success.

I was warmly welcomed by David Frost on the programme but with an opening designed to trip me up from the outset: "Good morning, Charles. This sounds like amazing news, good news, did the Prime Minister OK the mission?"

"Yes, the Prime Minister has taken a close interest in it."

"So, he's okayed it?"

"Yes, he's okayed it."

In May 2000, the Sierra Leone Government had requested our help. A civil war had been raging in the country since 1991, but things had taken a turn for the worse. A mob of machete-waving tribal thugs called the Revolutionary United Front (RUF) were about to overrun the country. Sierra Leone was of limited strategic value to the West, but the stability of West Africa mattered. Diamond and gold mining were the main sources of income, two natural resources that attract corruption and play havoc internationally.

There was a huge UN force in the country from 28 countries; however, as I had ruefully witnessed in the Balkans, all were reliant on what their national governments said they could or could not do. Frankly, getting 28 countries to agree on anything is nigh impossible, and the rebels were quickly in the ascendant. Kofi Annan, the UN Secretary-General, was humiliated. It was not the first time that the UN found itself powerless to act.

After military advice, Tony Blair decided to take action. Many people have criticised Blair for his robust doctrine of humanitarian intervention. They have done so largely because of the invasion of Iraq in 2003. On Iraq their criticism (albeit in hindsight, given the catastrophic aftermath) is justifiable. But it is easy to forget what Blair did get right, and what happens when the West turns a blind eye. The Rwanda genocide in the summer of 1994, when 1,000,000 people were slaughtered, is but one example.

We flew a force of battle group strength to Sierra Leone under the command of the experienced and gifted Brigadier David Richards who, ten years later, was to become CDS. The 1st Battalion Parachute Regiment were the core of the battle group under the command of another first-rate soldier, Paul Gibson, who was later to become my military assistant.

I had every confidence in our intervention, but it has always been my business to see for myself what was going on, rather than reading reports from the comfort of an armchair in the MOD or to look at a screen. I went out with Peter Westmacott, whom I already knew to be an outstanding diplomat from the Foreign Office and who subsequently served as our ambassador to Turkey, France and Washington. We were met by David and briefed on the state of play, and then went down country in a Chinook helicopter accompanied by Paul Gibson to get a sense of things. I remember landing near a local village where the women were on the riverbank washing clothes. The backwash from the helicopter caused havoc with their washing.

Our intervention in Sierra Leone prevented the fall of Freetown and routed the RUF. There was, however, a nasty sting in the tail which could have ended very badly indeed. It was this incident that caused me to appear on the *Frost Show*. Another mob of lawless hoods who called themselves 'The West Side Boys' had kidnapped soldiers from the Royal Irish Regiment and their Sierra Leone Army liaison officer. They were being held captive in Gberi Bana on the opposite side of a treacherous creek.

The West Side Boys were vicious and prone to extreme violence, fuelled as they were by drugs, booze and various other stimulants. They brutalised their opponents by chopping their limbs off with machetes. Tony Blair was on holiday, so I authorised the SAS to get on with the detailed planning on getting the hostages out alive and safe.

It was an extremely complex operation given the terrain and lack of intelligence. The UK Chief of Joint Operations, an admiral whose operational experience amounted to the Royal Yacht *Britannia* and the Royal Navy Presentation Team, tried to stick his oar in. I gave him short shrift and left the SAS to get on with it.

Once again, I went out to Sierra Leone to see for myself. Perhaps, with my retirement six months away, I wanted to give myself one last hurrah, that sense of excitement and adventure for which I had joined the army 40 years before. I met the SAS commanding officer and the squadron commander who would command the ground operation. For a brief period – not exactly part of the remit of a CDS – I was back to the glorious days in which I had served with the SAS. We all made our assessments of how we would conduct the operation. To my pleasant surprise, we found that we all agreed that a rapid helicopter assault and diversionary attack by elements of the Parachute Regiment was the most plausible course of action.

I asked to see Tony Blair immediately on his return from holiday. It was a brief discussion as I set out the military's recommended course of action to extract the kidnapped soldiers. He asked, "Are you guys up for it?"

Blair must have known that was a needless question. After the operation, I called him at his flat and told him the operation had been a complete success except for the death of one SAS soldier, Bradley Tinnion, who was hit by machine gun fire. Blair was genuinely moved by his loss.

Sierra Leone was a good example of the kind of liberal military invention, similar to our role in Kosovo, that gave our military a good name and a renewed sense of self-worth. For that, Blair deserves praise.

There was just one occasion when I had to rein Blair in. That was on the question of Zimbabwe, where the original white settlers were being murdered and their lands confiscated at the hands of President Robert Mugabe. Mugabe was the sort of ogre that Blair and many others detested, not helped by Mugabe's absurd referral to Blair's government as "a gangster regime using gay gangsters". This was a blatant attack by Mugabe on the courageous gay activist Peter Tatchell, who had challenged Mugabe on his persecution of gay people in Zimbabwe. I was pleased that the Labour government lifted the ban on gay men and women in the services in January 2000. This was finally enshrined in law with the Armed Forces Bill in 2015–16.

Any attempt to try to overthrow Mugabe was on a hiding to nothing. Our colonial past would have been thrown in our face, with the whole of Africa united against us. I remember saying to him, "Hold hard, Prime Minister, or you'll make it a lot worse."

I was blessed throughout my four years as CDS with a wonderful team. Eve Milne, my PA back in the MOD who had been with me since I became CGS, was exactly what you would wish for in a PA: fun, efficient and quite used to facing down self-important officers or civil servants whatever their position or rank. The phrase "lunch is for wimps" escaped me. I ensured that, with Eve's magnificent diary control, I never had a wasted lunch. Press barons, defence editors, publishers, captains of industry, top civil servants, politicians – indeed anyone who could influence and help the armed services in any way were – and should be – an essential part of any CDS's network.

I had three exceptional personal staff officers in Richard Shirreff, John Ponsonby and Paul Gibson. You spend a good deal of time with your personal staff, and it made a big difference to me to have companionable colleagues who didn't flap, understood my way of working and what was important to me. Richard went on to become a four-star general and John a two-star in the RAF.

My three ADCs, all young promising Welsh Guards captains during my CDS years – Guy Bartle-Jones, Pierre Morgan-Davies and Harry Legge-Bourke (the double-barrelled names are pure coincidence and not a prerequisite for an ADC) – had different temperaments. I know the experience stood them in good stead in their later lives. I gave them enough rope for the usual ADC cock-ups: wardrobe malfunctions – arriving in a suit when I should have worn white tie; map-reading disasters; chatting up the prettiest girls in the room at the expense of other guests; failing to book the right transport at the right time. But they were always fun to have around.

The time had come to select my successor as CDS. The accepted practice was for the serving CDS to put forward his recommendation(s) to the Defence Secretary, who would then forward them to the Prime Minister. He or she will then interview the prospective candidates to decide which one they could work with. The final recommendation then goes to Her Majesty the Queen for approval.

Since the Second World War, the practice had become 'Buggins's turn'. That meant rotation between the three services, rather than selection on merit. Air Marshal 'Chocks Away' Buggins, General 'Up and at Em' Buggins, or Admiral 'Salty Sea Dog' Buggins may get the job to which they are ill-suited.

Over the last 30 years that practice has changed. It is no surprise that since 1990, seven of the last 11 CDSs have been from the army. That is because we have had the broadest and most demanding operational experience: the two Gulf Wars, the Balkan conflict, wrapping up the Troubles in Northern Ireland, and Afghanistan.

There was an outstanding candidate in General Sir Rupert Smith; however, Rupert marched to his own drum. The navy had been miffed that Admiral Sir Jock Slater had not been made CDS instead of me. Their time came as my successor was Admiral Sir Mike Boyce, a submariner. We were chalk and cheese in experience and temperament. Patrols under the ice cap for up to three months commanding a nuclear-powered submarine require a very different style of personality and leader. Mike Boyce had a fine intellect with a penetrating eye for detail, a prerequisite for commanding a submarine armed with nuclear missiles. In temperament he was taciturn, a characteristic I have noted in many submariners. Six months under the polar ice cap does not lend itself to too much bonhomie.

My last visit as CDS was to Oman. I felt it was important that Mike Boyce should meet the Sultan, who was such a key strategic ally of Britain.

I suspect by then I was getting a little demob happy, as was my ADC, Harry Legge-Bourke, who was due to leave the army. On the morning of our return to the UK, we were all at breakfast, but Harry had not yet made an appearance. Eventually he appeared looking a little bleary-eyed, put his arms on my shoulder and said, "Morning fatso, sorry I overslept." Boyce's jaw hit the table, as did that of his Royal Marine ADC.

My PSO, Richard Shirreff, later overheard Boyce take his ADC aside, saying, "If you ever address me like that, your career will be at an end." When I heard about that later, I couldn't help smiling.

I took off my uniform for the last time in March 2001. I had completed 42 years of service.

21

The Hinterland

*I was more than happy to retire from my job but
determined not to retire my mind.*

After 42 years I was ready to leave the army. But at the age of
62, I was not ready just to reminisce, walk the dog, or spend
an evening under a lamp with the photograph album.

I was grateful for my army pension, but Kate and I had
gone out of our way to entertain as best we could during my
time in high command. When I was Commander-in-Chief
in Germany, we would on average entertain 250 people to
dinner a month. It was important to show people you cared
and to thank the men and wives from the NATO Alliance for
the work they did. Inevitably, we exceeded our small army
budget for entertaining, and precious little was put aside.
When I retired, I needed to earn some money.

Evelyn de Rothschild approached me. "Charles," he said, "I
wonder if you would like to be Chairman of Rothschilds for
Latin America? The thing is," he continued, "Latin American
presidents don't pay much attention to bankers, but they do
listen to generals."

I had first met Evelyn through his wife, Lynn Forester. She
was a polymath: a highly successful American businesswoman

and entrepreneur who had done much to foster dialogue between the US and Europe. She had also done a great deal for charity. Lynn had become a good friend to Kate and me through her charity work, and because I had a strong interest in furthering US and European relations. It seems trite to say it, but Evelyn and Lynn were the original power couple. They had been introduced to each other by Henry Kissinger and spent their wedding night, courtesy of the Clintons, in the White House.

Evelyn was right. Latin American presidents do listen to generals, rather than bankers. It is an unwise president who does not keep a watchful eye on his military. Regime change is never far away. A sensible president will ensure that his ambitious generals are kept busy hounding down left-wing rebels, or the more extreme Marxist-Leninist sympathisers that bedevil so many Latin-American states. What few people realised, however, was that right-wing paramilitary groups were responsible for just as much violence, if not more. Vested interests, if threatened, are ruthlessly protected.

Rothschild & Co astutely describes itself as a global advisory firm. I would never describe myself as an investment banker, but I certainly felt able to give advice, particularly to Latin American presidents with pressing internal security issues. Ironically, it was my SAS experience rather than strategic defence advice which proved to be most useful, as I discovered on my first trip on behalf of Rothschilds to Colombia.

I was met at El Dorado International Airport in Colombia's capital, Bogota, by a cavalcade of motorcycle outriders and a bullet-proof limousine. I was then whisked to the presidential residence, the *Palacio de Narino*, where I was warmly greeted by President Alvaro Uribe.

Alvaro was a good man with an obvious social conscience and a determination to end the Colombian armed conflict. What was meant to be a 48-hour visit turned into a three-week stay. Rothschilds business was mentioned only in passing.

President Alvaro rang Tony Blair direct to ask his permission for me to advise Colombia on how to tackle the *Fuerzas Armadas Revolucionarias de Colombia* (FARC) guerrillas; and, more controversially, how to get rid of the right-wing paramilitary groups who were up to their necks in corruption and drug-trafficking.

Plan Colombia, as the President called it, wasn't short of funds, with $2.8bn in direct foreign aid from the USA. I quickly discovered that a fair bit of that sum was finding its way into the wrong hands. The President's generals, who ran Colombia's administrative districts, thought they all should receive kickbacks. They lived high on the hog with fleets of Mercedes cars and other indicators of unearned opulence. On my advice, they were all removed from their positions.

My SAS experience in kidnapping drills was well received and easy to implement in a society where the matriarch is held in respect. "Always ensure that if the kidnap threat is high, you have a hysterical mama close to hand in the household," I said to a group of Colombian special forces operatives. "The more hysterical she is, the better. It rattles people more than the sound of gunfire." Once again, I found myself drawing on past lessons as a young SAS officer rather more than anything I had to offer as a former CDS.

I would always try to take Kate on my business trips to Latin America. Her talent for discovering what was actually going on was invaluable. Her avenue for this detective work was gossiping with Rothschilds executives and their wives, invariably late at night as it was customary not to start dinner before 11pm. I found out through Kate that, not only did most of the Rothschilds executives in Brazil hold down other jobs, but they also trousered a huge amount of money selling indifferent wine and labelling it 'Chateau Mouton Rothschild'. Evelyn was a true guardian of the great name of Rothschild, and he was furious. Wide-scale changes were made.

I may paint a colourful picture of how business is conducted in Latin America, but it is a part of the world for which I have great affection. You will never find warmer people, or where the obligations of friendship and family are observed with such care.

Rothschilds continues to flourish in Brazil and Mexico, the most powerful Latin American economies. I have always attributed Rothschilds' enduring success to Nathan Rothschild's famous dictum: "Buy when the cannons are firing, and sell when the trumpets are blowing."

After seven years as CGS and CDS, it was only natural that I should feel the odd tinge of regret that I was no longer in the thick of it; but my relationship with Tony Blair was neither transitory nor dependent on the office I had held. We continued to talk quite frequently about the security matters that were exercising his and the Labour government's mind. I made a point of never pontificating from the comfort of my armchair. But I would always put my head above the parapet on the services' welfare, or the risk to servicemen and women facing liability for their actions in the heat of combat at the hands of opportunist lawyers.

I did not proffer any advice on Iraq and the so-called weapons of mass destruction. I was not privy to intelligence on the matter. I do remember, however, saying at the time that the US invasion of Afghanistan with its allies in October 2001 was the right decision. It denied al-Qaeda a safe base of operations. But we would have to stick at it for the long haul. Any wavering or weakness on our behalf would be pounced upon by our enemies. There would be consequences for Western security and credibility if we were to vacillate.

I became used to entering through the back door of No. 10 Downing Street to avoid setting off any hares or upsetting my successor as CDS, who had yet to find his land legs.

One problem that was becoming of increasing concern to Britain was the tension between two nuclear powers, India and Pakistan.

I had first met President Musharraf of Pakistan when he was a student at the Royal College of Defence Studies in Belgrave Square. I had given a lecture – I forget the topic – but he came up to me at the end and introduced himself. We struck up a friendship and I took him out to lunch at the Beefsteak Club. He was good company, clever and cultured; I could tell he would rise to high office.

Musharraf told me something I had not realised before. President Zia of Pakistan in the 1970s had made the grave error of linking Pakistani nationalism to strict Islamic doctrine. Zia's decision to emphasise Pakistan's role in Islam radicalised Pakistan, heightened tensions over Kashmir and worsened relations with its nuclear-armed neighbour, India.

Musharraf said to me over lunch, "Pakistan's politics is about nuclear weapons and Kashmir. Remember that Zia said that Pakistan would develop nuclear weapons even if Pakistanis had to eat grass."

It was only after 9/11, however, that my friendship with President Musharraf acquired a wider relevance. Musharraf was in a tricky spot. He had to work with the Taliban government in Afghanistan, but in some way keep a grip on the porous borders between Pakistan and Afghanistan through which flowed all the Taliban's and al-Qaeda's trappings of terror. I flew to Islamabad a number of times to get a sense of Musharraf's intentions.

He was easy to deal with and forthcoming. I was only dismayed with his insistence that I should always be fed what he considered to be traditional English fare. This was invariably Brown Windsor soup, roast beef and Yorkshire pudding and baked Alaska. He introduced me to his chef who took great pride in showing me his most cherished books: *A Guide to Cooking for English Gentlemen* and *A Taste of Empire*.

The problem was that Afghanistan was a failed state. The Taliban had taken over and they allowed extremism and al-Qaeda to grow unchecked. My view – and this was shared by Tony Blair and Musharraf – was that we should have stuck at it in Afghanistan after we launched Operation *Enduring Freedom* in October 2001. We had achieved a degree of success and the Taliban had collapsed by the end of 2001.

I had time enough to reflect ruefully on the first principle of war: selection and maintenance of the aim. Afghanistan was the right aim but we did not maintain our commitment. Iraq and the so-called Weapons of Mass Destruction issue took over. The Taliban returned with a vengeance.

Musharraf achieved a little more success in his relations with India. There was at least dialogue – trains and cricket matches resumed between the two countries – but there was nothing that endured. I did my bit as I had an equal affection for India.

I had planned to visit when I was CDS, but that trip had to be cancelled when the Labour Foreign Secretary at the time, the fizzing and over-exuberant Robin Cook, suggested that Britain's colonial knowledge and expertise might have a part to play in the resolution over Kashmir. That went down badly.

Rothschilds had an office in Mumbai. It was the perfect conduit to visit India and do what I could to dampen down tension between India and Pakistan. All I can remember was that, after three days, I had to have a new suit made to take on the vast numbers of visiting cards pressed into my hands.

In June 2001, I was elevated to the House of Lords. The term 'elevated to' sounds somewhat grandiloquent, but I was glad of the honour as it allowed me to be a Crossbench Peer who, by tradition, has no political affiliation. I felt I still had a contribution to make on wider matters of defence and Britain's role in the world.

There was the usual palaver with the Garter King of Arms at the College of Arms to agree my title and coat of arms. The process was not unlike the popular BBC programme *Who Do You Think You Are?* We settled on Lord Guthrie of Craigiebank. Craigiebank is a district of eastern Dundee in Scotland. Needless to say, in the USA the Clan Guthrie is flourishing, with some 500 Guthrie families who have joined together to promote and preserve our common heritage. They even sponsor a quarterly newsletter headed by the rhyme, "Guthrie o' Guthrie and Guthrie o' Gagie Guthrie o' Taybank an Guthrie o' Craigie".

Anyway, it was a point of amusement amongst friends and colleagues who thought my Celtic origins were Welsh rather than Scots. The Guthrie family motto is 'Neither Timid Nor Rash'. I have never been one for too much self-reflection, but it has always struck me as a good summary of the way I have tried to conduct myself.

I made my maiden speech on 17 December 2001, flanked by a phalanx of former Chiefs of the Defence Staff and two former Secretaries of State for Defence. I may have done important jobs in my life, but I have always been mindful that we are all equal as human beings.

I started my speech by saying, "I seem to have served in the army with a surprising number of doorkeepers at the Palace of Westminster and one with whom I joined the Welsh Guards over 40 years ago."

Much of the rest of my speech was devoted to Afghanistan, praise for President Musharraf and the outstanding work of the BBC World Service, which I knew was listened to by 70 per cent of Afghan households (although women were not permitted to listen to the radio in Afghani homes).

Unlike the rowdy and sometimes ill-tempered House of Commons, the House of Lords is given to elaborate courtesy. It took time to get used to hearing phrases such as "the noble and gallant Lord Guthrie", "outstanding speech", "incisive and well-chosen words", "a great asset", "much to contribute" and other such compliments.

If I had anything to contribute it was on the wellbeing of the services. I was particularly incensed by Gordon Brown's continuing refusal to fund our equipment needs in Afghanistan adequately, and the risk to servicemen and women facing liability for their actions, particularly over the Iraq invasion.

I was often asked for my views on nuclear weapons. My views have not changed since I was MA to Field Marshal Lord Carver, who described nuclear weapons as "either bluff or suicide".

My view is that there must be a continual drive towards multi-lateral nuclear disarmament and non-proliferation; but we must have a voice to achieve this. Our nuclear capability gives us that voice.

I shall be resigning from the House of Lords in December 2020. I do not agree with my friend Max Hastings, who wrote, "Forget the rabble that is the Lords", but he does have a point insofar as it is surely time for wholesale reform. There are now 811 peers; only the People's Congress of the People's Republic of China is larger. To many it has become a national embarrassment. The seemingly inexorable increase in the membership of an unelected parliamentary body continues to undermine its reputation.

As a practising Roman Catholic ('devout' or 'staunch' would be stretching it in my case) I was inevitably asked to become president of several charities. I try never to turn things down if people have gone to the trouble of seeking my support.

By 2010, I was involved with 25 charities. One which was particularly close to my heart was Action Medical Research, founded by my uncle Duncan Guthrie in 1952. Duncan raised £4m that year in his quest to find a cure for polio which had affected his daughter and my first cousin, Janet Guthrie. Since then, it has spent close to £120m on projects; many of them have been ground-breaking, such as the importance of folic acid in preventing spina bifida. I also became President of the Federation of London Youth Clubs, which has done much to improve the lives of young people in London.

Henry Kissinger once said, "The reason that university politics is so vicious is because the stakes are so small." It is an observation that you can apply to many walks of life, and one I came to recognise in some of the work in which I became involved after the army; none more so than in my acceptance to become Chairman of the Trustees for the Hospital of St John and St Elizabeth in St John's Wood.

The hospital, founded in 1856, had strong links to the Knights of Malta. This is a Catholic order and the oldest surviving order of chivalry with origins in the Crusades. I became a Knight of Malta shortly after I became a Catholic. The hospital owned a chapel in which the knights have historically worshipped.

I had cause, however, to ban three knights who failed to carry out child-protection procedures which had affected one of the chapel's young sacristans. I also sacked the hospital's board. I was right to do so, as there had been a transparent failure of leadership. I had become increasingly concerned about the Catholic Church's failure to acknowledge and stamp out abuse.

My decision almost produced a schism within the British Association of the Order of Malta. The counter-attack was led by the son of a field marshal who had become Grand Master of the Order in Rome. He saw my decision as part of a wider conspiracy to reduce the Order of Malta's influence over the hospital and its chapel. This was surprising to many, as the Order neither owned the hospital nor the chapel. It all became rather tawdry, with poison pen letters flying around. The Grand Master was forced to resign by Pope Francis a few years later when he tried to prevent the use of condoms to help in the battle against AIDS and child pregnancies in Africa.

I am glad to say the British Order of Malta is now in much better shape under Richard Fitzalan-Howard's leadership, whose father (Michael) I had succeeded as Colonel of The Life Guards.

'Who Dares Wins', the SAS motto, proved to be as much as a pull in my business adventures as it had been in my military career. I also found I was attracted to working with frontiersmen engaged in wildcat exploration. I was lucky enough to strike up a friendship and business relationship with two such men, Simon Murray and Peter Hambro.

Simon Murray was a former French Foreign Legionnaire who had fought in the Algerian War. Although he came from a well-to-do background with a tradition of military service, his father inexplicably abandoned the family early on in Simon's life. His uncle paid his fees at Bedford School.

Simon learnt to be self-sufficient. From the time he left school, he was drawn to a life less ordinary. He became the oldest man to reach the South Pole unaided, at the age of 63. The French Foreign Legion has never quite left him. Still sinewy, his hair *en brosse*, his energy and enthusiasm for life remains undimmed.

As a businessman, Simon achieved extraordinary success and wealth in the Far East. He started a mobile phone company called Orange, a global brand in its day, which he sold for $36bn. He then changed tack and applied his formidable energy to mining and became chairman of Gulf Keystone Petroleum (GKP), the operator of the Shaikan Field, one of the largest developments in the Kurdistan region of Iraq. It was a joint venture with the Kurdistan Government.

Simon asked me to become a non-executive director of GKP. I knew precious little about mining, but Simon thought I would be useful in his dealings with the Kurdistan Government. Like all wildcat exploration companies, it was like riding a big dipper. At one stage, we were producing 40,000 barrels a day when the oil barrel price was $100 a barrel. We became the darling of the stock market for adventurous investors.

But like all these things, the good times never quite last. The Kurdistan Government had problems of its own, and made fewer and fewer payments. There was a downturn in demand. Fortunately, a Norwegian oil explorer with deep pockets and an eye for the long term took it off our hands.

Simon's unswerving loyalty to France and the French Foreign Legion was rewarded with his award of the Order of Merit of the French Republic. He is also a Chevalier de la Légion d'Honneur. In part this was due to a stroke of luck in 2016 when Simon and I came across the Free French flag kept by General de Gaulle in Carlton Gardens during his exile in London during the Second World War. We were able to return it to the French Government, who were indebted to Simon for this greatly prized symbol of the Free French under de Gaulle and their wartime resistance. Simon is a guest of honour at the annual Bastille Day military parade in Paris to which he has often invited Kate and me. The parade is on a much grander scale to our own Trooping the Colour and is a moving testament to '*la Gloire de la France*'. To hear the French National Anthem, '*La Marseillaise*' at the beginning of the parade never fails to foster a frisson of patriotic pride.

Peter Hambro, a scion of the Danish banking family, was cut from the same cloth as Simon Murray. Peter had trained as an accountant, but that was the extent of his desire to conform. He worked for a bullion house before he and Pavel Maslovskiy founded Peter Hambro Mining plc. Peter had gold in his blood and carried with him a money clip fashioned from two American gold coins. This, he felt, would always guarantee him safe passage anywhere in the world.

Peter Hambro Mining plc was later renamed Petropavlovsk plc to give it a more Russian feel. Given the banditry and corruption rife in Russia, the name was ill-chosen.

Petropavlovsk plc was an Anglo-Russian venture to develop a highly prospective, under-developed gold project in the far east Russian region of Amur. It is a remote region of bewildering beauty and home to the rare Amur (Siberian) tiger. Once again, I found myself attracted to a venture where risk and reward were two sides of the same coin.

I flew to Moscow to join Peter on a couple of occasions. We then flew seven time zones eastwards to Komsomolsk-on-Amur. We then flew in Russian Hind 24 helicopters, piloted by ex-Russian military pilots, to the site of the gold mines. I once said to Peter that it would be interesting to travel on the Trans-Siberian express to Vladivostok and then helicopter in from there. Peter looked at me and said, "I think after seven days you might grow tired of silver birch trees, and nothing but cabbage soup."

Peter was a man of integrity, a true trailbreaker who treated his Russian workforce fairly and transparently. If anything, he was a touch naïve about the Russian system, particularly in Putin's Russia. They do not like foreigners making money in their country. Success was bound to attract trouble. And where there is no rule of law, dishonest men flourish.

The story plot of Petropavlovsk plc followed a similar pattern to most highly prospective ventures. There is initial scepticism; then good news begins to leak out; there is a wild scramble to invest; share price rockets to an all-time high; and then greed and fear try to face each other down as the price of gold collapses and mysterious Russian tycoons swoop in to seize control.

Peter lost control and was ousted in a boardroom coup. He was an admirable man in a great country that had slid into the shadows.

My other non-executive directorships were tame by comparison. I had kept up my friendships with my US military colleagues who had also retired. Most of them retired to the middle of nowhere. They seemed quite happy to draw down their pensions and play golf in places like San Antonio in Texas, which had a good country club and was close to the Audie Murphy Veterans Hospital. Audie Murphy was the most highly decorated US soldier of the Second World War. I remember when I was a cadet at Sandhurst that anyone who did anything foolhardy was invariably met with the instructor's refrain, "Who do you think you are – Audie Murphy?"

I was introduced as a non-executive director to Colt Defence LLC by a former US Marine general. Colt handguns were an historic household name with their provenance stemming from the Mexican-American War of 1847, and Custer's last stand at the Battle of Little Big Horn in June 1876. Its most iconic brand, the Colt .45, used by ranchers, lawmen, sheriffs and storekeepers in the Wild West, was known as 'The Peacemaker'. Colt moved on from the .45 and developed grenade launchers and the M16, its future seemingly secure with lucrative contracts from the US Marine Corps.

Unfortunately, an illustrious provenance can often lead to complacency. I had pointed out to Colt's board that they faced fierce competition from the German Heckler and Koch, the Austrian Glock, the Italian Beretta, the Israeli Uzi and other brands. They listened, but poor financial management and a disastrous foray into financial restructuring led to Colt going bust in 2015.

I can count on a number of men and women in my life whose counsel I have often sought; but none more remarkable than Ronnie Grierson, who I felt deserved a special mention in my memoirs. Ronnie was German-born with a Jewish grandfather who started a paper mill in Bavaria. The family got out of Germany as soon as they saw what was about to happen under Hitler. Ronnie was educated at Balliol College, Oxford, joined the British Army after a brief period of internment and went on to become a lieutenant colonel in the SAS. He spoke half a dozen languages and changed his name from Griessman to Grierson. By the end of the war, he had impeccable British credentials.

Many German Jews who escaped Nazi Germany made a huge contribution to Britain's financial and cultural renaissance after the war. Ronnie joined SG Warburg on the invitation of his friend, Sir Siegmund Warburg, another German-born Jewish businessman of great influence and outstanding ability. Ronnie was effervescent, sociable and the consummate networker. When I was CGS and CDS, Ronnie would ask me to lunch at the Savoy three or four times a year. He told me everything I needed to know about geostrategic trends, UK politics, business and the arts. "Forewarned is forearmed," he would say to me.

My life-long desire for travel and excitement found a natural outlet in my business ventures abroad, but I did not lose sight of my charitable commitments at home. Weston Spirit was a charity started by a remarkable former Welsh Guardsman, Simon Weston, who had been very badly burnt in the Falklands campaign. Simon's long recovery from his awful injuries was heroic. I had remembered him from my time commanding the Battalion in Berlin. He was certainly spirited then, and regularly appeared before me for some misdemeanour or another.

Simon's charity was to help young people acquire the skills and training to build a successful life. I hosted a number of lunches and dinners to attract investment and favourable publicity. It was a great success, but charities require careful financial management. Understandably, this was not Simon's strength. He was poorly advised and Weston Spirit folded in the 2008 credit crunch.

In the spring of 2012, I received a telephone call from Sir Christopher Geidt, the Queen's Private Secretary, to say that Her Majesty wished to confer on me the rank of Field Marshal. The Queen was also to promote the Prince of Wales to Field Marshal in recognition of his support for the Queen as Commander-in-Chief.

The size of the British Army no longer really justified the rank of Field Marshal, so Sir Christopher's call took me by surprise. "Of course, you will have to acquire a Field Marshal's baton," Geidt said. "Spink & Son can make you one."

I took his advice and made my enquiries, only to discover that a new baton would set me back £75,000. Fortunately, not long afterwards, I met Prince Philip on another matter and mentioned that the cost of a baton was pretty steep. "Oh, I'm sure there must be a few lying around somewhere," he said.

A couple of days later I received a call from his Private Secretary to say that indeed one had been found in some attic and the Palace was quite happy for me to have it.

My academic career had never amounted to anything, but Liverpool Hope University saw fit to ask me to be their Chancellor. Liverpool Hope, with just 5,000 students, grew from three Christian teacher training colleges and retains a strong ecumenical tradition. I spent ten happy years as Chancellor there. In my last three years as Chancellor, it rose

77 places in the *Guardian* league table and received a gold medal for its teaching excellence.

I am not sure my influence had anything to do with its dramatic rise in the league tables, but I took great pride in its achievements. It was also good for deflating my academic friends whose conversations were often peppered with, "Now when I was at Cambridge…"

In May 2009 I received a telephone call which stopped me in my tracks. It was from Tom Bonas, the Welsh Guards Regimental Adjutant, to tell me that Rupert Thorneloe, commanding the Battalion in Afghanistan, had been killed in actio.n. Rupert was an officer of great promise. His death shook our family Regiment to the core. There was some disquiet from the Army Board over Rupert Thorneloe's replacement as commanding officer. The Regiment was unequivocal in its choice of Charles Antelme, an outstanding Welsh Guards officer who had served with distinction in the SAS and had won the Distinguished Service Order for his leadership. Some staff officer in the office of the CGS, General Dannatt, remarked, "Antelme may be the right man for Afghanistan but is he the right man back in the UK?" I could hardly believe my ears when this was told to me. Fortunately, the Army Board saw sense and Charles Antelme was appointed.

The Regiment's tour in 2009 was costly. The Armed Forces Covenant introduced by David Cameron's government was sound in principle, but less so in practical help. It was left to each Regiment to raise funds to support the families of those wounded or killed in action. Post-traumatic stress disorder amongst veterans will remain a long-term call on the financial resources of all regiments.

'Walk on Wales' was an initiative to raise funds for the Welsh Guards' Afghanistan Appeal. It was started by Jan Koops, a much liked and respected young officer of mine who had served with me in Berlin and South Armagh. As a field marshal and 'Father of the Regiment' ('Grandfather' would have been more apt), I was called upon to walk the last 9 miles of the 870-mile tour around the Welsh coast with a triumphant finish in Cardiff.

I was 75 and I found I had to muster every ounce of willpower to complete the 9 miles. The going was slippery underfoot and I limped in with as much dignity as I could muster to the cheers of present and former Welsh Guardsmen. After a few beers and genial banter, I was put on the train back to London. I had hoped to snooze all the way back to London, but the train was full of returning Welsh Guardsmen who thought it would be discourteous not to engage me in conversation. A few were good enough to accompany me to the taxi rank at Paddington as my legs seemed to be on strike.

As I approached my 80th year I went with Kate, Andrew and David and their families to Thailand for Christmas. I fell ill with double pneumonia from which I recovered, only to have a more serious setback when I was thrown from my horse at Trooping the Colour in June 2018. I landed on my head which, miraculously, was partially protected by my helmet. It could have been a great deal worse. My doctor was unequivocal: a third setback was not an option.

Epilogue

Life is not over but the story is.

George Orwell once said, "Memoirs are only to be trusted when they reveal something disgraceful. A man who gives a good account of himself is probably lying."

I am sure I have done things I have regretted nor am particularly proud of, but I trust I have written an honest account of my life. I hope whoever reads this memoir will accept that in my military career and retirement, I count myself lucky enough to have met many colourful and engaging people from every walk of life.

In time, this book will gather dust in the Regiment's archives but not, I hope, in the minds of my descendants. I wish I had known more about the lives of my grandparents and great-grandparents, and the times and circumstances in which they lived.

I write this epilogue on Armistice Day 2020. I read that the current CDS has said that robot soldiers could make up a quarter of the British Army by the 2030s. That may come to pass, but mine has been a soldier's story, a human story, at a time when the British Army was emerging from the relative certainties of the Cold War in the last decade of the 20th century to face a more complex and dangerous world.

ST DAVID'S DAY, I MARCH 2020

The Battalion and the Regimental family meet each year on the feast day of Saint David, the patron saint of Wales. In 2020 we came together at the Regiment's new barracks in Windsor, more or less unaware that only a fortnight later the country would be placed in lockdown after the Covid-19 pandemic took hold.

I March marks the first day of spring, but the long shadow of winter was still with us as Kate and I made our way to the Holy Trinity Church in Windsor. It was an unusually poignant service. As we had come to the Regiment's new home in Windsor, we witnessed the re-dedication of the Falklands memorial cross. The cross commemorates those members of the Regiment who lost their lives in the Falklands campaign.

Over the last 60 years since I joined the Welsh Guards, there have been only a handful of occasions when I have been unable to celebrate St David's Day somewhere in the world. I have always taken the time to make a silent tribute and salute to the Regiment and to its great gift of friendship and family.

It is our custom to hold a parade after the church service where we are presented with a leek. The leek is one of the two national emblems of Wales; the other is the daffodil. British Army regiments may be idiosyncratic and sometimes eccentric in their uniforms and headdress; the leek was chosen as the Regimental symbol of the Welsh Guards, and it is also our distinctive cap badge.

I have been with the Regiment, formed in 1915 on the command of King George V, for well over half of its life. In that sense, if nothing else, I suppose I have earned the honorary title of 'Father of the Regiment'. This *nom de guerre* has its advantages for someone of advancing years. First, at the reception after the parade, a comfortable chair is found for you and strategically placed so that you do not miss any of the day's theatre. Second, people come to chat to you to wish you well, but do not linger too long when they see others hovering behind them.

However reassuring it is to see old friends and familiar faces, I take most pleasure from talking to the Regiment's young officers. This year the commanding officer, Henry Llewelyn-Usher, spoke of how lucky we were to have such a promising and varied mix of young officers. Over the last two years, many had served in Afghanistan, Belize and the Falklands and had tested themselves in many adventurous training expeditions.

People often ask me about the changes I have witnessed over my 60 years as a Welsh Guardsman. They often expect me to say something to do with technology; but when I speak to today's young officers, I see that it is societal change that has had the most impact. There are constants, of course; officers today yearn for the same things I did in 1959: travel, sport, excitement, friendship, the desire to escape the shackles of modern life or, worse still, the looming prospect of 'working from home'.

But young officers nowadays are drawn from much wider strands of society than in my day, when a handful of public schools made up the pool of my contemporaries. Today's officers are every bit as good as we were, if not better. I am absolutely confident of their ability to lead the Guardsmen under their command.

I am not sure whether it was politeness or heartfelt interest but, despite my wish to ask about their lives, they mostly seemed intent on asking me about my life and times in the army. Higher command was of scant interest to them at the early stage of their careers, and I suspect many had heard my war stories before. But they did not seem to tire of hearing about a bygone age and anecdotes from a more light-hearted and less censorious time.

"Sir, did you ever meet the Nazi war criminal, Rudolf Hess, when you were commanding the Battalion in Berlin and the Battalion took turns to guard him in Spandau prison?"

"Field Marshal, someone said you took your SAS patrol in Aden to lay up in a cemetery next to dead bodies left to the vultures as nobody would suspect your presence."

"Sir, how did fighting the IRA during the Troubles compare with fighting communist guerrillas in Malaya?"

As Kate drove us back to London later that afternoon, the gentle murmur of the car radio jolted me out of a quiet doze. Kate turned up the volume. The news from Italy and Spain was gloomy. The Covid outbreak was becoming serious. I looked at Kate and said, "That doesn't sound too good, does it?"

Kate didn't reply for a moment and then said, "No, it doesn't; but we've been so fortunate and blessed in our lives, so I'm sure we'll get through to St David's Day next year."

Acknowledgements

My memory is the only diary I have kept. When I decided to write my memoirs, I discovered that some years had slipped like sand through my fingers. Although 2020 was a year of precious few blessings, for the first time in many a year, I found I had time on my hands to look through the 60 photograph albums that Kate and I have kept over the last 50 years. They have been a great prompt.

I have always tried to keep my friendships in good repair. Fortunately, the many officers, non-commissioned officers and soldiers with whom I served have been a great help in reminding me of the detail of the events during my 42 years' service. I have found it a little easier to retrace the footprints of the two decades since I left the army; but, here again, friends and family have often helped to jog my memory.

On my particular little stage, I should like to thank the following players without whom I would not have been able write these memoirs. First, my gratitude to Major General Richard Stanford, Colonel Tom Bonas, and the Regimental Trustees of the Welsh Guards for commissioning the book and convincing me that my memoirs would be of value to past, present and future Welsh Guardsmen.

My thanks to the team at Bloomsbury and Osprey Publishing. In particular, Nigel Newton, Marcus Cowper, Michael Fishwick, Emily Neat, Christelle Chamouton, Julie Frederick, Gemma Gardner, Joanna Narain and Stewart Larking.

My time as a Harrow schoolboy was brought to life by my old friend and Harrow contemporary, Dale Vargas. His excellent book, *The Timeline History of Harrow School*, was invaluable.

Aden in 1965–66 was such a formative part of my career that I was able to recall a good deal. Nevertheless, my thanks to Brigadier Peter Williams and Lieutenant Colonel Ray Evans for the finer points. Mickey Senior, Jamie Robertson, Christopher James, Angus Wall and Peter Cheney reminded me of how, as Adjutant, I struck fear into the hearts of newly joined officers.

My four years in the SAS were equally memorable. Here, I am grateful to Major Alastair Morrison, OBE, MC, for his friendship and for prompting my memory.

Reminiscing about the battle of Snugville Street in the Northern Ireland tour of 1971 and my time as a company commander in Münster, Germany, was made much easier thanks to David Mason. David was one of my platoon commanders and became a highly successful author in later life. I owe him particular thanks for his exceptional copy-editing skills.

General Lord Ramsbotham, who was my immediate boss at the Ministry of Defence, reminded me of the trials and occasional pleasures of working for Field Marshal Lord Carver.

My time as second-in-command and commanding officer of the Welsh Guards in Cyprus, Berlin and South Armagh was one of the happiest periods in my life and not difficult to recollect. I should like to thank, however, Lieutenant Colonel Charles Stephens, Brigadier Aldwin Wight, MC, Vyvyan Harmsworth, Rhydian Vaughan, Robert and David Mason, William Prichard, David Pritchard, Peter Drummond (Royal Scots Dragoon Guards), Julian Peel Yates, Nigel Hanbury, Alun Powell, Lieutenant Colonel Rhodri Traherne, Simon Rhodes, Julian Sayers and Colonel Sir Alexander Malcolm, for sharing their individual memories.

Major General Andrew Cumming, Major General Robert Gordon and Major Alan Braithwaite were able to recall and jog my memory of my time at 4th Armoured Brigade. Carl Kefer, my House Sergeant, has been a great prompt for domestic mishaps.

My ADCs warrant special thanks: Colonel Hugh Bodington, Lieutenant General Sir Ben Bathurst, Major General Richard Stanford, Mark Carr, Pierre Morgan-Davies, Guy Bartle-Jones and Harry Legge-Bourke.

Brigadier Alan Mallinson, a friend, and whose outstanding book *The Making of the British Army* was just the right reference book for the challenges the British Army faced during my career. Sir Max Hastings, also a friend and the pre-eminent military historian of my generation, has always encouraged me to retain an independent view but keep loyal to government decisions. David Soskin reminded me of the importance of not making assumptions about people's knowledge of events long past.

I should like to thank General Sir Richard Shirreff, Air Vice Marshal John Ponsonby and Brigadier Paul Gibson, not only for their outstanding service as my staff officers but, more importantly, for reminding me of the highlights and occasional low points during my time in high command. Eve

Milne was my wonderful PA when I was in the MOD as Chief of the General Staff. I was equally fortunate in Jacqui Saunders as my PA when I became Chief of the Defence Staff. Jacqui was a formidable woman. Both Eve and Jacqui have remained good friends to Kate and me. Lieutenant General Sir Bill Rollo shared a story from Kosovo with me, long forgotten, which reminded me of what could be lost in translation in multinational alliances.

A miscellany of Welsh Guardsmen: Lieutenant Colonel Guy Stone, Lieutenant Colonel Henry Llewelyn-Usher, Captain Orme Clarke and Simon Weston have all been helpful. Yvonne Brown, Christopher Enraght-Moony and Sergeant Laing at Regimental Headquarters, Welsh Guards, have all done useful research work. Major Martin Browne has proofread the memoirs with unerring accuracy. Nicholas Drummond, Tommy Macdonald-Milner and Peter Craig-Cooper have overseen the project with professionalism and encouragement.

Shawqi Sultan from Oman shared with me many happy memories from the time I have spent in that wonderful country.

The Life Guards, never reluctant to put forward their claims, and a Regiment to whom I was privileged to be the Colonel for 20 years, had three fine advisors in Brigadier James Ellery, Lieutenant Colonel Giles Stibbe, Colonel Simon Doughty, and Lieutenant Colonel Ralph Griffin.

I am entirely indebted to Captain Paul de Zulueta, who has been with me throughout 2020 to help me plan, research, organise and write my memoirs. Without his dedication, enthusiasm and support there is no way I could have completed this book.

My family has encouraged me for some time to record my life, in particular my dear brother James and my two spirited sons, David and Andrew. My sister-in-law, Sue Lewis, and my brother-in-law, Peter Worrall, have both added stories now enshrined in the family's folklore.

On behalf of the Regiment, I should also like to thank HRH The Prince of Wales for graciously writing the Foreword to my Memoirs. The Prince of Wales took over from his father, the late HRH Prince Philip, Duke of Edinburgh, as Colonel of the Welsh Guards in 1975. He has been an outstanding Colonel of the Regiment and an inspiration to all Welsh Guardsmen, both past and present.

My last word of thanks must go to Kate, whose encouragement, support and love throughout our married life, but particularly during this year of the global pandemic, has been invaluable.

Index